Eastern Approaches to Western Film

WORLD CINEMA SERIES

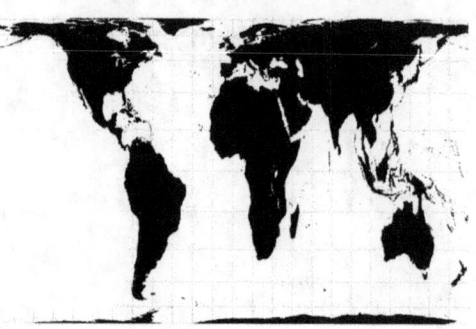

Series Editors:
Lúcia Nagib, *Professor of Film at the University of Reading*
Julian Ross, *Research Fellow at the University of Westminster*

Advisory Board: Laura Mulvey (UK), Robert Stam (USA), Ismail Xavier (Brazil), Dudley Andrew (USA)

The *World Cinema Series* aims to reveal and celebrate the richness and complexity of film art across the globe, exploring a wide variety of cinemas set within their own cultures and as they interconnect in a global context. The books in the series will represent innovative scholarship, in tune with the multicultural character of contemporary audiences. Drawing upon an international authorship, they will challenge outdated conceptions of world cinema, and provide new ways of understanding a field at the centre of film studies in an era of transnational networks.

Published and forthcoming in the World Cinema series:

Allegory in Iranian Cinema: The Aesthetics of Poetry and Resistance
By Michelle Langford

Animation in the Middle East: Practice and Aesthetics from Baghdad to Casablanca
By Stefanie Van de Peer

Basque Cinema: A Cultural and Political History
By Rob Stone and Maria Pilar Rodriguez

Brazil on Screen: Cinema Novo, New Cinema, Utopia
By Lúcia Nagib

The Cinema of Jia Zhangke: Realism and Memory in Chinese Film
By Cecília Mello

The Cinema of Sri Lanka: South Asian Film in Texts and Contexts
By Ian Conrich and Vilasnee Tampoe-Hautin

Contemporary New Zealand Cinema
Edited by Ian Conrich and Stuart Murray

Contemporary Portuguese Cinema: Globalising the Nation
Edited by Mariana Liz

Cosmopolitan Cinema: Cross-cultural Encounters in East Asian Film
By Felicia Chan

Documentary Cinema: Contemporary Non-Fiction Film and Video Worldwide
By Keith Beattie

Documentary Cinema of Chile: Confronting History, Memory, Trauma
By Antonio Traverso

East Asian Cinemas: Exploring Transnational Connections on Film
Edited by Leon Hunt and Leung Wing-Fai

East Asian Film Noir: Transnational Encounters and Intercultural Dialogue
Edited by Chi-Yun Shin and Mark Gallagher

Film Genres and African Cinema: Postcolonial Encounters
By Rachael Langford

Impure Cinema: Intermedial and Intercultural Approaches to Film
Edited by Lúcia Nagib and Anne Jerslev

Latin American Women Filmmakers: Production, Politics, Poetics
Edited by Deborah Martin and Deborah Shaw

Lebanese Cinema: Imagining the Civil War and Beyond
By Lina Khatib

New Argentine Cinema
By Jens Andermann

New Directions in German Cinema
Edited by Paul Cooke and Chris Homewood

New Turkish Cinema: Belonging, Identity and Memory
By Asuman Suner

On Cinema
Glauber Rocha
Edited by Ismail Xavier

Palestinian Filmmaking in Israel: Narratives of Memory and Identity in the Middle East
By Yael Friedman

Performing Authorship: Self-inscription and Corporeality in the Cinema
By Cecilia Sayad

Queer Masculinities in Latin American Cinema: Male Bodies and Narrative Representations
By Gustavo Subero

Realism in Greek Cinema: From the Post-War Period to the Present
By Vrasidas Karalis

Realism of the Senses in World Cinema: The Experience of Physical Reality
By Tiago de Luca

The Spanish Fantastic: Contemporary Filmmaking in Horror, Fantasy and Sci-fi
By Shelagh-Rowan Legg

Stars in World Cinema: Screen Icons and Star Systems Across Cultures
Edited by Andrea Bandhauer and Michelle Royer

Theorizing World Cinema
Edited by Lúcia Nagib, Chris Perriam and Rajinder Dudrah

Viewing Film
By Donald Richie

Queries, ideas and submissions to:

Series Editor: Professor Lúcia Nagib –
l.nagib@reading.ac.uk

Series Editor: Dr. Julian Ross –
J.Ross1@westminster.ac.uk

Publisher at Bloomsbury, Rebecca Barden –
Rebecca.Barden@bloomsbury.com

Eastern Approaches to Western Film

Asian Reception and Aesthetics in Cinema

Stephen Teo

BLOOMSBURY ACADEMIC
LONDON • NEW YORK • OXFORD • NEW DELHI • SYDNEY

BLOOMSBURY ACADEMIC
Bloomsbury Publishing Plc
50 Bedford Square, London, WC1B 3DP, UK
1385 Broadway, New York, NY 10018, USA
29 Earlsfort Terrace, Dublin 2, Ireland

BLOOMSBURY, BLOOMSBURY ACADEMIC and the Diana logo are trademarks
of Bloomsbury Publishing Plc

First published in Great Britain 2019
This paperback edition published in 2021

Copyright © Stephen Teo, 2019

Stephen Teo has asserted his right under the Copyright, Designs and Patents Act,
1988, to be identified as Author of this work.

For legal purposes the Acknowledgments on p. xi constitute an extension
of this copyright page.

Cover design: Charlotte Daniels
Cover image © Kim Novak in Vertigo (1958) (© Courtesy Everett Collection / Mary Evans)

All rights reserved. No part of this publication may be reproduced or transmitted
in any form or by any means, electronic or mechanical, including photocopying,
recording, or any information storage or retrieval system, without prior permission
in writing from the publishers.

Bloomsbury Publishing Plc does not have any control over, or responsibility for, any
third-party websites referred to or in this book. All internet addresses given in this
book were correct at the time of going to press. The author and publisher regret any
inconvenience caused if addresses have changed or sites have ceased to exist, but
can accept no responsibility for any such changes.

A catalogue record for this book is available from the British Library.

A catalog record for this book is available from the Library of Congress.

ISBN: HB: 978-1-7845-3982-5
PB: 978-1-3501-9476-2
ePDF: 978-1-3501-1331-2
eBook: 978-1-3501-1330-5

Series: World Cinema

Typeset by Deanta Global Publishing Services, Chennai, India

To find out more about our authors and books visit www.bloomsbury.com
and sign up for our newsletters

Dedicated to all students, East and West

Contents

List of Figures	x
Acknowledgments	xi
Introduction	1
1 Star Wars Eastern Saga	21
2 *Vertigo*, Hitchcock's Chinese Riddle	49
3 Orson Welles's *The Lady from Shanghai*	79
4 *Le Samouraï*, Eastern Action in the *Milieu*	103
5 Robert Bresson, French or Daoist?	129
6 Dreyer's *Vampyr*: Wandering in the West	153
7 Eastern Principles in Sam Peckinpah's Westerns	179
8 *Make Way for Tomorrow*, America's Confucian Classic	205
9 John Ford and Asian Family Values	231
Conclusion	255
Glossary	263
Bibliography	265
Index	280

Figures

1.1	Yoda, a metaphor of Daoist transformation	32
1.2	Light sabres, a product of "Techno-Orientalism"	34
1.3	Darth Sidious projects "force lightning" on Luke Skywalker	41
2.1	Madeleine enclosed by "double happiness" symbols	51
2.2	Madeleine in red and the mandala	54
2.3	The lovers and the backdrop of the "bitter sea"	61
2.4	Scottie rescues Madeleine from the water	67
3.1	Michael and Elsa steering the wheel	88
3.2	Elsa at the opera theater	91
3.3	Elsa, the vulnerable femme fatale	92
3.4	Michael leaves Elsa to die	95
4.1	The "floating cloud" scene	109
4.2	The woman in the car	116
4.3	Jef uses a gun as a samurai uses a sword	122
5.1	The donkey Balthazar and Zhuang Zi	136
5.2	Gerard and his "action painting"	141
5.3	Nie Yinniang and her donkey	146
6.1	Gray, the fisherman and vampire hunter	161
6.2	Symbols associated with the vampire	169
6.3	Gray and Gisele walk toward the light and out of the West	174
7.1	Cable Hogue and the lizard	184
7.2	The Bunch walking into the tiger's lair	191
7.3	Bennie rising from the grave	198
8.1	The family at the beginning of *Make Way for Tomorrow*	212
8.2	The public listens in on Lucy Cooper's phone conversation with Barclay	215
8.3	A renewed courtship	218
8.4	The Coopers with the car salesman	223
9.1	The return of Tom Joad	233
9.2	Tom Joad and his family	235
9.3	The patriarch and his family	239

Acknowledgments

The idea for this book came to me in a conversation with Professor Tim Bergfelder over a dinner in Glasgow where I was attending the Screen Conference in June 2016. He suggested that it would be a great idea to write a book analyzing Western films from a Confucian point of view. At the time, I nodded favorably without being really convinced that such a book could be written. However, the seed was planted in my mind so that when the time came to write a book proposal to submit to the publisher, I was ready with some concrete ideas for chapters. The scope had widened to include not just the Confucian viewpoint but a whole "Eastern approach." Effectively, this meant including a Daoist outlook, and for that, I am indebted to my old friend and classmate Chia Khiong Fatt whose belief in Daoism was always inspirational to me and had enthused me over the years to look for Daoist motifs in films.

I am grateful to my chair of school, Professor Charles T. Salmon, for his support of this project by freeing up some time from my teaching for me to do the hard writing necessary for this book. I am also grateful to the three anonymous reviewers of my manuscript. Their comments and suggestions guided me to reformulate my introduction and revise the texts and introduced new ideas in my analyses. For material support, I thank Lee Sangjoon, Eternality Tan, Adrian Danks, Shanti Rajamani, Xavier Lum, Junainah Binte Abdul Latif, and Wanda Ramadhani Kurniawan. Above all, I thank my spouse Lim Bea Fung for her unstinting backup and assistance in the research, editing, and rewriting of the chapters.

Introduction

The Eastern approach

The main function of this book is the adoption of an "Eastern approach," certain arguments following principles of Eastern thought, to apply to the contents and narratives of Western films of my choice, all classics, made in Europe and America by a selective group of auteur directors. The approach is a synchronic application of Eastern concepts as a kind of mind exercise along the line of a freewheeling Daoist "wandering" proceeding from contact with the Western object. This is an intervention that has no precedence and historical context. Thus, I own up to the fact that this may be an entirely idiosyncratic collection of polemical essays. Be that as it may, the methodology is as follows:

Each chapter assesses the case study by seriously engaging with the criticism on record (written by mostly Western scholars) regarding the specific case. Great care is taken to scrutinize the films for their Eastern content, and the films are backed up by references to the particular Eastern philosophy or set of philosophies cited. All these references can be readily verified as long extant and influential texts. As far as possible, I refer to reputable translations, although on some occasions I resort to my own translations. The actual work of interpretation and analysis is undertaken based on the scrutiny of certain inscriptions of Eastern motifs and themes embedded in the films. It is not undertaken without any foundation for the invocation of Eastern precepts as the tools of analysis, however far-fetched it may seem on the surface of it. This involves a comparative method that I borrow from the ancient Chinese text, the *Guigu Zi*, and it is the principle of *xiangbi*, meaning semblance or likeness (*xiang*) and contrast or comparison (*bi*).[1] *Xiangbi* is a methodology of trying to know one's opposite or an interlocutor in any form of cross communication. In my approach, therefore, it involves finding appropriate correspondences and matches of Eastern precepts to Western themes. The approach, then, is fundamentally a reconceptualization of reading film classics, giving an alternative interpretation that is, because of its emphasis on an Eastern cultural underlayer, "proximate" to the Western texts.[2]

The analysis involves not just our readings of the narrative texts of the films but also reassessments of the established critical writings, or at least the more important criticisms pertaining to the specific cases, to address certain lapses or "blind spots" in understanding or interpretation and ultimately to add to the record. What is idiosyncratic is the conceptual approach based on an "Eastern" perspective. I aim to demonstrate that such a perspective can enrich the understanding of the films, hopefully achieving a more equitable balance in East-West cross-cultural communication which has tended to tilt overwhelmingly toward the West, that is to say, overwhelmingly Eurocentric. The approach marks an attempt to change one's ways of observing and analyzing film by discerning Eastern characteristics, motifs, and philosophical elements which have the potential to entirely renew and readjust one's view of film. It represents an effort to reformulate and reexamine the established views of the classics chosen for analysis which have been overwhelmingly appraised and analyzed from Eurocentric theoretical and philosophical perspectives. Eurocentric theory has essentially guided the international discourse on film not just on films made in the West but also films made in the East. Much academic and journalistic writing have taken this practice as the standard. This book thus goes against the grain of this practice. It seeks to inject an alternative, Eastern philosophical perspective into the film literature and to provide an addendum and corrective to Eurocentric, or America-centric, analyses.

An explication is now in order about the term "Eastern." It is a word I happily embrace, along with the title of the book (not my original choice). I used it in my previous book, *Eastern Westerns*,[3] a title that was also suggested to me (I had preferred "Asian Westerns") and it would seem, in that instance, that with the publisher's preference for the word "Eastern" over "Asian," the reader could immediately grasp the essence of the term. It is so commonly used that no explanation would seem necessary. Perhaps because it is so common I should now have to further comment on the use of it and on its theoretical implications for this project. First, I should proceed by speaking about my own Eastern roots. I was born in Malaysia, of Chinese descent.

As a Malaysian, I am compelled to live with a mixture of Asian cultures and traditions, principally Malay, Chinese, and Indian—the three main population groups in Malaysia (there are also other minority groupings composed of Eurasians and indigenous ethnicities). Due to the colonial era I was born into, I was educated in the colonial language of English and it is the language that I write in, but my Malaysian nationality allows me other choices of languages (Chinese and Malay). I am a Southeast Asian, with roots in Chinese tradition, language (Mandarin and other dialects), and culture; there is also close familiarity with other Asian cultures and languages. This is my "Eastern" background.

At the same time, because of the hybridizing nature of colonialism and the thrust of Western developmental modernism that befell Malaysia, and most Southeast Asian countries, I may also be considered "Western." Am I more Eastern than Western? This is an identity conundrum that bedevils a lot of Malaysians and I am not immune from this crisis. Although the question is somewhat beside the point of the analysis of this book, it may serve to illustrate the theoretical compulsion for the whole project as well as what some have perceived to be its central problem. Some of my reviewers have decried the approach of this book, reliant, as it is, on an East-West binary that to them is untenable, having been "problematized by decades of postcolonial theory." My book, however, is not prepossessed by postcolonial theory, and it does not set out to argue any position within that field of theoretical study. That the East-West binary is perceived to operate in the book arises more as a condition of my Eastern approach adopted for the interpretation and analysis of Western films. I would argue that my approach presents no clear opposition between East and West but analogous comparison, and that I merely bring out what Western films have already received and absorbed of Eastern characteristics. If there is a binary, it is a rather blurred one. On the other hand, postcolonial scholarship has also brought out evidence of "bidirectional interpenetration" of Eastern and Western cultures and religions in the colonial context, as J. Jeffery Franklin has uncovered in his study of the interpenetration of Christianity and Buddhism in nineteenth-century Ceylon (now Sri Lanka).[4] This kind of "interpenetration" may be a theme of postcolonialism as Franklin discusses it, but it is an old doctrine of Buddhist thought, expounded in the *Avatamsaka Sutra* as "All in One, One in All." It is a doctrine that may be taken as our lodestar, but if a binary is operative in this book, it is only because there is a need to make evident the Eastern in the Western, so often hidden and deferred in analysis.

The fundamental contradiction in postcolonial societies is the objective condition of neocolonialism. The state of postcoloniality, as Homi Bhabha asserts, "is a salutary reminder of the persistent 'neo-colonial' relations within the 'new' world order and the multi-national division of labour."[5] Theoretically speaking, postcolonialism involves not just a "decolonization" process but also one of "deimperialization," according to Kuan-Hsing Chen. Both movements "intersect and interact, though very unevenly."[6] Chen notes that imperialism is far from being "a historical ruin"; it "expresses itself in a new form" through an "ongoing process of globalization" while former colonies undergo decolonization, which "can be a painful process involving the practice of self-critique, self-negation, and self-rediscovery" and deimperialization "which is no less painful and reflexive, is work that must be performed by the colonizer first, and then on the colonizer's relation with its former colonies."[7]

From my Malaysian perspective (and as a postcolonial subject), "deimperialization" imposes a greater moral burden on the West, and the West's failure to "deimperialize" in the context of postcolonialism therefore hardly suggests the redundancy of the East-West binary, although I must reemphasize that my book does not hold up the binary in the framework of postcolonial theory but as a dualistic device for the sake of comparative film theory. To many of us living in Southeast Asia, postcolonialism has exacerbated an identity crisis within many modern Asians in the form I have described above. Some may cope better than most and find no problem with it (in Malaysian English, a response for such a conundrum could well be "Same-Same," stating the issue of sameness from the Malaysian or Eastern perspective). While this may suggest that the binary is of no great import to some, it is necessary for Asian intellectuals and scholars to complement the process of "deimperialization" as a moral imperative for both East and West for the sake of a greater peace in the world. In this process, Chen proposes that scholars ought to engage in a discourse employing "Asia as method." This implicates an Asian scholarship that "requires a different sort of knowledge production" from the kind of Euro-American knowledge products on Asia.[8] I confess to being inspired by Chen's arguments and his thesis of Asia as method. My Eastern approach may in some way fall into his theoretical grid though with a more modest aim of trying to loosen the grip of Eurocentrism in film studies.

Issues of the East

I acknowledge that the "Eastern" terminology has some problematic ambiguities as does the term "Asian" (I use the two terms interchangeably), but I will now forgo the latter term to focus on the more serious implications of the "Eastern"—or "the issues of the East," as an anonymous reviewer of my manuscript has put it. One of these "issues" is that of Orientalism. Orientalism is entrenched in some of the films discussed, as in the Star Wars Saga, the subject of chapter 1. It is addressed in the chapter itself, but here, I wish to address the issue as an intrinsic problem in my Eastern approach of analyzing Western films, but first, to preface my remarks, I have to say that when I was writing this book, I was never conscious of being an Orientalist at all or that I was using that particular approach in any specific way. Yet, there may indeed be aspects of Orientalism in my approach which I may put down to my postcolonial subjectivity. The problem relates to Orientalism as an ideological Eurocentric tool of analysis and as a legitimate form of intellectual discourse, using Eastern ideas and philosophy to measure and assess Western works. That my book is open to a charge of being Orientalist reveals the nature of the approach itself, which is, of course, an "Eastern approach," and that it attains value through its semblance and contrast with Western content. This is the sine qua non of the book.

However, the charge presupposes that Eastern thinking must adopt modern or current Western values and Western thinking to be free of the Orientalist stain—Orientalism as distortion, bad practice, or bad epistemology. Western films should be interpreted only according to the Western European intellectual tradition (which may actually include Western norms of Orientalism). To this extent, my "Eastern" approach is, in fact, a "Western" approach. Such a standpoint does not contemplate that Orientalism can be a positive endeavor from the perspective of the Eastern intellectual, a self-Orientalism, to be sure, but nevertheless one that adopts a corrective tweaking toward the expression of an Eastern perspective or identity. Arif Dirlik observes that by the twentieth century "orientalist conceptions had no distinct geographical origin,"[9] which suggests to me that the idea of Orientalism is not loaded by geographical terms and that the issue is one of proportionality and balance in the comprehension of the values of East and West as well as the appropriateness and validity of the ideas applied.

The real essence of my Eastern approach, then, is to seek a balance of East and West. In the *Zhuang Zi*, it is written, "If we recognize that east and west, though opposites, cannot be without each other, their shared merit will be fixed."[10] The Eastern approach is meaningless if it is not applied to Western creations, or, in other words, it must be balanced (compared, evaluated, offset) with the Western practice. The Western works would also benefit from being balanced with an Eastern analytical outlook. The idea of balance is crucial to my own evolution as an intellectual and writer. If I am guilty of Orientalism, I am equally guilty of what some might call Occidentalism. A few years ago, I wrote a paper on a Chinese film in the Western genre with the editorial stipulation that I had to adopt a Deleuzian approach. Here then is the reverse of this book's proposition of the Eastern approach whereby I analyze an Eastern film for its incorporation of Western elements—in this instance "Western" referring both to the geographic West and the cinematic genre of the Western. Half of my book *Eastern Westerns* is based on this reversal, and so I do know from where I have come in tackling this present book.

The next pressing issue concerns the broadness and ambiguity of the Eastern terminology. This is more like a pitfall which I happily fall into, in the spirit of Daoist wandering and acceptance of the broadness or limitlessness of any entity. Perhaps this is a good principle to grasp the abstract scope of this book. While this is a problem for some scholars, I see the issue through the lens of my Malaysian eyes. All Malaysians essentially settle down into a generic Asianness, underscoring "Asian" values of courtesy, tolerance, harmony, sociality, and, yes, broadmindedness. Being a Malaysian of Chinese ethnicity, if I were to cite Chinese cultural references in a multicultural context, I am happy to say that they are Eastern or Asian in the spirit of a pan-Asian "interpenetration" of cultures. Thus, the word "Eastern" is used in this spirit. On the other hand, it has been pointed out to me that because I have used more Chinese philosophical references in my analyses for this book, I am prone to the charge of Sinocentrism. This charge comes from the opposite of broadness or ambiguity, and it is yet another pitfall which I have obviously fallen into, and it would be necessary here to address it in some breadth.

In my analyses, I mainly invoke Daoist and Confucianist ideas and beliefs borrowed basically from the *Zhuang Zi* and the *Analects* (also from other Confucian texts such as the *Mencius*). These comprise of ethical principles, philosophical ideas, and certain lifestyle values that I apply to the films in terms of story themes and new interpretations of narratives. In a nutshell, Confucianism usually points to ethical obligations in social institutions like the family. Obligations involve respect for one's elders, taking care of aged parents, friendship, and loyalty. The obligations govern relations in an ordered and hierarchical manner so long as there is proper observation from all, and on a macroscopic level, this embraces the relationship between the ruler and the ruled. The form of propriety may be important to ethical behavior in social institutions but in practice should bring out the substance of ethics. The Confucian philosophy emphasizes social responsibility as an implicit duty of all citizens, and it is up to each one of us to fulfill this duty with earnest sincerity. Daoism represents more philosophical abstractions of values and life choices. The individual seeks to follow the *dao* (the path) to achieve transcendence in a way that accounts for how one immerses oneself in the physical world and conducts relations with material things. This may seem paradoxical and, indeed, Daoism suggests dialectical interactions between the self and the material world. A practice in Daoist thought is *wuwei* (nonaction), trusting to one's mind in discovering natural and unpremeditated principles of action to respond to material conditions and freely flow with the *dao*.

As I see it, both schools of thought, with their ethical and metaphysical outlooks on life and death, duty and freedom, are completely pertinent to the series of films that I analyze in the following chapters. My approach is broad and general and does not address in detail the philosophical foundations of the schools of thought so cited because I do not expect that my readers are specialized in Eastern thought or philosophy but are more attuned to film studies and criticism. After all, the approach is applied to programmatic themes and motifs contained in the films I have selected and must operate within the parameters of the art of film so deployed and their particular narratives as well as the published criticisms.

I also invoke some Japanese and Indian philosophical ideas, but there is no symmetry in these invocations. All my chapters mark different instances of one school of thought being more applicable than the other, depending on the stories and themes of the films. Thus, for example, a film like *Make Way for Tomorrow* invokes more Confucianist principles than, say, Hindu thought; the Star Wars Saga is more Daoist than Buddhist but does not exclude the latter; similarly, *Vampyr* has a more Daoist outlook, but the film contains marvelous passages that immediately remind me of Indian rasa theory; *Le Samouraï* contains Japanese Bushido philosophy as well as correspondences to the myths and actions of Chinese *wuxia* and with Daoism; and so on. This may be a piecemeal approach, but it is like wandering through a maze and encountering different varieties of narratives embedded into the hedgerow and you use what is applicable in Eastern theory along the principle of *xiangbi* (semblance and contrast) to interpret them at each moment of the turn around the maze.

I do not seek to approach the films with a preconceived set of Eastern theory that is a single, authoritative, and well-structured entity. No doubt, this is a manifestation of my own limitations, but I have made my choices based on my own personal predilections and interests, and, from that perspective, it is practically impossible for me to apply the entirety of Eastern sources of thought, from West Asia to Japan. The charge of Sinocentrism also reflects the problem of how to define the Eastern. At the same time, my use of Japanese and Indian ideas in some cases also accentuates Sinocentrism, according to the critics. This confuses what is meant by the "Eastern." The confusion is regrettable, but at least the attempt to be inclusive has not been entirely disregarded. The sense of confusion is probably a side effect of the previous charge of ambiguity and broadness, which are not in themselves negative (I have said they ought to be embraced). I revert to my Malaysian background, its version of the broad church. Different races coexist and try to get along, and there are implicit ambiguities in understanding each other—an effect of inclusiveness—slow turns and careful negotiations in a dance of the races.

In the Malaysian context, it is implicitly understood that not all Asians think alike—a useful point to bear in mind too, in reference to another opinion that not all Asian viewers will use Daoism, Confucianism, or Buddhism, which

I mainly invoke, to approach the films of Europe and Hollywood (in fact, they will think like Westerners and that is the problem that I am trying to redress here). The Muslim Malay and the Hindu Indian will not be overjoyed with my Chinese interpretations, but on the other hand, there is always space in the Malaysian polity for mutual understanding and interaction across cultures. Such a space may be called Eastern, and when it is conjoined to the Western space (and here we may think of East and West as a unitarian space, no longer a binary), there is even greater room for cross-cultural exchange and communication. In this great ocean of space, I tend to see the charge of Sinocentrism as a minor issue, although one should always be mindful of the Chinese proverb under such circumstance, "One pole can sink the whole ship" (*yi ganzi da fan yitiao chuan*): the single stroke of criticism that seeks to sink the whole project. What matters is whether the ideas and arguments can shape up to a dialogue and a connection between cultures, and I leave it to the readers to judge whether they shape up.

The charge of Sinocentrism is a counterintuitive, over-generalized imputation of bad epistemology rather than an indictment of being part of a longstanding or impending trend of undue Chinese predominance over the whole field of Asian/Eastern studies or international film studies, of which there is no evidence in fact. It is more like an occupational hazard for an Asian scholar of Chinese culture and cinema. I have been accused of Sinocentrism even when I was writing about Chinese films and genres, such as *wuxia*, and I find it paradoxical but where the intent is an attack on my scholarship, needless to say, I stand by my scholarship unwaveringly. Here, it would be necessary for me to say that I make no apologies for citing Chinese references and invoking Chinese thought. Criticism about my use of them suggest that they do not fit the material, are out of place, and somehow, not totally belonging to the East. This last point is something that I comprehend very well, being Malaysian with a "Western" mentality (or more accurately, someone with a Western subconscious) and therefore someone who must constantly grapple with the idea that the East is not really part of us. I have no rhetorical skill to make as if I am not part of the East even as I partake of an "Eastern" approach. This book is tantamount to a self-discovery. The Chinese allusions are an integral part of me—and an integral part of the "Eastern." Much thought and energy has been expended to ensure that they fit the material of this book.

The Eastern viewpoint

The next issue concerning the Eastern is that in fact it is all made up by the West. While acknowledging some truth to this proposition, which is essentially Said's thesis in *Orientalism*, I am not put off by it nor do I see it as an obstacle (in fact, it can also be exploited for our purposes because not all of it is "bad epistemology"). There is an East made up by the East and one needs to carefully uncover it. My methodology of Eastern investigation tries to look at the original sources even if it is reliant on translation—and on translated texts. I try to be scrupulous with the translations and with my choice of texts, ensuring as best as I can that they are accurate to the original sources (e.g., *Zhuang Zi*, *Analects*). Another method is to try to be dense with quotes from these sources and to include some vernacular, folkloric references to popular proverbs. Thus, careful choices and scrutiny of Eastern sources present a veritable set of theory that can justifiably be applied to Western material—an Eastern approach to Western matter. As someone tied to two poles, I have exerted much effort to align the East with the West through the comparative process of *xiangbi*, referred to earlier, matching and corresponding Western matter with Eastern thought. This sort of matching does not preclude the possibility that the East may contain certain Western inscriptions. This entails some negotiation with the correspondences and respect for the Western material. In the *Guigu Zi*, the engagement of opposites is always one of *fanying* (reactions and responses), a matter of reciprocity. In essence, my Eastern approach reciprocates the Western material I receive as a viewer.

The East has undoubtedly learned much from the West. We can certainly say that the West has gifted the East with Western knowledge, science, and technology, likewise with Western films, a repository of entertainment, art, and culture, offering a rich source of learning. With the Eastern approach, it is only proper that the East reciprocates with its own knowledge and ideas, cognizant of the Western substance it has received. I make no claims about the "purity" of the East. However, if there is that impression, it probably stems from my attempts to find the original Eastern resources to get around the idea that the East is an invention of the West. This idea, of course, ignores that dimension of the East as an invention of Eastern intellectuals and others, not to mention that group of "orientalized Westerners" pointed out by Arif Dirlik, people like the Jesuits of China and Lawrence of Arabia "who sought to live as Chinese or Arabs."[11] In fact, there is another whole dimension of the "Oriental West" referred to by the political scientist John Hobson in his book, *The Eastern Origins of Western Civilisation*, where he demonstrates that the West had received and assimilated "Eastern 'resource portfolios' (e.g. Eastern ideas, institutions, and technologies)" through a process of "oriental globalization" that took place from 500 to 1800.[12] Moreover, "Western imperialism after 1492 led the Europeans to appropriate all manner of Eastern economic resources to enable the rise of the West."[13] Colonialism (the deeper form of imperialism), therefore, was the condition for the further integration of Eastern resources into the Western worldview, Western culture possessing and incorporating Eastern elements.

It is ironic, from our point of view, that the West that exercised hegemony over the East through imperialism and colonialism and plundered its resources has traditionally looked to the East for knowledge and wisdom. Thus, one of the principles of the Eastern approach is that in interpreting the films of the West from an Eastern perspective, we are in fact doing nothing more than disclosing what the West has took from the East, absorbed and integrated into their images and ideas, at the same time reimposing a state of balance by pointing out what is Eastern in Western films. The films that are analyzed and interpreted in this book contain Eastern signs and inscriptions that point to the aesthetic and philosophical influences of the East, suggesting that there is a more thorough integration of East and West than previously thought or imagined. The task at hand is to point out and make apparent the Eastern signs which are effectively buried in a Western cultural veneer that they do not seem obvious. The principle of the "Oriental West" can also produce an attenuated view of the East in that it is so thoroughly assimilated into the West that they do not seem Eastern anymore. In my research for this book, some of the literature on the films that I discuss refers to Oriental philosophical themes and ideas, as well as the presence of motifs, symbols, and colors, without mentioning and recognizing their Oriental provenance. They are all taken for granted as part of the Western province of knowledge and creativity. The "attenuated East" is a kind of motif in Western films that makes the Eastern approach possible. More knowledgeable Western critics do acknowledge the Eastern sources of influence on the films but doing so not from a specific Eastern point of view. Their interest lies not so much in adopting an Eastern approach of analyzing Western films but in discussing the films as essentially Western creations coming out of Western minds.

In writing this book, I do not wish to suggest that I am alone in the endeavor of trying to break the mold of Eurocentrism in film studies through a refocusing on Eastern theorizing perspectives or use of Eastern philosophy. I acknowledge other contributors in the field, and here I principally take note of Victor Fan's book, *Cinema Approaching Reality: Locating Chinese Film Theory*,[14] which is impressive for its investigation of early Chinese theorists and filmmakers looking at questions of film ontology. The book makes clear that the Chinese theories are developed with a view of applying them to film practice in China. Thus, the scope and character of my book is quite different from Fan's. My book does not deal with a historical investigation of Chinese film theory nor do I invoke any specific Asian film theory (Chinese, Japanese, or Indian) but rather Eastern thinking broadly derived from philosophical ideas and vernacular proverbs, maxims, or aphorisms, and I apply them to Western films rather than to suggest that these exist primarily within Asian or Chinese films.

This book continues the theoretical direction of my previous two monographs *The Asian Cinema Experience: Styles, Spaces, Theory* (2013) and *Eastern Westerns: Film and Genre Inside and Outside Hollywood* (2017), both adopting an Eastern analytical perspective on film and genre. *The Asian Cinema Experience* suggests that we can see films made in Asia from an Asian perspective and that Asian films contain intrinsic Asian styles and theories. *Eastern Westerns* is a study of a specific genre, Westerns, made by Asian film industries and by Hollywood itself and other industries. I adopt a comparative analytical framework in analyzing Asian Westerns and Westerns made by Westerners, seeing these films through Asian eyes, evoking and employing Asian philosophical ideas and value systems (such as Confucianism and Buddhism) and ancient literary classics from India (the *Ramayana*, *Mahabharata*), as well as ancient dramaturgical theory (rasa theory from the *Natyasastra*). This book continues this Eastern framework of analysis by extending it to films of a broader range of genres in the canon of European and American cinemas. The Eastern approach then is a wider application of Eastern theory on the greater field of Western cinema, inclusive of both popular films as well as more esoteric art cinema, and of old classic films as well as recent productions.

Chapters

The focus mainly on classic films is deliberate because of my predilection for older films made by favorite "auteur" directors. In this enterprise, I have chosen the classics to show the Eastern has long been present in Western films, and the various auteurs have more or less consciously evoked Eastern themes and concepts. While I am offering the approach as a new application of theory, the presence of Eastern influences and elements in Western films is not a new phenomenon. I begin with the Star Wars Saga, which crosses both the "classical" and contemporary eras (its first episode was released in 1977 and the series is still ongoing) and it is generally recognized by fans and critics as a storehouse of Eastern philosophical influences, advancing tenets of Daoism, Buddhism, and Confucianism. At the same time, the films feature Eastern-like settings, costumes, and characters. It also invokes Eastern genres such as the Japanese *jidaigeki* and Chinese *wuxia*. The theme of the family and its generational conflict between father and son would already justify an Eastern approach. It is the best example in the cinema of the "Oriental West." The chapter lays out the Eastern elements and its philosophical themes that are now familiar as generic conceits of science fiction cinema due to the series' popularity and widespread cult worship.

I move on to Chapter 2 by analyzing Hitchcock's mystery murder thriller *Vertigo* (1958), where Chinese motifs, colors, and philosophical themes are transparent and some of which are referred to in the dialogue. Yet the vast literature on Hitchcock (or on the film) does not discuss these Chinese elements in any depth, therefore not really acknowledging their presence and role in determining the content as well as the imagery of the film. The chapter brings out the details and analyzes precisely the role of these Eastern parts and components, which feature as motifs in the layers of the narrative and as ethical and philosophical factors in the characterizations of both protagonists Scottie (James Stewart) and Madeleine (Kim Novak). Once again, *Vertigo* is an example of the "Oriental West," or even, an exemplary model of its time (and of all time) due to the sophisticated way in which the Oriental motifs, colors, and themes are embedded in the narrative and personified in the characters by Hitchcock.

Chapter 3 focuses on *The Lady from Shanghai* (1947) by Orson Welles, which bears a resemblance to Hitchcock's *Vertigo* through its Chinese references that are inscribed in the dialogue and in the story. Welles's film is thriller-like in the film noir manner with a memorable femme fatale characterization by Rita Hayworth in the title role. The "lady from Shanghai" is a walking symbol of the "Oriental West" and thus the Orient is conspicuously present in the film, with a theme that the East is corrupted by the West. That the lady from Shanghai appears so completely Western in her guise is the central Eastern mystery which I unravel in the chapter. It helps that Welles himself is thoroughly conversant with Eastern philosophy, part of his infatuation with the mysterious East, and that he therefore relies not just on Western thought and dramatic structures to construct his thriller but also on Eastern culture (note, for example, his use of Chinese opera in a crucial moment) and beliefs. Despite being recut by the studio, Columbia Pictures, the film's Eastern quality and theme comes through in an innovative, refreshing style.

Jean-Pierre Melville's sublime action film *Le Samouraï* (1967) is the topic of Chapter 4, the first of a focus on European art cinema in the book (the chapters following will deal with Robert Bresson's *Au hasard Balthazar* and Carl Dreyer's *Vampyr*). The title of Melville's film already reveals what is Eastern in the film, and in the character Jef, but this has been hardly touched upon in the literature, hence the necessity of a more incisive Eastern approach in analyzing the film here. Melville's style, which contains an abstract element of Eastern spirit, in fact incorporates Eastern concepts of heroism and action, which has in turn been influential on Asian directors (such as John Woo and Johnnie To). Melville reinterprets the traditional Japanese samurai figure as a Western persona in the guise of the taciturn professional assassin-hero played by Alain Delon who effectively functions as the walking Eastern symbol of the film, much like the lead character in Welles's *Lady from Shanghai*. I analyze the character's unmistakable Eastern characteristics (formed by Daoism and Zen) and denote how Melville also reinforces his Eastern dimension.

Chapter 5 seizes on Bresson's *Au hasard Balthazar* (1966) as a far from obvious Western model of a film that can be interpreted in an Eastern way.

On the surface, there is nothing about it to suggest any connection with Eastern philosophy. Yet, it lends itself quite readily to a Daoist reading, as I will show, and it therefore comes across in fact as a rather typical European art film full of Eastern characteristics and meaning. It can be said to be the most Daoist of Western films through its employment of materialistic objects and emblems. The film's uniqueness rests on it being a French manifestation of Daoist thinking, based on Zhuang Zi, using animal and human models to achieve Daoist transcendence. Bresson's distinctive, singular style has always seemed to be misunderstood when commented on by Western critics. I analyze his filmmaking style as one that converges with Daoist Eastern essence of nonaction and quietude despite his seemingly entrenched French background and roots in European culture.

Chapter 6 offers an Eastern revisionist reading of Carl Dreyer's majestic horror film *Vampyr* (1933). Like Bresson, Dreyer is quintessentially European, but this is deceptive. I point out the Eastern roots that underpin his vampire narrative. The vampire hunter of his tale is exposed as a Daoist itinerant and his journey west is a journey into the underworld of the dead, a quest of Daoist transcendence. Dreyer employs several Eastern motifs, such as the spectacular dance of shadows seen on a wall in the vampire lair and various symbols scattered throughout the film, which are explicated in the chapter. The film's conceptual bearings are inevitably more Eastern than Western when most Western commentators think of it as difficult to follow. The film also shows certain "Oriental West" criteria due to its grounding in psychology so evocative of Jung, whose influence on the film is implicit and whose debt to Eastern philosophy is inherently entrenched in the film's very structure.

Chapter 7 switches back to Hollywood cinema with an analysis of Sam Peckinpah's Westerns. The chapter demonstrates Peckinpah's evocations of Eastern philosophy, as for example, the Daoist "straw dogs" principle, as well as other motifs found in heroic literature and films of the East, to shore up his unique brand of Western violence and chivalric manner. Elegiac moments in his Westerns are also analyzed as Chan (Zen) poetic conceits. The Westerns of Peckinpah are transformative models of East and West, challenging and revising conventions within the Hollywood Western form through his adaptation of heroic-chivalric motifs from Eastern convention. As such, his Westerns are the most expressive models of mutual East-West reciprocity in the cinema of the West. There seems no doubt to this writer that Peckinpah actively invokes Eastern philosophical ideas to augment his worldview in the Western genre form, but they are not as apparent because the form belies the substance, thus making it all the more necessary to elucidate what is Eastern in the Western.

Leo McCarey's 1937 masterpiece *Make Way for Tomorrow* is the topic of Chapter 8. The film is truly exceptional as an example of a Confucian lesson on family, parent-child relationships, and filial piety produced by the old Hollywood studio system and directed by McCarey who is in many ways the extreme opposite of a Confucian moral instructor. A conservative Catholic and better known as a director of slapstick and screwball comedies, McCarey directs the film sensitively as a tragic melodrama. He etches out the themes of filial responsibility and the problem of the aged and makes a pitch for caring for and respecting the old. As a result, this is a very Confucian work in a very American social context, reflecting age-old Confucian obsessions about filial piety and reverence of old people. McCarey elicits brilliant performances from his actors playing the aged parents and their children, therein perfectly illustrating the Confucian essence of family and filial piety.

Finally, Chapter 9 explores the films of John Ford with a stress on the family (*The Grapes of Wrath*, *How Green Was My Valley*, *The Quiet Man*). Ford is analyzed as a director with deep convictions about family and sympathy for society's underdogs. This strain of his work can be regarded in Eastern terms as respect for family values and a natural sympathy for the Other. The chapter complements my other writings on Ford where I focus on his Westerns (in my previous book, *Eastern Westerns*). Ford's Asian values, which are seen in his Westerns, are even more evident in his non-Westerns about the family and these films are taken up for closer inspection in this last chapter. As such, while I end this book with Ford, I also pick up from where I left on Ford in my last book. Ford's work is prolific and traverses a wide range of genres, which are all open for more interpretations under our Eastern approach.

Indeed, the task here of viewing the films of the West from an Eastern perspective is unfinished because many works by the directors assessed in this book are still open to further evaluations and I have had no opportunity to explore them in any depth (just to cite a few examples: Dreyer's *Michael* and *The Passion of Joan of Arc*, Bresson's *Lancelot du Lac*, Welles's *Chimes at Midnight* and *The Immortal Story*). Thus, the Eastern approach of this book represents a preliminary stage of application, and there is still much left to explore. Indeed, I may discuss more films in future books encompassing the works of other auteur directors in the canon of Western cinema. In the conclusion, I raise questions of how the Eastern approach may develop into the next stage and what its prospects may entail in the current state of unbalance in film studies. Ultimately, the idea of an Eastern approach must involve its own negation in the sense of the Daoist concept of *wu*, or nonbeing, but only when balance has become nonessential. The Eastern interpenetrates into all approaches and is so integrated and assimilated that it melts into nonbeing, implying no necessity for its identification. We may consider this as the final essence of the Buddhist doctrine of "All in One and One in All."

One final word about the chapters. A criticism may be made about my choices of all male directors and that there is an overwhelming whiff of masculinity emanating from my focus on "masculine genres" (action, the Western, film noir, the thriller, horror). Such criticism is misplaced. I deal as much with women and femininity in my analysis and readings, as in the chapters on *Vertigo* (where I also touch on gender identity), *The Lady from Shanghai*, *Au hasard Balthazar*, *Make Way for Tomorrow*, and Ford's family films. Some of the genres in question such as film noir, the thriller, and horror are not just male genres, they are bisexual. In any case, my Eastern understanding of genres does not emphasize any proclivity toward any particular genre nor does it limit my choice of genres due to predetermined questions of gender equality or group identity. It is outside the scope of this book to give a Weberian-style critical judgment about aspects of Eastern philosophy when they are perceived to run against modern Western liberal values. I do not put on shackles in using my "Eastern approach" and it would be absurd to expect that I would do so. With this approach, I enter into a contract with the reader to discover its applicability and suitability to the material, and above all, its potentialities and capabilities for broadening understanding. Eastern philosophy contains its own vastness of thought and diversity, and there are both good and bad things which might need a sense of periodicity and an objective view of history to fully comprehend. It is hoped that the reader will abide by a sense of being just and even in judging the material of this book.

Notes

1. The *Guigu Zi* is generally considered to be a work about the art of persuasion or rhetoric. The term *xiangbi* comes from chapter 2, "Fanying" ("Reactions" or "Responses"): "Language has semblance (*xiang*), and actions have comparisons (*bi*), and thus we see what comes from one's words and actions. Semblance means a likeness to a thing, and comparisons is the equivalence of words. From that which is shapeless, we seek to give voice to our words" (my translation). While the extract quoted may point more to an oral tradition of persuasion, I am captivated by the word *xiang*, which can also mean image. Obviously, I employ the notion of *xiangbi* in relation to moving images which is like a language and how we may read these images from Western films like words that could function as an analogue to certain precepts of Eastern thought. The Chinese text of the *Guigu Zi* may be accessed online: see https://ctext.org/gui-gu-zi/zhs.
2. I borrow the term "proximate" from Alexander Zahlten in his study of film in Japan that has undergone tremendous transformations "in the systemics and experiences of the film and media ecology" from the 1960s onwards. Zahlten speaks of a form of reading films and genres "that is not fully close nor distant but that we might instead call proximate." See Alexander Zahlten, *The End of Japanese Cinema: Industrial Genres, National Times, and Media Ecologies* (Durham, NC and London: Duke University Press, 2017), p. 2.
3. Stephen Teo, *Eastern Westerns: Genre Inside and Outside Hollywood* (London and New York: Routledge, 2017).
4. See J. Jeffery Franklin, *Spirit Matters: Occult Beliefs, Alternative Religions, and the Crisis of Faith in Victorian Britain* (Ithaca, NY and London: Cornell University Press, 2018), p. 86.
5. Homi K. Bhabha, *The Location of Culture* (London and New York: Routledge, 1994), p. 6.
6. Kuan-Hsing Chen, *Asia as Method, Toward Deimperialization* (Durham, NC and London: Duke University Press, 2010), p. 4.
7. Ibid., pp. 3–4.
8. Ibid., p. 2.
9. Arif Dirlik, "Chinese History and the Question of Orientalism," *History and Theory*, 35 (4), 1996, p. 108.
10. Victor H. Mair, *Wandering on the Way: Early Taoist Tales and Parables of Chuang Tzu* (Honolulu: University of Hawai'i Press, 1994), p. 155. I will rely on Mair's

excellent translation of the *Zhuang Zi* for my other quotations deriving from this Daoist text in the rest of this volume.
11 Arif Dirlik, "Chinese History and the Question of Orientalism," p. 101.
12 See John M. Hobson, *The Eastern Origins of Western Civilisation* (Cambridge: Cambridge University Press, 2004), p. 2.
13 Ibid.
14 Victor Fan, *Cinema Approaching Reality: Locating Chinese Film Theory* (Minneapolis and London: University of Minnesota Press, 2015).

1

Star Wars Eastern Saga

The force is the Dao

This chapter focuses on the Star Wars Saga as the best known template of the incorporation of Eastern elements in the cinemas of the West. It sets the tone of this book in identifying and analyzing the Eastern concepts that are present but not usually perceived or studied in Western films as a matter of course. The basic theme is that the East has been an embedded part of the films of the West but that current film theory and criticism, Eurocentric and narcissistic, has obscured this material. The book intends to bring this material to light through analysis of a series of films by canonical Western directors ultimately to demonstrate an Easternized West in the films of the West. While Eastern motifs, designs, characters, and concepts appear in some films of the West in a transparent fashion, they are not as obvious in others. The Star Wars Saga is the most transparent example of the "Oriental West" in the contemporary Western cinema. The Saga refers to a franchise produced in Hollywood that is the most popular and financially successful of Western cinematic narratives told and constructed in a serial fashion over the past forty years. At the time of writing, it consists of the official eight films thus far released, including the original trilogy, a prequel trilogy, and the first and second episodes of a sequel trilogy (another film, a spin-off from the Saga, has also been released).[1]

The Star Wars Saga is representative of the fundamental integration of Eastern elements and archetypes in Western narratives. This is not a new discovery, and the current literature on Star Wars both online and in print reveals that this basic truth is widely recognized. Many writers and scholars have attested to the Saga's evocation and use of Eastern philosophy, elements, and characteristics, and some have decried them as Orientalist.

I will address this Orientalist tendency in greater length below while acknowledging a serious attempt by Hollywood filmmakers at an East-West synthesis of character, story, and concepts. The Orientalism, after all, is in time-honored Hollywood tradition. One of the most predictable influences on the Saga was the serial *Flash Gordon*, popular in the 1930s, which featured the Oriental Emperor Ming as the space villain who seeks to destroy Earth, saved invariably by the Occidental hero.[2] Mainly, however, I will consider the significance of the "Eastern" in three ways. First, as a notion distinctive from "Orientalism," which is, to take a cue from John Hobson, a concept that is interchangeable with Eurocentrism;[3] second, as an inherent quality in the West—what Hobson calls the "Oriental West"—and I will cover this in more detail in the next section; and third, the didactic dimension of the Eastern. There is a lot of moral teaching in the Saga, as its primary creator George Lucas has confessed: "I wanted it to be a traditional moral study, to have some sort of palpable precepts in it that children could understand."[4] Many of the precepts are reminiscent of the pithy teachings found in ancient Chinese texts, such as those attributed to Confucius, Lao Zi, and Zhuang Zi. The Force is one such precept, now regarded as generic to the whole mythical-religious structure of the Star Wars Saga, and it has become the single most identifiable concept of the whole franchise. Its "high concept" definition is "a cosmic energy source that incorporates and consumes all living things."[5] Sounding abstract and accessible at the same time, one could regard it as prototypical of 1970s' American New Age esotericism arising out of the imagination of George Lucas. However, I will make clear that it springs from Eastern sources of thought that have influenced Lucas.

The Force is suggestive of the Dao, the Eastern philosophy that seems closest to its substance. Kevin J. Wetmore Jr. had earlier stated as much in his article "The Tao of Star Wars, or, Cultural Appropriation in a Galaxy Far, Far, Away," published in 2000. He remarked that "the language the various characters use to describe the Force suggests Taoism."[6] In the recent offshoot of the franchise, *Rogue One* (2016), whenever we hear the refrain "The Force is with me, I am one with the Force," exchanged by two Chinese Jedi knights (played by Donnie Yen and Jiang Wen), it is immediately reminiscent of the Daoist idea of being one with the Dao and that all things come from the Dao. (The fact that it is also uttered by two Chinese knights also heightens the association between the Force and the Dao.) The description of the Force as a "cosmic energy force" is, more specifically, a description of the vital energy contained in the Dao, which is *qi* (literally, breath).[7] Walter Robinson sees the Force largely in terms of its application to the martial arts philosophy of the Jedi knights in which *qi* is a vital energy that sustains one's power as a martial arts warrior. However, Robinson also notes that the Force is "central to the *Star Wars* mythology."[8] It is a complete system of thought which has inspired a new religion, Jediism, described by Markus Altena Davidsen as the "Force religion of the Jedi knights," acquiring a universal "theology, ethics, and spiritual practice."[9] Davidsen questions whether the Force "is monistic or dualistic in nature" even if it is "usually presented as dualistic, with both a light side (Ashla) and a dark side (Bogan)."[10] The dualism of the dark and light sides suggests the Daoist origins of the Force with its yin (or dark side) and yang (or light side) conjoined into a circle.[11] Davidsen recognizes influences from "Christianity and Westernized Buddhism and Taoism."[12] From our perspective, the Force is much more akin to the Dao. Both are ethereal in nature, but the Force is only a kind of Dao, of course, transmuted by the space-frontier environment and narrative contexts of the whole Saga.

Lucas has admitted to the influence of Carlos Castaneda's stories in the "Don Juan" books, *The Teachings of Don Juan: A Yaqui Way of Knowledge*, published in 1968, followed by two sequels, and a further book, *Tales of Power*, published in 1975.[13] In *Tales of Power*, the narrator experiences a "life force" summoned into him through the knowledge of the Indian shaman, Don Juan, who also speaks of "the warrior's freedom." Castaneda's Don Juan is reminiscent of the Daoist warrior. The tales of the book are like Zhuang Zi's instructions for his disciples to follow the natural force of the Dao (the Way), as written in the *Zhuang Zi* (partly attributed to the master himself but mostly written by his followers). Through Castaneda, the Dao has seeped into the Star Wars Saga. The Indian sorcerer, Don Juan (the Zhuang Zi-like figure), is the main influence on the character of Obi-Wan Kenobi and his relationship with Luke Skywalker. Obi-Wan Kenobi is the Daoist warrior cognizant of the arcane ways of the Dao (Force) and stresses that what matters to a warrior "is arriving at the totality of oneself," achieving this by immersing oneself with the Dao/Force.[14] We may say that the Force is Lucas's Western methodology of "knowing" the Dao, concretizing the Dao as an "energy field created by all living things that binds the universe together," and when the Jedi knights tap into this field of energy it gives them "the status of magician/warriors."[15]

It is generally acknowledged that the Star Wars Saga draws on ancient Eastern traditions of moral, spiritual, and lifestyle teaching. This is not to suggest that the Saga is interested in proselytizing any particular Eastern religion, although it might have inadvertently promoted its own religion of Jediism out of its syncretization of Eastern religions. As Dale Pollock tells us, Star Wars is "a metaphor for the tenets of Christianity, Buddhism, Judaism, and Islam."[16] We can now add Daoism to the mix, as many writers have already denoted a greater influence of the teachings of the Dao on the Saga.[17] That all these religions stem from the East is justification enough for our identification of the whole series as an Eastern Saga although some may argue that its Eastern ideology is nothing more than shallow Orientalism. The Saga is also a modern myth and fairy tale based in outer space which is expressive of an advanced Western technological society. Its surface features and many of its characters are "Western." As the architect and scholar David Beynon explains, "The surface of a thing contributes to, if not helps to determine, its content."[18] The surface of the Saga is innately Western, and its mythical trappings suggest a completely Western tradition of classical myth and epic poetry. In an essay entitled "*The Return of the Jedi*: Epic Graffiti," published in 1987, Todd H. Sammons analyses the application of the European epic poetic mode to Episode VI of the Saga, *The Return of the Jedi*, and we may extrapolate from this the essentialist relevance of European epics to the entire legend as it now stands. Sammons tells us that "every single scene in *Jedi* has an analogue in the European epic tradition," and he gives an impressive list of epics that have influenced the film, including Homer's *Odyssey*, Virgil's *Aeneid*, *Beowulf*, Dante's *Divine Comedy*, Ariosto's *Orlando Furioso*, Tasso's *Gerusalemme liberata*, Spenser's *The Færie Queene*, and Milton's *Paradise Lost*.[19]

Sammons goes on to demonstrate how the characters and events in the film relate analogously to these epics, but there is a deceptive layer to the allusions of all these seemingly Western poetic myths. Sammons also demonstrates how Lucas has transformed them. Lucas was making a science fiction adventure series wherein the scientific and futuristic conceits would demand a New Age if not postmodern approach to the material (the European epics would otherwise be just too medieval to be accessible). Sammons describes

Lucas's approach as "epic graffiti" in that he utilizes "epic analogues in *Jedi* the same way he uses songs in *American Graffiti*."[20] This is Lucas's own cinematic form of transformational grammar, which gives rise to a surface structure of the medieval European epics. It has resulted in a film that Sammons dubs "*epic manqué*," "the 'epic' tone guaranteed by the pastiche of epic motifs."[21] In a sense, the European tradition remains largely suppressed by this approach. Undoubtedly, the approach is highly eclectic and leads not just to the Saga's incorporation of European epics but also Eastern elements, which give it a more prominent Eastern visage. In fact, the Saga looks so very much like Orientalist art in its costumes, in its settings, and in many of the characterizations (including the use of nonhuman characters) that the Western surface is effectively effaced. This is ironic if we put ourselves into Sammons's perspective, which is a Eurocentric view of the Star Wars films, but the point to make here is that Orientalist motifs already infuse the European epic tradition that Sammons cites, perhaps notoriously exemplified by Dante, although Virgil, Ariosto, Tasso, Spenser, and Milton are all implicated. (It is beyond the scope of this chapter to review the Orientalism implicitly or explicitly present in all these works.)

Orientalism and Oriental West

The Orientalism in the classics mentioned by Sammons implies that the epic tradition that Lucas is transposing into "cinematic epic" is intrinsically European.[22] Sammons, however, does not acknowledge the Orientalism that is integrally part of this European tradition. He questions whether a film like *Jedi* is truly epic from the point of view of the European tradition. What is then the real significance of the European tradition? To Sammons, it seems to justify Lucas's epic graffiti method, European epic poems being the only one among other traditions that Lucas draws upon (the others are Westerns, war movies, and Freudian fables). The epics would suggest a "retrograde movement," a tendency in science fiction when conceiving the future and thinking "beyond [one's] horizon," as the director Paul Verhoeven has commented.[23] Such retrogressive creativity reveals a European essentialism underpinning the Saga, though Sammons does not say as much. His questioning whether *Jedi* is a true epic does not belie its evocation of the European epics as an essentialist marker of epic form and cultural identity (epics in other cultures have the same function). From our perspective, the European epic tradition affords Lucas a resource from which to draw on its Orientalism. One might say that Lucas naturally shares a greater affinity with the European tradition and that the Orientalism of the Star Wars films is very European in outlook. (His penchant to cast British actors in the more Orientalized roles is such an indication.) As such, the Western features display the European essentialism of the Saga and denote what is essentialist about its narratives.

How should we then view the Orientalism of the Saga? There is no doubt that Orientalism is an ingrained component in the Saga's structure and that it is reflective of a Eurocentric tradition. It would be easy to criticize and dismiss it for being a shallow if not a deficient expression of Eastern beliefs and conventions. However, there are many Orientalisms (middle-Eastern, far-Eastern, anti-Islamic, "Yellow Peril," etc.), and all embrace both negative and positive inflections. There are multiple ways of understanding Orientalism, not to mention its multiple facets on display in the Star Wars films, such that it is imperative to grasp their implications for considering how Orientalism ultimately turns the Saga into a legitimate Eastern epic.

Lucas's graffiti method presupposes a diverse world and imposes a unifying outlook on diversity, integrating the East with the West, or muddying them in his outer space melting pot. There are no absolute opposites, and East and West are fundamentally similar. We can take this in a Daoist sense. As stated in the *Zhuang Zi*, chapter 2, "On the Equality of Things," "Heaven and earth were born together with me and the myriad things are one with me."[24] As the creator of the Saga, George Lucas operates on this principle. In another passage from the same chapter it is stated, "'this' is also 'that'; 'that' is also 'this.'" "Where 'this' and 'that' cease to be opposites, there lies the pivot of the Way."[25] It would be true to say that Lucas's graffiti approach is that pivot where East and West cease to be opposites. From the Daoist point of view, Lucas's approach conforms to the natural "Way," a holistic outlook and manner of living. However, whether Lucas's graffiti methodology delivers more than meets the eye may be another matter. This methodology is not without its critics. For example, Sammons has commented that the intellectual content of *Jedi* is "thin, despite all the 'philosophy' about the Force, and destiny, and choice."[26] Michael Pye and

Linda Myles, writing about the first Star Wars film (Episode IV), refer to the "vague pantheism" of the Force as not very coherent.[27]

> *Star Wars* talks much of the Force, a field of energy that permeates the universe and can be used for good and evil. It is passed on, with a sword, just as the sword Excalibur is passed on in Arthurian romance; the influence of chivalric stories is strong. But when the Force is used by Luke Skywalker to help him destroy the monstrous Death Star, he is urged only to relax, to obey instincts, to close his eyes and fight by feeling. The Force amounts to building a theology out of staying cool.[28]

This initial criticism may not hold any longer for the Saga as it now stands. The "vague pantheism" of the Force in Episode IV may now have developed into a more systematic ideology pervading the Saga in its present entirety, and much of its coherence, I would argue, comes from the association between the Force and the Dao. The second film in the series, *The Empire Strikes Back*, already spouts much mystical wisdom from the mouth of Yoda, a character that might have come out of the *Zhuang Zi* (as I will later demonstrate), and Luke Skywalker's conflict with Darth Vader manifested far darker elements antithetical to "building a theology out of staying cool." *The Return of the Jedi* consolidates the theology of the Force by restoring "balance back to the Force," as Walter Robinson notes: Anakin Skywalker shedding off his Darth Vader mask and therefore reverting to the side of light.[29] By appearing first in sequence of release, the middle trilogy actually sets the tone for the whole Saga primarily from its relative intermixing of the dark and light sides, a concept inherent in Daoist cosmology, interpreted through the conflict between Luke Skywalker and Darth Vader, the dark side of the Jedi knight Anakin Skywalker. This would then be the nub of the series' Orientalism, which we can now grasp more positively as a central orientation of ideological substance in the idea of the Force. Indeed, the middle trilogy is the kernel of the Force, the three films together forming the tabernacle of its new religion, Jediism.

The charge of "vague pantheism" certainly hints at the first film's Orientalism now pervading through the whole series. As Abigail De Kosnik informs us, the series' "use of Orientalism actually began in its first installation," but De Kosnik mostly analyzes the Orientalism as a contextual lens mirroring the political landscape rather than the spiritual mood of the time—the film contains "a legion of Orientalist and techno-Orientalist references that address, in coded ways, the crises of its time."[30] I cite De Kosnik in order to bring up another variant of Orientalism, namely Techno-Orientalism, which I will expand on later, but as to the Orientalist references, De Kosnik sees unambiguous allusions to the Vietnam War. Originally released in 1977, two years after the end of the Vietnam War, the first installment of the Saga reflected the war as a space allegory, detailing "a clash of two war strategies and two uses of military technology" in which the Rebellion (North Vietnam) defeated the overwhelming might of the Empire (the United States).[31] According to Wetmore Jr., "Lucas's Asian appropriations suggest an East/West binary in which the Empire is Western and the rebellion is Eastern."[32] Wetmore Jr. therefore pushes the allegory even further, taking in the whole Third World. "A colonial discourse is apparent," he writes, in which the postcolonial theories of Frantz Fanon are placed "in outer space," thus adding the Jedi struggle against the Empire "to Fanon's Algerian insurrection, to the Mau Mau war of Kenya, to the Boxer Rebellion of China, and to dozens of other armed uprisings against politically, militarily, and economically dominant empires."[33] Stephen McVeigh gives supporting analysis of the middle trilogy as Vietnam War allegory and sees the prequel trilogy as another different allegory—of America's wars under new circumstances and conditions, namely the Global War on Terror (centered in Afghanistan and Iraq).[34] Such allegorical aspects of Orientalism with their politically charged motivations ascribed to Lucas must be set off against the perceived Fascist undertone felt in the first film, which resulted in the "critical confusion" of many critics, according to Pye and Myles. The fascism was implicit from the "images that parallel the finest documentary of Nazism, Leni Riefenstahl's *Triumph of the Will*."[35] These images of "geometrically massed people," in the words of Robert Kolker, are of the Rebellion celebrating their victory over the Empire.[36] The allusions to Nazism are "both good and bad": the Rebellion celebrates their victory in Nazi fashion and the Empire is obviously a wicked Nazi-like organization, with Darth Vader's storm troopers "armored in white" and Darth Vader himself in black.[37]

Might Lucas have overreached himself in his graffiti method by drawing generically on cinematic influences as well as influences from literary sources? Obviously, Lucas takes a rather polyglot view of all his influences such that he conflates Orientalism, Colonialism, and Nazism in his heterogeneous conception of Star Wars as space opera and *bildungsroman*. The point of

Lucas's approach, as Jonathan Rosenbaum has insightfully submitted, "is to make all the myths it plunders equally trivial and 'usable' as nostalgic plot fodder, even if most of the emotions are absent."[38] Accordingly, Lucas draws on nostalgic serials to make dispassionate use of archetypes. They are all "equally trivial and 'usable.'" As with the Nazi archetypes, the Orientalist models are "both good and bad." Noble Jedi knights, played by European actors, jostle for screen time with the treacherous Neimoidians, an alien space race of humanoids who "speak slow, broken English with slurred accents, suggesting Asian—specifically Japanese—speakers" recalling the Japanese stereotypes in the Second World War movies.[39] Rosenbaum speaks of a "knowing mindlessness" in Lucas's "shrewd" use of "racial ideology," alluding to "the styling of the Jawas as stingy Jewish merchants," while the Orientalist types seem not to exude "any sort of embarrassment."[40] This is because Orientalist pigeonholes have long been structural manifestations of Hollywood science fiction (the Emperor Ming in *Flash Gordon* is its central icon). They are certainly fair game for Lucas in his graffiti approach. The Orientalism of Star Wars certainly reflects "racial ideology" in East-West fashion. There is more to this racialism, as I will later show, in Lucas's treatment of the dramatis personae throughout his space saga since his racial types run a gamut and include not just humans but space aliens, animals, and robots. More interesting to us is the way in which Western actors and their physiognomic features embody and epitomize Orientalist archetypes. Rather than being entirely negative Orientalist stereotypes, I submit that they form the spectacle of the "Oriental West": the view that the West has already absorbed the Orient into its arts and sciences and physically embodied the Orient in all but the face.

Proposed by John Hobson, the theory of the "Oriental West" is meant at "countering the Eurocentric myth of the pristine West," as it is put in the title of the first chapter of his book, *The Eastern Origins of Western Civilisation*, published in 2004. In this view, "Eastern resource portfolios had a significant influence in each of the major European turning points," referring to the European medieval agricultural revolution after 600 CE, and after 1000,

> the major technologies, ideas and institutions that stimulated the various Western commercial, production, financial, military and navigational revolutions, as well as the Renaissance and the scientific revolution, were first developed in the East but later assimilated by the Europeans. After

1700, the major technologies and technological ideas that spurred on the British agricultural and industrial revolutions all diffused across from China. Moreover, Chinese ideas also helped stimulate the European enlightenment. And it is precisely because the East and the West have been linked together in a single global cobweb ever since 500 that we need to dispense with the Eurocentric assumption that these two entities can be represented as entirely separate and antithetical.[41]

Hobson has advanced the theory to undermine "the Eurocentric notion of the triumphant West that lies, either latently or explicitly, at the heart of the mainstream accounts of the rise of the West."[42] I have applied the notion of the "Oriental West" to the Saga for a close reading of its Orientalism, which is multileveled and multifaceted. It is far more intricate and complex than the Orientalism of, say, *Flash Gordon*. A close reading is necessary to rediscover the Eastern roots of the Saga that suggests how Western films are fundamentally reinvocations and reinterpretations of Eastern thought. Thus, with the notion of the Oriental West to reorientate our understanding of the Saga, the European (British) actors playing Oriental roles represent the Western assimilation of Eastern character types. First and foremost, there are the Jedi knights, whose character profiles and names like Obi-Wan Kenobi and Qui-Gon Jinn are recognizably Eastern. The "Jedi" name derives from the Japanese *jidaigeki*, per Walter Robinson, the term referring to historical period dramas, including those that feature samurai action.[43] One of the seminal influences on Lucas "right from the very beginning" when he was writing the treatment of the first Star Wars film was Akira Kurosawa's *jidaigeki* classic *The Hidden Fortress* (1958).[44] *Jidai*, which comes from the Chinese *shidai*, means, literally, the time of the ages, a notion well captured by Kurosawa's film, which is more like a fairy tale. This is contrasted with *xiandai* (in Japanese, *gendai*), which means the time of the present. In a sense, timeless Eastern philosophy and values, not just those of the Dao but also Confucianism, Buddhism, and Zen, are predetermined as the driving vital elements of the Force.

Yoda, another Eastern-sounding name, is the abiding pedagogue of the Eastern core wisdom infusing the Saga. His appearance and countenance (long-pointed ears, elf-like droopy eyes, and a face that looks isometrically flat from ear to ear with only impressions of depth in a high forehead, bulging eyes, and protruding lips) raises the issue of identity, one based on a nonhuman conception of the world. His small size and unusual face suggest a certain physical deformity that makes him cute, like a panda or a Pokémon. Thus, he may be a product that arises out of the culture of cuteness in the East (Chinese *keai*, Japanese *kawaii*), and as such, his physique represents a "creepy juxtaposition of cheerily bland flatness and bodily deformity in cute characters."[45] We might see this as a tradition from the *Zhuang Zi*, a great resource to inspire nonhuman forms that spout sagely wisdom. In the *Zhuang Zi*, there are characters with names like "Old Longears," "Old Master Chenopod," "Gnaw Gap," "Master Rushcoat," "Skyroot," "Boreal Wind," "Longbrand Redwand," and "Spidersight," to use Victor Mair's superb transliterations in his translation of the *Zhuang Zi*.[46] These characters or representations suggest deformity or mutilation to destroy the illusion of an objectified self. Thus, "Zhuangzi's praise of mutilated persons," Eske Møllgaard writes, "and his valuation of the incomplete over the complete are aimed at undermining [one's] identification with the whole body (*shen*), or the objectified self inscribed in the realm of man (*ren*)."[47] One can perceive the same aim in the Saga, evident in the representations of many secondary characters. Yoda is one such representation, a makeover of some of the characters mentioned in the *Zhuang Zi*, like Old Longears and Old Master Chenopod, transformations of Lao Zi, which makes Yoda probably the first prototype of the philosopher in the films of the West. Yoda is a metaphor of transformation. A parable in the *Zhuang Zi*, chapter 6, instructs us to prepare for transformation (Figure 1.1).

> Now, the Great Smelter casts his metal. If the metal were to jump up and say, "You must make me into Excalibur!" the Great Smelter would certainly think that it was inauspicious metal. Now if I, who have chanced to take on human form, were to say, "Man! I must remain a man!" the Great Transforming Creator would certainly think that I am an inauspicious man. Now, once I accept heaven and earth as the Great Forge, and the Transforming Creator as the Great Smelter, I'm willing to go wherever they send me.[48]

The transformation of things is a theme in Daoism that presupposes a non-anthropomorphic universe and the human form is inconsequential. "Slough off your bodily form" is one of the exclamations of wisdom in the *Zhuang Zi*.[49] "Being embodied is our nature as earth-born creatures," writes John Gray, and more's the pity since it gives rise to our preoccupation with the human

Figure 1.1 Yoda, a metaphor of Daoist transformation.
The Empire Strikes Back, Producer: Gary Kurtz.

form.[50] Crucially, the Star Wars Saga has shed off this preoccupation in its many representations of alien or subhuman characters even though, one could argue, it is actually half-hearted in such representations by making them, ultimately, anthropomorphic-friendly. Yoda is one such model, but we should consider him an incomplete model, only a surface representation of the non-anthropomorphic being. He goes beyond racial typing although he still suggests an Eastern type in nature and philosophy. Yoda is a unique transformation, an East-West synthesis of a character that emerges out of the minds of Western filmmakers and storytellers. Thus, he is an East-West "transformation" in the spirit of the Oriental West but he is yet a Hollywood-fabricated character with unmistakable Orientalist proclivities (his antediluvian character and speech, his grotesque alien-ness of look, a squat, misshapen physique, his inscrutability).

Techno-orientalism and spiritualism as technology

At this stage, we should briefly reconsider whether the Oriental West is fully applicable to how we understand the Saga's Orientalism. Yoda is a test case of the Oriental West. Is he truly an Eastern resource? Or is he an odious product of an Orientalist mind? How does he express Eastern wisdom and how does the West assimilate this wisdom? Such questions may reflect the ongoing ambiguity of the East-West interconnectivity of modern globalization and suggest a skepticism of the Oriental West due to the overpowering Eurocentrism that still pertains in the present time. The main hurdle of the Oriental West, as we might see it here, is its readjustment of modernism, or its pre-Colonial temporalization of the West's historical development. Modernism, identified with the rise of the West, locates Orientalism as one of its classical enterprises, which rests on the historical colonization of the East by the West. In the post-colonialist age, the West's strength, its superiority, lies in its tremendous advantage of technological and military might. We might draw on this fact to postulate a standpoint of the "Technological West" countering the idea of the Oriental West—that the West has driven technological progress and the East has copied and absorbed all that the West has offered in the field of science and technology in the modern era. The Technological West is the foundation of the Star Wars Saga, its Orientalism being an outflow of this reality.

The Oriental West as applied to the Saga raises an interesting problem in timeline and its synchronization with technology. The chronology of the Saga itself is inverted, a postmodern collapse of primitivism, modernism, and futurism into one millennial era that can go on for tens of thousands of years (the war between the Empire and the Rebellion is really to dominate time as well as space). Its stories transpire "a long time ago in a galaxy far, far away," which would seem to suggest the past (*jidai* time, synchronous with the Jedi knights and their use of swords as light sabres). However, the science fiction materialization of technological prowess in the form of space ships, robots, gadgets, holograms, laser guns, and other scientific thingamajigs suggests the modern and the future. How does the time factor of the Saga's narratives match up with the Oriental West timeline? The Oriental West, as Hobson sees it, is a notion based on Eastern cultural, technological, and scientific advancement—an Eastern modernism achieved during an earlier age, which thence stimulates the West into its own historic turning points. The stories in the Saga preconceive a West not just technologically advanced but triumphant above the East and everyone else. As such, the Saga seems to push the temporal zone of the Oriental West well into the future thus displacing its logic. There is a necessity to reconcile the "modern" era of the East according to the Oriental West proposition and the "postmodern" *tempores* of the Saga in our analysis of how the Saga has assimilated the Orient. What are the terms and conditions of this assimilation? In considering the move of modernism into postmodernism, Rey Chow has spoken of the West's "increasing technologizing of culture" in its process of modernization, referring to photography and film as her example.[51] The perfection of such technologies turns the visual into "a kind of dominant discourse of modernity" which "reveals epistemological problems that are inherent in social relations and their reproduction"; and Chow emphasizes that such problems "inform the very ways social difference...is constructed."[52] Here, we may return to the Eurocentric foundations of modernity reflected through the technology of the visual, and for Chow, the displacement of the modern into postmodernism must be addressed with such foundations in mind. As such, Eurocentrism poses the intractable problem of epistemology over modernism (Figure 1.2).

The Star Wars Saga is exemplary of this Eurocentric "visual modern," if I may call it that, and it would be to our interests to ponder over how the Saga constructs the "social difference" of the East and the West. Does the Oriental West play a role in the Saga's interpretation of this social difference, where the stakes are quite high over the visual modern—the technologization of culture? In truth, the Saga has projected a Techno-Orientalist outlook from its science fiction premise of technologization—Orientalism being fashioned by and interacting with the high technological accessories and sci-fi special effects showing a modern West overpoweringly strong in science and technology. Techno-Orientalism does not necessarily override the concept of the Oriental West, as I will demonstrate shortly, but first, we should briefly consider the underlying contexts of Techno-Orientalism and its relevancy to the Star Wars films. Originally applied to America's phobic perception of Japan as a rising

Figure 1.2 Light sabres, a product of "Techno-Orientalism."
Return of the Jedi, Producer: Howard Kazanjian.

technological power in the 1980s,[53] "Techno-Orientalism" may in fact be an outgrowth of the Vietnam War. In his book, *American Myth and the Legacy of Vietnam*, published in 1986, John Hellmann claims, "America's discomfort with its transformation into a technological society was crucially bound up in its initial dreams and eventual nightmare of Vietnam."[54] The Star Wars films of the middle trilogy were a way of ushering Americans "through a traumatic experience, analogous to Vietnam, toward a reconception of their character and destiny."[55] Techno-Orientalism was really a reactive process aimed at recapturing "the lost landscape of American myth" in the post-Vietnam era.[56] At the same time, it reacted against technological change, which diminished the effect of myths. No doubt, Techno-Orientalism has evolved as the Vietnam War has faded into memory and technology has stamped an ineradicable mark on culture and continues to do so. It has lately been defined as a phenomenon "of the West's project of securing dominance as architects of the future, a project that requires configurations of the East as the very technology with which to shape it."[57] In its emphasis on the future, Techno-Orientalism presents a vision of a more advanced Asia that could threaten America in economics, the military, and cyberspace. Over the years, America's relationship with Asia has grown stronger due to trade and the amazing growth in the economies of big Asian countries, such as China and India. Thus, "Techno-Orientalist speculations of an Asianized future have become ever more prevalent in the wake of neoliberal trade policies that enabled greater flow of information and capital between the East and the West."[58]

Techno-Orientalism, then, reflects the frictions and the fear of America vis-à-vis Asia. There are frictions over trade and geopolitical strategy, and fear that Asia (Japan in the 1980s, China at present) may surpass and replace the United States as the supreme economic power. This is the basic theme of *The Phantom Menace* which reflected "the tenor of late nineties American foreign policy and its concern with globalization," as Stephen McVeigh points out.[59] Uncannily, it is even more resonant today. The trade dispute in the galaxy between the Trade Federation and the planet Naboo can obviously stand as a metaphor of the current state of frictions in American foreign policy, the turn against globalization under President Trump and his initiation of the trade war against China. Thus, the Star Wars films have evolved in their allegorical content representing America's trauma in Vietnam to fear of Asia's rise and losing dominance and influence over the global system of trade. However, if phobia is the key measure of its Techno-Orientalism, there is a sense that the Star Wars films reflect a greater confidence in the technological might of the United States than in its spiritual development. The Orient may be the source of fear if not evil, but it is also the source of much wisdom. Techno-Orientalism also epitomizes Hollywood's greater cultural engagement with Asia—Asia being a huge market for Hollywood blockbusters and their merchandising products. Conversely, while Hollywood may be an instrument of American foreign policy, some have argued that the Star Wars films are more like "expensive *independent movies*."[60] If there is an intent to propagandize American values and foreign policy, the effect is rather neutral. After all, the Empire is a parallel of the United States, equated with technological might—and the Trade Federation's levy of trade routes in *The Phantom Menace* is eerily prophetic of the massive tariffs now levied by the Trump Administration on China and other trading partners of the United States.

One can rewire the Techno-Orientalism of the Star Wars Saga to the temporal currents of the Oriental West theory as far as spiritualism is concerned. In this way, we may grasp the Oriental West concept more appropriately. The East may be technologically backward but far advanced philosophically and spiritually. The West has absorbed the spiritual strength of the East, manifested as generic Orientalism in the Saga. Indeed, the Orientalism powers its theological and spiritual elements, working as a kind of orthodoxy. The light sabre is a symbol of the Oriental West, a weapon developed by the scientifically advanced West out of the Eastern sword. It is the weapon of the Jedi knights, who spout the wisdom of the Force (Dao). Yoda is another symbol, a unique representation of Western assimilation of Eastern wisdom, a pure essence manifested as a "techno-cute" character-object produced out of Western minds. The archetypes of Yoda and the Jedi knights (such as Obi-Wan Kenobi and Qui-Gon Jinn) all fall into "a nostalgic Asian premodernity," a notion raised by Betsy Huang, "that apotheosizes rather than vilifies the Orient through idealized characterizations of ancient Eastern philosophies and texts."[61] Hence, the Eastern past may also be the Eastern future, a fluidity the East expresses through its ineffability and esoteric philosophy. The Daoist *wu* (emptiness) is the void that may project both the past and the future. Time is but a flow of nature and one's relationship with the Dao (the Way), and thus we may understand time as the infinite time of the universe that can sustain the Oriental West's applicability to the whole Saga.

The Daoist void may also find a parallel with space in case one might see a certain incompatibility with the science of space and the Oriental West. Space is the original emptiness from which the "myriad things" (*wan wu*, literally, "ten thousand things") are drawn. The "myriad things" are the thingamajigs of the Star Wars science fiction as well as the aliens, creatures, robots, and the like that populate the galaxy. The planets and all the life-forms in the galaxy are part of "the myriad things." "Nothingness" in Dao is "the source of the origin of existents," and there is a "cosmogonical dimension" in the nothingness of Daoism.[62] Thus, space is not discordant with Chinese philosophy. When applied to the science fiction context of Star Wars, Eastern philosophy in the guise of the Dao fits into the religious schema of the Force, attesting to what John D. Caputo calls the "mystico-scientific power that runs through all things" in the Force and which Caputo recognizes is "rather more Eastern than Judeo-Christian."[63] The scientific theory of Dao is quite explicitly put forward in chapter 23 of the *Zhuang Zi* ("Gengsang Chu") which discusses space and time as an equation of the universe (*yuzhou*, in Chinese), and likens man to the universe. "He goes forth but has no root; he enters but has no opening. He has a kernel of reality, but it is not located in a place; he has duration, but no origin or conclusion."[64] This is a description of the universe as man, or of man as universe. "Having a kernel of reality but not being located in a place is his spatial dimension. Having duration but being without an origin or a conclusion is his temporal dimension."[65] In the original Chinese, the spatial dimension is *yu* and temporal dimension is *zhou*. When enjoined, they make up the universe. Later, the passage refers to the "gate of heaven" where one enters and goes forth without revealing one's form. "The gate of heaven is nonbeing. The myriad things come forth from nonbeing. Being cannot bring being into being; it must come forth from nonbeing, and nonbeing is singularly nonbeing."[66]

Being must come forth from nonbeing. From this, we may see that the Dao represents both ontological and cosmogonical approaches to life, or *sheng*, a central concept in both Daoist and Confucianist metaphysics (*sheng* infers "begetting, generating, giving rise to").[67] The Force emulates both approaches. When characters say "The Force is with me," this implies a cosmogonical source of energy enervating the self, and when they say "I am one with the Force," this implies an ontological condition of living and surviving. The

Jedi knights clearly rely on an admixture of both approaches to sustain their conception of morality (as well as evil) in the universe. In his duel with Darth Vader in Episode IV, Obi-Wan Kenobi deliberately lets his guard down and Darth Vader kills him. In Episode VIII, *The Last Jedi*, Luke Skywalker repeats this same gesture in his duel with Kylo Ren. Obi-Wan's body as well as Luke's literally evaporates into nothingness, leaving behind only their robes and light sabers. The body is extinguished "yet a kernel remains," and under such circumstance, "it is the unity of his ghost," in the words of the *Zhuang Zi*.[68] In death, Obi-Wan Kenobi becomes more powerful than Darth Vader can possibly imagine. "You can't win, Darth," Obi-Wan says, a conviction that comes out of his knowledge that the Force prevails through a balance of light and dark (yin and yang), of existence by enjoining oneself with the cosmos. Darth Vader's darkness unbalances him in his way to the Force (which guarantees his defeat). Obi-Wan's participation in the Rebellion is really a way of fighting to keep the balance and to prevent the dark side/the Sith from upsetting the Force.[69]

The character of Darth Vader has a Daoist ontogenesis. He is the dark side of ex-Jedi knight Anakin Skywalker. As Darth Vader he is clad in dark armor and a dark mechanical mask, which hides his burnt face and body. Not entirely extinguished, Anakin Skywalker has not given up his ghost, so to speak; he is half-dead. There is no kernel and no unity of his ghost. To acquire his ghost, he must acquire death. Because of his past as a Jedi warrior, Darth Vader knows about the power of the Force and is suspicious of the Death Star's power. "Don't be too proud of this technological terror you have constructed. The ability to destroy a planet is insignificant next to the power of the Force," he tells Admiral Motti. Ironically, Darth Vader himself is a "'technological terror', a human reduced to living in a mechanical body," as Wetmore Jr. describes him.[70] Wetmore Jr. analyses him as an Eastern character corrupted by Western ways. "Vader is the philosophy of the East perverted, mechanized, and imprisoned by the West," he writes.[71] Technology subsumes and overcomes his weakness, giving him strength. As such, he is the symbol of the Technological West and its might, but this strength is an illusion since it keeps him on the dark side. Where Daoism emphasizes *qi* (the breath) such that "one must breathe 'correctly' in order to be one with the Tao," Darth Vader breathes through a machine.[72] Luke Skywalker ultimately defeats

Darth Vader, who is his father, through the power of the Force, not through superior strength as such. This is the cosmogonical power of the Force, which ultimately drives the ontological condition.

Darth Vader's weakness is an ontological weakness. He depends on technology to become strong, not the will to be morally strong. Luke Skywalker loses a hand during his first duel with Darth Vader and is thus conferred the father's same sign of weakness (though not sharing the same symptoms). Similarly, technology makes him whole and he is able to function as though he has not lost his hand. Weakness is an Eastern theme deployed to show the cosmogonical, religious sense of the Force, and in this, it mitigates the notion of the Technological West. Technology is the antithesis of the Force in as much as it compromises the cosmogonical purity of the Force. If there is a technology to the Force, it is the power of the will for goodness, which can make one strong even in weakness. The theme of weakness and a correspondence with technology actually has some precedence in the films of the East, particularly martial arts movies. The Hong Kong cinema is especially evocative in this regard. Luke's losing his arm is reminiscent of *The One-Armed Swordsman* (1967), the Shaw Brothers martial arts movie directed by Zhang Che. In this film, the hero loses his arm but trains himself into a one-armed warrior. There is no modern technology to give him back an arm. Rather, he lives with his condition and becomes an even greater warrior with one arm through sheer will, training, and strength. The "technology" of the one-armed swordsman is that of inner spirit and strength, a matter of practicing and harnessing the *qi* within us.

In a spin-off of this same theme, Zhang Che directed another film *Crippled Avengers* (1978) featuring protagonists who are handicapped in various ways. Here, he expands on the question of technology and the spirit, contrasting technology as a hard science and as a soft science method of harnessing physical weakness as martial arts skill. One of the villains is a man who is himself handicapped, both his arms cut off but who is fitted with iron arms and trained in the martial arts by his father, a local tyrant. Clearly, there is a theme of using technology to outfit a man with prosthetic arms, which can fire hidden darts and stretch mechanically to surprise opponents, turning him into a malevolent warrior. The same technology supplies one of the "avengers" with artificial legs, who together with three others is trained as a martial arts expert to exact revenge on the tyrant and his son who had caused their physical debilities. Technology is utilized at the service of the martial arts for both good and bad. Naturally, by the standards of Star Wars, the technology in *Crippled Avengers* is old hat. It is the technology of the premodern East. Still, it involves engineering and mechanization. The theme of technology counterbalances the theme of relying on one's innate skills and goodness to defeat evil. "One may be physically handicapped but the mind (or heart) is not" is a line spoken by one of the avengers. Luke's condition echoes the theme, and it sustains him to his ultimate victory over Darth Vader and the restoration of Anakin Skywalker to the good side of the Force.

An interesting aspect of the technology in Star Wars is the light sabre and how it expresses the *qi* of the Force. Essentially, the light of the sabre is a projection of *qi* from the body through the hand, the sword being an extension of the hand. *Qi* also projects directly through the hand or through the fingers as in the case of Darth Sidious's malevolent *qi* ("force lightning," in Star Wars jargon) in his duel with Yoda in *Revenge of the Sith* and his clash with Luke Skywalker in *The Return of the Jedi*. The *qi* that flows out of one's hands is another reminder of the Chinese martial arts cinema. Anyone who has grown up watching Hong Kong Cantonese movies in the 1960s would be familiar with *Buddha's Palm*, a serial martial arts adventure released in four parts in 1964 (with a further spin-off released in 1965). In these cinematic offerings, the young hero does battle with an old villain with light rays emitting out of the palms of their hands. Such borrowings from Chinese films may not be readily acknowledged by Western critics unfamiliar with the tradition but they are all part of the Eastern mythmaking that is trivialized by appropriations in Hollywood Orientalism (in this sense, one can indict the Star Wars films for their generic perpetuation of Orientalism; Figure 1.3).

However, the Star Wars films are somewhat exceptional for exceeding banal expectations. From the Western point of view, much of what the films portray and signify may be "New Age nonsense and superstition," as John D. Caputo has written, but they are "a fascinating mélange of mysticism and science fiction that bears witness to a strange symbiosis of religion and post-industrial technologies."[73] From our point of view, they transcend the generic expectations of a Hollywood science fiction potboiler series by succeeding

Figure 1.3 Darth Sidious projects "force lightning" on Luke Skywalker. *Return of the Jedi*, Producer: Howard Kazanjian.

brilliantly in emitting Eastern messages of moral content and lifestyle values through its Orientalist veneer. No matter how trivial or contrived, Eastern myths and motifs in the Star Wars films present a revelation of the Eastern as a broad and open source of knowledge and wisdom. The science fiction basis of the films suggests a temporal reconfiguration of the Oriental West, the West technologized by the East in matters of the mind and the spirit which seeps into the hardware and the science of technology. A Technological West of hard sciences would hardly matter without soft Eastern substance. Hence, the films perform a synthesis of East and West as the future.

Conclusion

In conclusion, I have explained above how the Eastern conceptual vision of the Star Wars Saga makes it an exceptional manifestation of the "Oriental West." The Orientalism is both distinctive in its neo-religious dimension and complacently hubristic in its Eurocentric manner of Orientalist characterizations. The steamrolling nature of the Saga's development over a span of forty years has gathered denseness and much complexity to its subject matter. There are several facets of its vast Eastern frame that I have left unexplored. I will make a few remarks here concerning the father and son theme in the Saga. It assumes much Eastern Daoist resonance in its interpretations of filial piety, loyalty, and sacrifice. The plot that runs through the Saga involving Anakin Skywalker and his son Luke as well as Darth Vader's relationship with the Emperor (a theme that recurs in Episodes VII and VIII in the relationship between Kylo Ren and Luke Sykwalker) echoes this passage in the *Zhuang Zi*, chapter 12:

> The filial son who does not fawn upon his parents and the loyal subject who does not flatter his lord are the best kinds of sons and subjects. When a son assents to whatever his parents say and approves of whatever they do, it is the common opinion of the world that he is unworthy. When a subject assents to whatever his lord says and approves of whatever he does, it is the common opinion of the world that he is unworthy. But can we be sure that this is necessarily so?[74]

Episode VII, *The Force Awakens*, appears to uphold the question by reviving the theme of the father and son conflict, resurrecting the Darth Vader figure through his grandson Kylo Ren (the son of Han Solo and Leia). From Darth Vader to Kylo Ren, we see a cycle fixed or predetermined by the human inclinations to unbalance the Force (the Dao), or the inclinations of the young to be seduced by the dark side. Thus, a new cycle of conflict ensues. Fathers and sons, lords and subjects are fated to repeat the crises of filial duty and loyalty. In this chapter, I have mainly focused on the Daoist underpinnings of the Star Wars philosophy, referring primarily to the *Zhuang Zi* as the classical text that principally bears on the films. This is because, in my opinion, the Star Wars films show a startling resemblance to the *Zhuang Zi*'s philosophy and cosmology and even some of its characters seem to crop out of the *Zhuang Zi*.

There is still much to be said and analyzed about the Saga's Eastern content (this would take a whole monograph), particularly when we extend the scope of the Eastern to consider more specific Confucianist and Buddhist interventions in the narratives. The Confucianist order of the five relationships (those between lord and master, father and son, husband and wife, between brothers, and between friends) is a governing motif in all the relationships in the Saga, which, for lack of space, has fallen out of the scope of our discussion. With the Saga yet to be completed, we see a theme of perpetual conflict and war, a kind of Buddhist cycle of suffering due to the misbalance of yin and yang. The Eastern reading and analysis of this chapter is thus limited to the extent of the Saga's present editions (eight films plus an offshoot). What we may conclude from our analysis in this chapter is the exemplification of the

Star Wars films as an Eastern Saga of discord in the universe and its message of achieving balance. Hence, the Eastern lies in its essence of maintaining a balance of life forces. Furthermore, the Star Wars films are Eastern in their generic Orientalism—the overall look as well as the content. We have endeavored to analyze the Star Wars Saga as an exemplification of the Oriental West in the cinema, the notion that the West has assimilated the East. Although the Saga inevitably displays vestiges of Orientalism (Eurocentrism) in general tendency, its substance is inherently Eastern in terms of a deeper spiritualism, inspired by Daoism, which comes from the integration of the East with the West. Its Techno-Orientalist form reveals, on a closer reading, a technology of Daoist being from nonbeing. The nonbeing of the man of spirit is expressed thus in the *Zhuang Zi*:

> His spirit rises, mounted on the light,
> While his physical form vanishes,
> This is called "illumination of immensity."
> He fulfils his destiny and perfects his attributes.[75]

That the Star Wars films encompass this man of spirit as its central object of technology is a tribute to its Eastern origins.

Notes

1. The films in order of release (with their official titles as listed in Wikipedia) are *Episode IV: A New Hope* (1977), *Episode V: The Empire Strikes Back* (1980), *Episode VI: Return of the Jedi* (1983), *Episode 1: The Phantom Menace* (1999), *Episode II: Attack of the Clones* (2002), *Episode III: Revenge of the Sith* (2005), *Episode VII: The Force Awakens* (2015), *Episode VIII: The Last Jedi* (2017). The spin-off is *Rogue One: A Star Wars Story* (2016).
2. In his 1983 biography of George Lucas, Dale Pollock writes that Lucas had "borrowed liberally from the Flash Gordon serials he had watched as a child, transplanting video screens, medieval costumes, art deco sets, and blaster guns to *Star Wars*." While the acting "was awful and the special effects were cheap and crude . . . there was constant action, a quality he wanted in *Star Wars*." See Dale Pollock, *Skywalking, The Life and Films of George Lucas* (London: Elm Tree Books, 1983), p. 142.

3   Hobson, *The Eastern Origins of Western Civilisation*, p. 7. "Orientalism or Eurocentrism," Hobson writes, "is a worldview that asserts the inherent superiority of the West over the East. Specifically Orientalism constructs a permanent image of the superior West (the 'Self') which is defined negatively against the no less imaginary 'Other'—the backward and inferior East" (p. 7).
4   See John Seabrook, "Letter from Skywalker Ranch: Why Is the Force Still with Us?," in S. Kline (ed.), *George Lucas Interviews* (Jackson: University Press of Mississippi, 1999), p. 205.
5   Pollock, *Skywalking*, p. 139.
6   Kevin J. Wetmore, Jr., "The Tao of Star Wars, or, Cultural Appropriation in a Galaxy Far, Far, Away," *Studies in Popular Culture*, 23 (1), 2000, p. 94.
7   See Walter Robinson, "The Far East of *Star Wars*," in K. S. Decker and J. T. Eberl (eds.), *Star Wars and Philosophy: More Powerful than You Can Possibly Imagine* (Chicago and La Salle, IL: Open Court, 2005), p. 29.
8   Ibid.; emphasis in original.
9   See Markus Altena Davidsen, "From *Star Wars* to Jediism: The Emergence of Fiction-based Religion," in E. V. D. Hemel and A. Szafraniec (eds.), *Religious Language Matters* (New York: Fordham University Press, 2016), p. 382.
10 Ibid.
11 See Robinson, "The Far East of *Star Wars*," pp. 31–32.
12 Davidsen, "From *Star Wars* to Jediism," p. 383.
13 J. W. Rinzler, *The Making of Star Wars* (London: Ebury Press, 2007), p. 46. Another literary influence was Joseph Campbell's *Hero with a Thousand Faces* (see Rinzler, p. 47).
14 Carlos Castenada, *Tales of Power* (New York: Washington Square Press, 1974), p. 4.
15 Pollock, *Skywalking*, p. 140.
16 Ibid., p. 139.
17 See John M. Porter, *The Tao of Star Wars* (Atlanta, GA: Humanics Trade Group Publications, 2003). Wetmore, Jr.'s "The Tao of Star Wars, or, Cultural Appropriation in a Galaxy Far, Far Away" also expounds on the Daoism of the series. For more on the Daoist connection, see Jonathan L. Bowen and Rachel Wagner, "'Hokey Religions and Ancient Weapons': The Force of Spirituality," in M. W. Kapell and J. S. Lawrence (eds.), *Finding the Force of the Star Wars Franchise* (New York: Peter Lang, 2006), pp. 77–81. Bowen and Wagner also analyze the Buddhist and Christian influences in the rest of the article. Bryan P. Stone acknowledges that the Force is more like the Dao in his discussion of the Christian concept of the Holy Spirit and its likening to the Force: see Stone, *Faith and Film: Theological Themes at the Cinema* (St. Louis, MO: Chalice

Press, 2000), p. 135. For the Saga's associations with Buddhism, a close cousin to Daoism, see Matthew Bortolin, *The Dharma of Star Wars* (Somerville, MA: Wisdom Publications, 2005), and Christian Feichtinger, "Space Buddhism: The Adoption of Buddhist Motifs in Star Wars," *Contemporary Buddhism*, 15 (1), 2014, pp. 28–43. Walter Robinson's "The Far East of *Star Wars*" also discusses the Buddhist-Daoist characteristics. Daoism has long figured in Western science fiction. Betsy Huang has explicated how Daoist thought runs through the novels of Philip K. Dick, Ursula Le Guin, and others. See Betsy Huang, "Premodern Orientalist Science Fictions," *MELUS*, 33 (4), 2008, pp. 23–43.

18 David Beynon, "From Techno-cute to Superflat: Robots and Asian Architectural Features," *Mechademia*, 7, 2012, p. 137.
19 Todd H. Sammons, "*Return of the Jedi*: Epic Graffiti," *Science Fiction Studies*, 14 (3), 1987, p. 356.
20 Ibid., p. 366.
21 Ibid.
22 Ibid., p. 356.
23 See Christine Cornea, *Science Fiction Cinema, between Fantasy and Reality* (Edinburgh: Edinburgh University Press, 2007), p. 137.
24 Mair, *Wandering on the Way*, p. 18.
25 Ibid., p. 15.
26 Sammons, "Epic Graffiti," p. 356.
27 Michael Pye and Linda Myles, "George Lucas," in S. Kline (ed.), *George Lucas Interviews* (Jackson: University Press of Mississippi, 1999), p. 83.
28 Ibid.
29 Robinson, "The Far East of *Star Wars*," p. 32.
30 Abigail De Kosnik, "The Mask of Fu Manchu, Son of Sinbad, and Star Wars IV: A New Hope: Techno-Orientalist Cinema as a Mnemotechnics of Twentieth-Century U.S.-Asian Conflicts," in D. S. Roh, B. Huang, and G. A. Niu (eds.), *Techno-Orientalism: Imagining Asia in Speculative Fiction, History, and Media* (New Brunswick, NJ and London: Rutgers University Press, 2015), p. 97.
31 Ibid., p. 98.
32 Wetmore, Jr., "The Tao of Star Wars, Or, Cultural Appropriation in a Galaxy Far, Far Away," p. 97.
33 Ibid., pp. 96–97.
34 See Stephen McVeigh, "The Galactic Way of Warfare," in M. W. Kapell and J. S. Lawrence (eds.), *Finding the Force of the Star Wars Franchise* (New York: Peter Lang, 2006), pp. 35–58.
35 Pye and Myles, "George Lucas," p. 83.

36 Robert Kolker, *Film, Form, & Culture*, Third Edition (New York: McGraw-Hill, 2006), p. 227.
37 Pye and Myles, "George Lucas," p. 83.
38 Jonathan Rosenbaum, "The Solitary Pleasures of Star Wars," *Sight and Sound*, 46 (4), 1977, p. 209.
39 Wetmore, Jr., "The Tao of Star Wars," p. 102.
40 Rosenbaum, "The Solitary Pleasures of Star Wars," p. 209.
41 Hobson, *The Eastern Origins of Western Civilisation*, p. 22.
42 Ibid., p. 26.
43 Robinson, "The Far East of *Star Wars*," p. 36.
44 Rinzler, *The Making of Star Wars*, p. 9.
45 Beynon, "From Techno-cute to Superflat," p. 135.
46 See Mair, *Wandering on the Way*.
47 Eske Møllgaard, *An Introduction to Daoist Thought* (London and New York: Routledge, 2007), p. 129.
48 Mair, *Wandering on the Way*, p. 59.
49 Ibid., p. 99.
50 John Gray, *Straw Dogs, Thoughts on Humans and Other Animals* (London: Granta Books, 2002), p. 144.
51 See Rey Chow, "Postmodern Automatons," in J. Butler and J. W. Scott (eds.), *Feminists Theorize the Political* (London and New York: Routledge, 1992), p. 101.
52 Ibid.
53 See David Morley and Kevin Robins, "Techno-Orientalism: Japan Panic," in D. Morley and K. Robins (eds.), *Spaces of Identity: Global Media, Electronic Landscapes and Cultural Boundaries* (London: Routledge, 1995), pp. 147–73.
54 John Hellmann, *American Myth and the Legacy of Vietnam* (New York: Columbia University Press, 1986), p. 208.
55 Ibid.
56 Ibid., p. 211.
57 David S. Roh, Betsy Huang and Greta A. Niu, "Technologizing Orientalism: An Introduction," in D. S. Roh, B. Huang, and G. A. Niu (eds.), *Techno-Orientalism: Imagining Asia in Speculative Fiction, History, and Media* (New Brunswick, NJ and London: Rutgers University Press, 2015), p. 2.
58 Ibid.
59 McVeigh, "The Galactic Way of Warfare," p. 45.
60 John C. McDowell, *The Gospel According to Star Wars: Faith, Hope, and the Force* (Louisville, KY: Westminster John Knox Press, 2007), p. xiv. Emphasis is McDowell's.

61 Huang, "Premodern Orientalist Science Fictions," p. 24.
62 Zhihua Yao, "Daoism and Buddhism," in Xiaogan Liu (ed.), *Dao Companion to Daoist Philosophy* (Dordrecht: Springer, 2015), p. 516.
63 John D. Caputo, *On Religion* (London and New York: Routledge, 2001), p. 83.
64 Mair, *Wandering on the Way*, p. 232.
65 Ibid., p. 233.
66 Ibid.
67 Yao, "Daoism and Buddhism," p. 517.
68 Mair, *Wandering on the Way*, p. 232.
69 I am indebted to my student, Daphne Lin, for this insight.
70 Wetmore, Jr., "The Tao of Star Wars," p. 98.
71 Ibid., p. 99.
72 Ibid., p. 98.
73 Caputo, *On Religion*, p. 90.
74 Mair, *Wandering on the Way*, p. 115.
75 Ibid., p. 114.

2

Vertigo, Hitchcock's Chinese Riddle

Chinese red passion

There is a set of Chinese motifs and designs embedded right at the heart of the semiotic system of *Vertigo* (1958) which is hardly discussed in the critical literature on the film and on Hitchcock. It remains largely hidden in the massive cryptographic scheme hatched by Hitchcock and spread out over all his works. The title of Tom Cohen's two-volume book *Hitchcock's Cryptonymies* underscores Hitchcock's nature as a master serial cryptographer; yet, for all his exhaustive scrutiny of signature systems in Hitchcock's oeuvre, Cohen has missed these Chinese signs—or "Babel" markers, as he might label them—in *Vertigo*.[1] Another more recent book with a title relevant to our topic is D. A. Miller's *Hidden Hitchcock*, published in 2016. It deals with Hitchcock's cinematic game playing through his insertions of hidden pictures into his films. The objects are "visible *but not apparent*" (emphasis Miller's).[2] Miller, unfortunately, does not analyze *Vertigo*, which seems a pity for it is possibly the most exotic and mysterious example of what Miller calls Hitchcock's "secret style."[3] Perhaps for Miller, *Vertigo* contains no "*meaningfully* hidden meaning" even in its hidden Chinese secrets "since we see more or less the same meaning elsewhere in plain view."[4] The point is, though, that Chinese motifs are "in plain view" in *Vertigo* and that they constitute a Chinese puzzle which has not really been discussed at all in the literature (and *Vertigo* is probably Hitchcock's most analyzed work), its significance awaiting revelation and closer readings. This very fact discloses how Hitchcock plays his game of charades "unannounced," as Miller says, "and whose secret riddles are posed in secret, hidden under narrative camouflage until someone, accidentally falling into the game, simultaneously sees and solves one."[5] My task in this chapter is to decipher the significance of Hitchcock's Chinese riddle encoded in its exotic and erotic Chinese motifs.

I will start by focusing on the colors, first red and then green.[6] Red recurs throughout the film but what may be surprising is that we can actually see it as a Chinese denomination of red, a point not recognized by writers who have written on Hitchcock's color schemes, such as Richard Allen, Brigitte Peucker, and Eli Friedlander. In at least two or even three crucial scenes, Hitchcock specifically invokes red, as the Chinese would see the color: as a sign of marriage, prosperity, and good fortune. To Richard Allen, red and "red on white" (red in conjunction with the blonde Madeleine) "take on a pervasive meaning in relation to female sexuality" and he declares that the role of red "links female sexuality and danger."[7] This is the case only if we think of red as a color generically and conventionally associated with danger and if we have already in mind the plot devised by Gavin Elster to have Madeleine ensnare Scottie as the scapegoat in a murder scheme. (The viewer is not made aware of this plot until about two-thirds into the film.) Red therefore has other meanings, not all imputing female sexuality with danger. Hitchcock's use of red is in line with his use of red herrings and MacGuffins. He must present many variables to the audience before Elster's plot is revealed. The immediate variable is the love developing between the two protagonists, Scottie and Madeleine, that turns into what Noël Carroll calls "the impossible love."[8] To signal their mutual attraction and subsequent affair, Hitchcock applies red as a Chinese color.

Was Hitchcock conscious of using red in this Chinese way? Was he in fact conscious of inserting Chinese motifs at all into his film? We will never know for sure. However, there is some evidence to suggest that it was a careful design of his. Herbert Coleman, his associate producer responsible for logistics and production planning, revealed that he had picked, for Scottie's apartment, "a small house on a steep hill across the street from a grammar school where the playground was filled with Chinese children" and he further asserted that Hitchcock "liked the idea of tying the home to the Chinese school."[9] Dan Auiler's book *Vertigo, The Making of a Hitchcock Classic* states that the production designer Henry Bumstead remembered talking to "the Asian gentleman who lived in the apartment" to convince him "to change the ironwork that can be seen outside the door," presumably on Hitchcock's instruction, "although

Bumstead could not remember why they wanted to change the ironwork."[10] The apartment exterior as seen in the film has a red door and the ironwork on the balcony shows three "double happiness" (*shuangxi*) signs, traditionally used in Chinese weddings and to decorate bedrooms to symbolize the nuptial bond. These are seen in plain view in the scene where Madeleine goes to Scottie's apartment to give him a note: Scottie, who has been following Madeleine in his car, quickly pulls up and he gets out to meet her. That the motifs are seen in plain view constitutes the semiotic base of what Tom Cohen calls the "(a)materiality of letter itself"—except that these are Chinese characters.[11] This indicates, to my mind, that Hitchcock was consciously inserting Chinese motifs into the text. The question then is why?[12] (Figure 2.1).

The Chinese design changes the meaning of the scene. Scottie, the hardnosed detective following his client's wife is now transformed into an eager suitor. He places his hand on the balustrade showing the ironwork signs for a few seconds then withdraws it coyly as he engages Madeleine in conversation, thus highlighting the significance of the double happiness signage. Madeleine has gone to the apartment practically to present herself to Scottie and to lure him into an ever-deeper relationship. In fact, their relationship had begun the night before inside that apartment to which Scottie had taken Madeleine after her jump into San Francisco Bay near the Golden Gate Bridge. The bridge is colored red, suggesting a pattern of Chinese red that attunes us to Madeleine becoming the love obsession in Scottie's life.

Figure 2.1 Madeleine enclosed by "double happiness" symbols.
Vertigo, Producer: Herbert Coleman.

The scene inside the apartment plays on the Chinese red motif to signify the sexual relationship developing between Madeleine and Scottie. She has been undressed and is lying on Scottie's bed under a blanket; her bare shoulders suggest she is naked underneath. She is supposedly still in a state of shock, murmuring incoherently. Scottie goes into the room to answer the ringing phone which startles Madeleine back into consciousness. He gives her a red dressing gown lying on the bed. She puts it on and stands by the bedroom door looking sexually alluring in red. As she moves slowly forward on her bare feet, we get a near 3-D effect of the red almost leaping toward us, the viewers. It is as if Madeleine has come out of the bedroom after lovemaking, like a bride emerging from the bridal chamber (or *dongfang* in Chinese). This shot is essentially repeated later in Judy's hotel room where Judy performs the final touch to appear as Madeleine, but there she is "suffused in a green haze" as William Rothman has remarked.[13] Both scenes are basically related to each other through colors, one in red (at Scottie's apartment) and the other in green (at Judy's room). The contrast of these colors is especially poignant in as much as green in the latter scene signifies death and corruption, while red is fertility and life.

Red seen in the context of Scottie's apartment denotes not so much danger as ecstasy. At this point, the viewer is seeing the story as a married woman falling mutually in love with a private detective hired by the husband to tail her. But there is an earlier scene at Ernie's Restaurant where Scottie sees Madeleine for the first time, in which red also plays a significant role in denoting passion and ecstasy. Madeleine sweeps past in a black gown with a trailing black and green wrap over her shoulder. As she pauses for a moment, her face is seen in profile against a vivid purplish-red wallpapered background which glows a bright light at that exact moment. Richard Misek gets it right when he writes that the momentary surging of light "evokes a rush of blood to Scotty's head, hinting that his response to Madeleine exceeds his duties as a private detective. At the same time, the surging red also exceeds the narrative, burning directly into our retinas. Seen in a cinema, the effect is overwhelmingly sensual."[14] Herbert Coleman informs us that the wall covering was of ruby red silk, ordered by the owner of Ernie's especially for the set of the restaurant built in the studio by Henry Bumstead.[15] The red setting links Madeleine with Scottie, a linking that begins cerebrally, as in the scene at Gavin Elster's office where Scottie goes to discuss the case with Elster (red features in the floor carpet and leather chairs), and in other scenes where Madeleine is associated with flowers, some of which are red, in the flower shop scene and in the graveyard. All these scenes direct us, finally, to the image of Madeleine in red, denoting a "flesh-and-blood reality" of her character, to use a phrase from Stanley Cavell.[16]

Where Madeleine stands in red in Scottie's apartment, on the wall to the right of the screen hangs a gold-plated ornament, a mandala shaped in the form of a blossoming chrysanthemum (a flower symbol that complements other uses of flowers throughout the film).[17] Here, the flower and the mandala (the Sanskrit word for "circle") symbolize wholeness, the unity and harmony of objects, which falls into the same pattern of wedding union and conjugal bliss that the whole apartment is made to represent. Its golden color adds to the luster of the shot. There is certainly *jouissance* in the symbolism here. The problem for Scottie, at this point, is how to achieve it, for there is something illusionary, dreamlike, in this shot. Red, which translates Madeleine's spectral personality into a real figure, points to the possibility of desire and perhaps love. This is an important point. Scottie's green pullover complements the red robe and it suggests empathy, a reaching out, a need to connect with the object of desire. Madeleine's red as she walks toward Scottie reciprocates Scottie's green. She seems automatically drawn to him appearing to invite him sexually. Scottie is of course nothing less than a gentleman, but he does make a move later, by placing his hand on Madeleine's (even if this was accidental; Figure 2.2).

This whole scene in Scottie's apartment has been described by Robin Wood as "one of the cinema's most perverse (and most 'romantic') love scenes—so perverse it couldn't possibly be filmed." (Scottie has undressed Madeleine and put her into his own bed, "believing her to be unconscious, while in reality she is *pretending* to be unconscious," writes Wood.)[18] I suggest that the perversity would be felt even more if we were to see the scene through the Chinese lens of red. The use of red as Chinese wedding red is the rub of the imagery in its connotations of a sexual union as between husband and wife when Scottie and Madeleine have yet to achieve that status. The red points to a *promise* of this desire, as Scottie would see it. Invoking Freudian psychoanalytical theory, Wood refers to the "original desire" in Scottie which conflicts with "the reality principle," and thus "'original desire' can never be fulfilled in life."[19]

Figure 2.2 Madeleine in red and the mandala.
Vertigo, Producer: Herbert Coleman.

Nevertheless, I would say that Scottie sees the possibility of fulfilling it. The color red signifies this possibility, and furthermore, transforms Madeleine into a figure that invites such a possibility. Similarly, the use of green suggests Scottie's mind bordering on the perverse in its imagining of possessing Madeleine. Green, then, infers the theme of union, the joining of green with red, which is later visualized in the red and green hues of the redwood forest in which they later wander. The red of the forest floor is integrated into the green of the tree foliage, a wedding theme that also suggests longevity, in Chinese, *chang qing* (forever green).

Charles Barr, in his book-length study of the film, has described the scene at Scottie's apartment as "the pivotal one of the whole film" considering it "extraordinary in its dramatic and emotional complexity, sustained by acting, scripting and direction of great delicacy."[20] The emotional complexity stems exactly from the idea that Scottie imagines Madeleine as his paramour and effectively applies his imagination as a reality onto her. Red represents his imagination. Neither Barr nor Wood mentions the significance of red in the scene—a significance, moreover, conferred by Chinese connotations of red. Brigitte Peucker, in her essay "Blood, Paint, or Red? The Color Bleed in Hitchcock," has also ignored such red significance on Madeleine. Peucker does note that red "often functions as part of a complementary pair in Hitchcock" and in *Vertigo* red is seen in opposition to green.[21] This is the case in this scene where green is figured in Scottie through his pullover, which complements the red of Madeleine's robe. We can also note that other greens appear in juxtaposition to red in the apartment scene, for example, the green ice bucket seen next to Madeleine's red robed figure; the pale green cushions against the pale pink curtains. There's the dark red armchair. Even outside the apartment, where Madeleine and Scottie have a dialogue, the red door is contrasted with the pale green-blue of the door and window frames and door curtain, as well as the bright green conifers lining the balustrade. However, Peucker avers that "the greens associated with the ethereal Madeleine are noticeably opposed to the reds that adorn the earthy Judy."[22] This statement can be disputed on several counts, though to be fair to Peucker, her essay does not focus on *Vertigo* but on a generic use of red in Hitchcock's films.

First, Madeleine is not just associated with green. As I have discussed at length earlier, she was seen in red in Scottie's apartment, which has the effect of turning her into a more sexually alluring figure than if she had worn a green gown. (The effect is heightened when her red gown is accentuated by the golden glow of the fireplace by which she sits.) In this scene, it is actually Scottie who wears green and it is significant that it is he who gives Madeleine the red gown making him complementary to Madeleine's red. A role switching has occurred: Scottie wears Madeleine's green while she wears Scottie's red, each occupying the other's psychological color. Second, Judy is not really represented by reds as much as she is by green. When we first see her, she is in green and for the rest of her scenes, green is her natural color except for the scene at Ernie's where, dressed in a violet blouse, she is offset against the red wallpapered background of the restaurant. Judy is not seen anywhere else in red unless we identify Madeleine in the scene at Scottie's apartment as Judy, which does illustrate at least the "more complex juxtaposition" of the opposition of colors as both roles are played by the same actress, Kim Novak, "their difference produced through artifice and intensified by the disturbed imagination of James Stewart's Scottie."[23] However, the film is quite neatly divided between Madeleine's section and Judy's section, and in the Madeleine episode, we do not know that she is Judy. Thence, some circumspection has to be exercised when distinguishing the colors associated with each persona. Furthermore, if Judy is an earthy figure as Peucker says she is, she would be best represented in green rather than in red, which is in fact the case.

Judy's green resonates with the Chinese idea of reincarnation. Green indicates objects and other beings of nature taking human form, as in the eighteenth-century writer Pu Songling's story of "The Girl in Green" ("Lüyi nü"), about a green hornet appearing in the guise of a woman in green, falling in love with a man so that he may eventually save her from being caught in a spider's web.[24] Green therefore is the color of Judy's reincarnation, Madeleine's spirit in earthly form. Green is also the color of fear or anxiety. The girl in green of Pu Songling's story is frightened. When asked why, she quotes a saying, "A ghost that steals life must forever live in fear" (*tousheng guizi chang wei ren*). Green represents Judy as a ghost forever in fear because she has stolen life, and she is earthy that way. Otherwise, why should a ghost be frightened? The point, of course, is that she is not a ghost. Her green suggests a connection to earth. Both Madeleine and Judy are ladies in green. Peucker's contrast of the "ethereal" Madeleine in green with the "earthy" Judy in red is a misperception. Where red is associated with Judy, it is seen peripherally in small details, as for instance, when she holds out a red wallet to show her driving license to Scottie, and when she is made over to Madeleine, her rouged lips are seen in close-up, and later when she puts on the ruby necklace.

The contrast should rather be between the green Madeleine and the red Madeleine. The green Madeleine whom Scottie follows around San Francisco is like a ghost, possessed by Carlotta's spirit. In contrast, the red Madeleine takes on an earthly form when she appears in Scottie's apartment in the red dressing gown. She is suddenly a corporeal presence, in no small amount due to "the camera's insistence on the flesh-and-blood reality of the female actor," to return to Stanley Cavell's phrase.[25] One should rather say that the insistence is on red—red to concentrate the mind on the object, and to realize the object of contemplation as the object of desire. This overturns the Platonic idea of Madeleine as the ideal woman and corroborates Slavoj Žižek's assertion that *Vertigo* "is the ultimate anti-Platonic film."[26] Equally, it attests to Fredric Jameson's "opposition between private and public" and his claim that Hitchcock constructs a concept of the private, which lies beyond a film's closure and thus "beyond representation."[27] Red is the color of the private. The "ideal woman," like "ideal marriage," lies well beyond the closure of the film and is therefore beyond representation. To the practical-minded Chinese, red, representing fortune, luck, and happiness, is a materialistic sign, often taking the form of red packets of money given to well-wishers during Chinese New Year or on other auspicious occasions like weddings. The red Madeleine is such a "red packet," something to be literally touched or put into the hand.[28] There is, of course, more than a "touch" of romantic irony in this image.

In *Hitchcock's Romantic Irony*, Richard Allen writes that romantic irony "essentially turns on the ambiguous logic of affirmation and irony that is staged by a self-conscious narrator, in particular the affirmation and negation of the ideal embodied in romance."[29] Following this logic, Hitchcock has designed the scene in Scottie's apartment to represent the romantic longing of Scottie in what would be a surrealist manner whereby "the world of the ideal, or the more than real, becomes identified with reality itself."[30] However, the accent is on the ideal—something that is *more than real*; this then exposes the "dialectic of simultaneous affirmation and negation as a function of the activity of representation itself."[31] It is notable that Allen would mention romantic irony in terms of a representation, understood in a dualistic way, like a yin and yang of representation. When performed on the human form of Madeleine, this representation "at once embodies an uncorrupted ideal of a complete and timeless beauty, and yet also, through its very surface perfection, intimates the underlying decadence and corruption of human mortality."[32] There is a strong whiff of Eastern essence in what Allen says, which sits well with the Chinese red motif exhibited by Hitchcock. Red is Hitchcock's means to achieve the *more than real* and to reinforce the ideal of Madeleine as timeless beauty. We know that this is an illusion that is yet real, both in terms of the plot and in terms of what Hitchcock is illuminating, philosophically. This is an Eastern strand of philosophy, already foreshadowed by the signs of the Chinese motifs. The more than real accords with the words of the famous couplet from the eighteenth-century classic novel *Dream of the Red Chamber*: "When the false becomes real, the real is also false; and where nothing is located in something, nothing lingers in something" (*jia zuo zhen shi, zhen yi jia; wu wei you chu, you huan wu*).

In Chinese thought, then, there is a preoccupation with overlapping illusion and reality, nothing and something, each element lingering in the other as they interact. The famous case of the fourth-century BCE philosopher Zhuang Zi's parable about the butterfly—did Zhuang Zi dream that he was a butterfly or did the butterfly dream that it was Zhuang Zi?—attests to a long intellectual tradition of inquiring along this line. Hitchcock has incorporated this philosophical conceit into *Vertigo*, making it the one film in his oeuvre "in which the confusion of ontological registers—between reality and illusion—most poignantly takes center stage," according to Peucker.³³ His use of red is a marker of his poignant approach to the philosophical ontological theme. It also signifies the power of thought where thought itself gives shape to an idea through the merging of sight and mind. This rhymes with the Buddhist notion of thought, *xiang* in Chinese (a word made up of the characters for image and mind), which is defined as "seeing the form of the object as though it were right in front of oneself" (*fangfu ru du qirong zhi chuqian yue xiang*).³⁴ To think, then, is to see the object right in front of oneself. Madeleine in red is such an image. In Chinese Buddhist thinking, the concept of *se*, the word used to indicate color, is also meant to indicate form or matter, and what is more vivid than red to manifest Madeleine as human form, an object of desire or contemplation, in full Technicolor glory? The concept of color as form gives pictorial shape to the thought itself. Hitchcock's film is a virtual compendium of thoughts as images and thoughts as illusions or dreams. Robin Wood writes that "the cinema itself is a kind of dream, an escape world in which reality can be evaded and forgotten" and that *Vertigo* was made to satisfy escapist expectations in the audience to see a "'hero' . . . involved in romantic wish fulfillments."³⁵

We should see the film as a story about love that, following Noël Carroll, provides "the philosophical resources that can enable thoughtful spectators to develop insights into the nature of love."³⁶ The Chinese motifs compel a Chinese understanding of love: that the power of love is real in an illusionary world. This is stated in the *gatha* (Buddhist saying), composed by Feng Menglong in his preface to *Qingshi leilüe* (*A Classified History of Love*), published in the seventeenth century: "Where the four elements construct the world as illusion, only love is real, its nature neither false nor void" (*sida jie huanshe, xingqing bu xujia*).³⁷ Carroll calls the love between Scottie and Madeleine/Judy the "impossible love," and he gives a list of all those factors that make it impossible. Principally, he contends that the love is impossible because it is "rooted in the notion that the object of love is a set of properties transferable from one vessel to another rather than a unique particular with whom one has forged a historical bond."³⁸ Carroll is perhaps too preoccupied with the notion of the transference of love, that is, the impossibility of transferring love. The Chinese may say that to be in love is enough to justify its possibility because it possesses its own spiritual force and that *Vertigo* is a story about a possible love on the premise of its very impossibility, even though the result is tragic. This kind of love is obsessive, one of the categories of the *Qingshi leilüe*.

In her book *Enchantment and Disenchantment: Love and Illusion in Chinese Literature*, Wai-yee Li refers to one such story, "The Story of Wang," which tells of the love of a timber merchant, Wang, for a courtesan, Tang. She is later taken into the harem of the prince. Wang requests a meeting with Tang, and the prince agrees only if Wang castrates himself. After a long recovery, Wang finally meets Tang. Their meeting is only a "long, silent, tearful mutual gaze."[39] The self-styled "historian of love" (Feng Menglong) comments, "During this meeting, love is infinite; after this meeting, there is no other love" (*ci yijian shi, you wuqiong zhi qing, ci yijian hou, geng wu yu qing*).[40] This is an impossible love, a love no longer based on the "primacy of phallocentric desire"[41] but for its own sake, a love carried to its furthest extremity as a sensual experience. Scottie's love borders on this kind, based on the idea of the infinite love. (His physical affliction suggests a self-castration.)

Chinese romantic irony

We come more to the philosophical core of the Chinese element in *Vertigo*. Chinese thinking itself, driven by the color red, pervades the narrative and introduces a philosophical concern about illusion and reality on one level and on another level about love and "impossible" love, if we follow Noël Carroll's line on the film. The merging of the romantic theme with the conceit of illusion or dream strikes at the heart of romantic irony, or as Wai-yee Li puts it, "disenchantment," which is enlightenment through love, as well as the recognition of its impossibility while striving for some transcendental state of love nevertheless, as the story of Wang demonstrates. If enchantment is "the process of being drawn into another world that promises sensual and spiritual fulfillment," then "disenchantment is the awareness of enchantment as mere enchantment, a condition of limited duration subject to inevitable demolition."[42] *Vertigo* is a classic Chinese tale of enchantment and disenchantment, where enchantment is the illusion of Madeleine, and disenchantment, the discovery of Madeleine as illusion. Scottie follows the "illusionary" Madeleine on two visual planes quite different from each other but yet overlapping in their dreamlike nature. The first plane takes the motif of wandering, the second that of painting. Both are apprehensible in the Chinese spiritual and aesthetic sense.

First, wandering is a very Daoist notion. It is a form of spiritual exercise in which people wander in the way (*dao*) in order to experience a freedom that may bring them closer to nature and "the ceaseless self-emergence of life."[43] Hitchcock evokes wandering as a conscious motif in those scenes of Scottie following Madeleine, where both protagonists wander separately. Later, they wander together. The scene at the Mission Dolores (Scottie following Madeleine) shows both protagonists walking in a garden of flowers including a dense cluster of red flowers, allegorizing erotic desire. The scene is shot through a hazy filter rendering it dreamlike. The seventeenth-century Chinese manual of interpreting dreams *Menglin xuanjie* (*The Forest of Dreams: Explicating the Arcane*) contains a category "wandering the garden and encountering a beautiful woman" (*Youyuan yu meinü*) which is interpreted as auspicious, a meeting of a bride-to-be arranged not by a matchmaker but by chance or fate. The irony of course is that Scottie's "meeting" of Madeleine is far from a chance encounter. Later, Scottie and Madeleine wander into the redwood forest at the Big Basin. Here the dreamlike nature of their wandering takes on a darker shade of meaning. Despite the propitious symbolism of the trees ("always green, ever living"), Madeleine is disturbed by the thought of her mortality. They stop before the display of a cross section of a tree in which rings indicate historical timelines. "Somewhere in here I was born, and there I die," Madeleine points, speaking in a dreamy tone. Traditional Chinese believe forests to be the habitat of spectral beings, or "immortals" to use Daoist parlance. As if haunted by a spirit, Madeleine walks away in a trance, and for a moment disappears among the trees, literally engulfed by the forest. Scottie is alarmed and surges forward to find her. He asks her questions, and her answers point to her being possessed by the spirit of Carlotta. She pleads to be taken to "somewhere in the light."

They go to Cypress Point where the ocean backdrop is the key *topos*, possibly the most significant image of the whole film. It simmers like the bitter sea of samsaric suffering in Buddhist thought,[44] while Madeleine talks of her dream of walking down a long corridor where fragments of the mirror still hang and at the end of the corridor there is darkness. When she reaches there, she will die. She runs to the edge of the sea, an action that immediately captures the essence of the Buddhist saying *kuhai wubian, huitou shi an* (the bitter sea is boundless, turn back and repent). As the wandering becomes a metaphor for Madeleine's walk into the corridor, it is the imagery of the bitter sea that presages her destruction. The romantic irony cannot be more striking: an invented dream is set off against the reality of the bitter sea. The refrain "too late, too late," uttered by Madeleine and Scottie in their respective climaxes at the Spanish mission bell tower alludes to the bitter sea and the Buddhistic beseechment to turn back before one falls into it. It is too late for each character to turn back as they are already in the sea (Figure 2.3). The motif of falling that recurs in various scenes, notably in Scottie's nightmare sequence as well as the falls of Madeleine and Judy from the tower aligns with notion of the plunge into the sea. (The fall of the policeman in the post-credits sequence is also a key dramatic moment that begins the film and kicks off the theme of Scottie having vertigo.) Charles Barr observes that the trees and the ocean backdrops are appropriate for "the romantic scenario that (Madeleine) needs to keep encouraging" and that they seem to "impress and move her as much as they do Scottie."[45] The natural backdrops, in Daoist philosophy, function according

Figure 2.3 The lovers and the backdrop of the "bitter sea."
Vertigo, Producer: Herbert Coleman.

to their own laws and have no sense of *ren* (benevolence). They therefore exert their own inexorable force on Madeleine and Scottie. Such Buddhist-Daoist notions of Providence in *Vertigo* may be a touch unorthodox in Hitchcock when the conventional wisdom at the time, as per Rohmer and Chabrol, was that Christian dogma—and therefore Christian Providence—"runs through (Hitchcock's films) like filigree work."[46]

Next, we come to painting. Much has been said about the concept of Madeleine as a painting and Scottie's appreciation of her as a virtual entry into the world of her painting. Tom Gunning's article "In and Out of the Frame: Paintings in Hitchcock" is probably the definitive article on this topic. In *Vertigo*, the painting is that of Carlotta Valdes. "Hitchcock's fascination with portraits of women always raises the question of the power an image can exert on those outside the frame and, therefore, the image's ability to exceed its static and framed existence."[47] The scene at the gallery of the Legion of Honor where Madeleine sits in front of the portrait of Carlotta Valdes is analyzed in great detail by Gunning to show how Hitchcock deploys careful camera movements and framing to suggest "the fantasy of entering the world of the image, inviting *and* denying it simultaneously."[48] A Chinese precedent of exactly this kind of fantasy exists in Pu Songling's tale, "The Painted Wall" (*Huabi*). A young graduate, Zhu, and his friend, Meng, visit a Zen temple and are given a tour by an elderly monk. They come to a mural on a wall in which Zhu sees the detail of a young maiden "with unbound hair, a flower in her hand and a magically smiling face."

> Her lips seemed to move, and the light in her eyes rippled like water. Zhu stared at this maiden like a man transfixed, and was soon utterly transported by the vision. He was wafted bodily up on to the wall and into the mural itself. He felt himself pillowed on clouds, and saw stretching before a grand panorama of palaces and pavilions, a veritable fairy realm. He could see an aged abbot preaching the Dharma from a pulpit, surrounded by a throng of robed monks. Zhu was mingling with the crowd when presently he felt someone secretly tugging at his sleeve, turned to look, and saw the maiden with the unbound hair walking smilingly away from him.[49]

Zhu runs after the maiden and when they are alone, makes love to her. They have more liaisons for another two days. The maiden's hair becomes a subject of mirth among her companions since she is no longer a virgin. Hairpins and pendants are brought to put her hair up like a grown woman. The lovers' enchantment with each other is suddenly interrupted by the entry of a guard in full armor who has come to check on the girls and make sure that they are not harboring any men from the outside world. Zhu is asked to hide under the bed by his fleeing lover. He does so and anxiously waits for calm to return. At this point, Zhu's friend notices his absence and asks for his whereabouts. The monk says he is not far from there. He taps on the wall and calls out to Zhu, who is suddenly visible on the mural. He drifts down and tells the whole story to his astonished friend. Then, they look at the mural and see the detail of the maiden, her hair "no longer hanging down but had been dressed in fine coils on her head." When asked to explain, the monk says, "The source of illusion lies within man himself" (*huan you ren sheng*).[50]

Judith Zeitlin has noted that the change of the girl's hairstyle is "the final turn of the screw" and "in this last erotic twist, illusion has merged with reality."[51] This detail resonates with the painting of Carlotta Valdes and Madeleine's imitation of her hairstyle. Pu's story might actually have been based on a real wall painting at the Fahai temple in the outskirts of Beijing and its detail of a celestial maiden holding a flower. There is an uncanny connection with the portrait of Carlotta Valdes, such that one might well wonder whether Hitchcock knew of the story or the painting at the Fahai temple and drew inspiration from them. The detail of the hair is of course an important one in the film. Madeleine puts her hair up like Carlotta, as in the painting. The significance is that Madeleine is a married woman, not a virgin—an important point when we see her doing her hair up with pins at Scottie's apartment.

The story of "The Painted Wall" is a strong model for Hitchcock in the fantasy of entering the picture. "The Painted Wall" makes the fantasy entirely credible in that its frame is not as limiting as a painting hanging on a wall. It is a wall mural, suggesting a greater degree of immersion, a greater degree of possibility, like that of a cinema screen. Hitchcock's elaborate camera moves on the painting of Carlotta Valdes (as per Gunning's analysis) make it seem like the frame of the painting has turned into a cinema screen, enabling Scottie to enter. This was the effect of the shot of Madeleine at Ernie's where her face in profile is framed like a painting on the wall with red all around, seemingly immersing her in the wall, and we with it, or conversely, that she has come out of a painting, as Eli Friedlander suggests.[52] This is the major implication of Pu Songling's story if we see a direct connection between it and *Vertigo*.

Hitchcock's elaborate moves with regard to Carlotta's painting are perhaps only a metaphor to suggest that Scottie should treat Madeleine as a painting and enter *her* world. Scottie is thus invited to take this notion up in those scenes where he does see Madeleine like a painting, namely, the scene in his apartment where she wears a red dressing gown and the scene in Judy's hotel room where she is dressed in green. Indeed, in both scenes, we see his light blue eyes scanning her person as he would a painting. In the latter, I tend to see that famous moment—when the camera rotates around Scottie and Judy as they kiss, and he sees that he is back at the livery stable—as Scottie entering Madeleine's painting. This is the effect in "The Painted Wall" story; we might now call this the "painted wall effect." This "painted wall effect" is missing in the earlier scene of Madeleine in red at Scottie's apartment because the red sensation has turned Madeleine into "flesh-and-blood reality." The scene inside the apartment is nevertheless dreamlike and may be confused with an immersive painting. However, the idea is that the apartment itself is the vessel of the illusion, and Madeleine's red turns her into a virtual reality.

Chinese melodrama

The scene at Midge's apartment where Scottie is shown to be recuperating from his near fall in the opening sequence, establishes him as a vulnerable figure with a history of illness, suffering not just from the affliction of acrophobia but from other traumas, more emotional, which we infer from Midge's furtive glances. These glances are part of the melodramatic impulses that suddenly infringe on the text. They convey an inverse effect on the Midge-Scottie relationship, which is otherwise cordial. From the viewpoint of narrative construction, their relationship is the inverse of the Madeleine-Scottie relationship. The shots foreshadow a classic Chinese melodrama coming into play, establishing marriage and the idea of romantic predestiny (*yuanfen*) as the main themes of *Vertigo* rather than the detective and crime drama indicated by the opening sequence. The film develops into a fantasy of marriage and a tragic love story misbegotten by fate. Marriage is broached as a subject in the conversation between Scottie and Midge and she is suddenly put into a spot. Why is she not Scottie's wife? Her own furtive glances tell us that she is clearly unsuited. Midge's later attempt to provoke Scottie into a response to her by wearing a red blouse and painting a replica of Carlotta's portrait but substituting her own face for Carlotta's backfires miserably. That Midge is not Scottie's ideal woman is reinforced by her own nature as a mother-hen of a character: "She is too *explicitly* the mother," writes Wood (his emphasis), and she also "demystifies sexuality" ("for the romantic lover sex must always remain mystified").[53] These are personality traits in the Western sense. The Chinese would say that the two are simply not fated to marry. That Scottie flits in and out of Midge's apartment suggests the lack of romantic predestiny (*yuanfen*), a perennial theme of Chinese melodramas that carries intonations of romantic irony. If she was meant to marry Scottie, her home would be less accessible. Robin Wood makes an insightful comment about this: "She is finally disqualified by her accessibility."[54] This is borne out by the fact that Midge does not meet Scottie in *his* apartment ever. The nearest she comes to it is when she drives by and sees Madeleine coming out of his apartment and hastily driving away in her Jaguar. Midge then drives off after seeing Scottie at the porch looking in the direction of Madeleine.

Tania Modleski has referred to the Freudian notion of uncanniness, which is rendered "in a lengthy dreamlike sequence after Madeleine has been at Scottie's house." The next day, Scottie follows Madeleine in his car

> and she leads him on an especially circuitous route, while the camera, continually cutting back to his face, emphasizes his increasing perplexity. To his great surprise and puzzlement, they wind up back at his house, where she has come to deliver a note. Scottie's pursuit of the mysterious other, then, inevitably takes him to his own home, just as Freud has shown that the uncanny, the *unheimlich*, is precisely the "homelike," the familiar which has been made strange through repression.[55]

Seen from a Chinese perspective, this whole sequence displays the uncanniness of *yuanfen*, romantic predestiny, which leads Scottie to his own home. As we have discussed earlier, this home is a locus of romantic love signified by the red door and the double happiness symbols, both a literal representation of the Chinese phrase *shuangxi linmen*, meaning "double happiness comes to the door." Thus, Scottie meets Madeleine by the red door, quite literally. The red immediately tells us they are destined to be lovers (in Chinese folklore, a more common symbol is a red thread symbolizing the fated relationship of two lovers, leading to their marriage). Did Madeleine (or in fact Gavin Elster) know in advance of the red door? As Judy reveals in her letter to Scottie (which she tears up after writing it): "I fell in love. That wasn't part of the plan." That was, in fact, the part of *yuanfen*. If Hitchcock had not known about the principle of *yuanfen*, then it is truly uncanny that it would be signified anyway, first, by the red door, and then by the whole apartment as the *unheimlich*, a home weirdly representing (through its Chinese motifs) the ultimate destiny of lovers. If Scottie is directed by the fate of *yuanfen*, he ultimately rejects it because he "exists within the frame of a Hitchcock film" and therefore he does not have "the power or the freedom to keep Judy safe." (Judy, of course, is Madeleine, Scottie's predestined lover, and romantic irony compels that Scottie rejects Judy.)[56]

The red tower of the Golden Gate Bridge points to another significant Chinese melodrama motif, which is that of water. It is uncanny that Madeleine jumps into the water, of course, because water signifies woman. Another famous line from *Dream of the Red Chamber* puts it this way: "Woman is made of water, while man is made of mud" (*nüer shi shui zuo de gurou, nanren shi ni zuo de gurou*). The sequence in the apartment where Scottie takes her after rescuing her from the water is another illustration of this truism. Madeleine is still wet. Her wet hair is the tell-tale sign ("I tried to dry your hair as best I could," says Scottie). Then, there is the red dressing gown, which she puts on. Both the red robe and her still wet hair symbolize the water motif. Madeleine has literally come out of the water. The red gown is a color extension of the red tower of the bridge, linking Madeleine to water. The complementary factor of green seen on Scottie—his pullover—makes him the mud to Madeleine's water. Green signifies that Scottie has at last found his ideal woman, signified in red. The water motif points to another saying (Buddhist in origin) about romantic love: *ruoshui sanqian, zhi qu yi piao yin* ("from three thousand *li* of fragile waters, I only ladle once to satisfy my thirst"). The saying is often used as a metaphor of romantic choice where a man chooses the one woman to love, from a vast ocean of women. Scottie has found his one woman. He literally picks her up from the ocean (Figure 2.4).

Figure 2.4 Scottie rescues Madeleine from the water.
Vertigo, Producer: Herbert Coleman.

This water motif in *Vertigo* is very evocative in the Chinese sense, and it is significant that in the Chinese remake of *Vertigo*, Lou Ye's *Suzhou River* (2000), much is made of this water motif. The Madeleine figure in Lou Ye's film is turned into a mermaid, an act in a performing floor show in a sleazy bar. The mermaid act alludes to the water motif in the original even as it makes use of such a motif within Chinese culture. Jerome Silbergeld tells us that there is "a cluster of Chinese traditions that link female beauty with water, water with marriage-and-sacrifice or love-and-suicide, and these with a corporeal return-from-the-dead."⁵⁷ Though Silbergeld was writing about *Suzhou River*, he might just as well be describing *Vertigo*. We can treat *Vertigo* practically as a Chinese melodrama, where the female beauty, associated with water, eventually commits suicide for love, returns from the dead, falls in love once more, and dies all over again (a matter of double unhappiness, or romantic irony, Chinese-style). Hitchcock introduces the water motif to underscore the melodramatic nature of his own tale, in the tradition of Chinese melodramas. *Vertigo* can then be appreciated as a Chinese-style melodrama of sexuality, marriage, and love with both characters acting in an "Oriental" or quite typically Eastern manner that has been deliberately fashioned by Hitchcock.

To press the point about *Vertigo*'s Chinese melodrama motifs even further, we might say that there is a gender element at play in the film. From the Chinese perspective, green on a man can be an unflattering image. This is the notion of the cuckold, green in Chinese representing the mark of an inferior man who is betrayed by a woman. The Chinese expression *dai lü mao* (to wear a green hat) is symbolic of this inferior nature of a man betrayed by his wife or lover. In the scene with Madeleine inside his apartment, Scottie wears a green pullover and not a green hat, but it has the same import, perhaps of an even heavier significance since one can easily throw away a hat but it is not as easy to remove a garment. The green pullover thus has the effect of transforming Scottie into another gender identity, and hereon, we may say that Scottie has become more feminine. The scene in the apartment is striking for the color coding of both Scottie (in green) and Madeleine (in red) as characters who are complementary, yet divergent. Green on Scottie at this point signifies that he will be betrayed by Madeleine, and red on her points to her eventual betrayal of Scottie. Scottie's status as a man is certainly made more vulnerable by his green garment. Susan White makes the point that Scottie "undergoes a metamorphosis during the course of the film."[58] This metamorphosis is most conspicuous in this sequence, marked by the green pullover, which has the effect of feminizing Scottie as he interacts with Madeleine's presence. Scottie's femininity is already on show in the scene at Midge's apartment that I style as the true opening. Tania Modleski points out the connection between the heroes of *Rear Window* and *Vertigo*, both characters physically impaired at the start (and both are played by the same actor, James Stewart).[59] "Scottie is placed in the same position of enforced passivity as L. B. Jefferies, a position that the film explicitly links to femininity and associates with unfreedom."[60] Scottie discloses that he is wearing a corset and that when it comes off, he will be "a free man."

> It is as if at this early moment in *Vertigo*, the film is humorously suggesting that femininity in our culture is largely a male construct, a male "design," and that this femininity is in fact a matter of external trappings, or roles and masquerade, without essence. This is an idea that the film will subsequently evoke with horror.[61]

Actually, Hitchcock has laid out an elaborate groundwork to evoke Scottie's femininity through the set of Chinese motifs that are hidden at first. In the scene at Midge's, we can already see some "hidden" qualities of Chinese design. Toward the end of the scene, Scottie is about to go. He stands near the door of the apartment, partially concealed by an Eastern-looking screen. Visible on the roof is a Chinese lantern. This partially hidden Chinese motif is a trigger that sets off Scottie's sudden urge to overcome his acrophobia. He stands on a three-rung stool (given by Midge) but alas falls down on the top rung when he looks down and is embraced by Midge. This is the first classic image of Scottie's femininity, expressed as physical vulnerability. In his scenes with Madeleine at Scottie's apartment, his femininity comes to the fore, the result of his green pullover. Here he is vulnerable in a gentlemanly, dandy-like way. At times, he is also strong—touches of masculinity coming through, which shows in effect that the pullover subsumes only half his personality (the other half is his tough detective persona).

In effect, this testifies to what Susan White says about James Stewart's performance, that it "projects gender ambiguity played to its extreme"—a statement that I would rephrase to "gender ambiguity played to both (masculine and feminine) extremes."[62] If Scottie represents the male gaze, I agree with Modleski's assertion that the male spectator "is as much 'deconstructed' as constructed" by the film in question.[63] I would argue that this is done through the association of Scottie with a "Chinese" identity, his green pullover representing the incarnation of this identity. In fact, both Scottie and Madeleine are projections of Eastern identity in the film, as I have already intimated, Scottie in the guise of a Confucian gallant (*ruxia*), and Madeleine in that of a high-class concubine. Scottie's *ruxia* status emphasizes both a masculine side and a feminine side. The masculine emanates from the fact that he is an ex-policeman and now a private detective. The feminine stems from the *ru* or scholarly component, evident through his use of Chinese motifs in his apartment and his quoting of a Chinese proverb to underscore his gallant nature connecting him to Madeleine: "The Chinese say that once you have saved a person's life, you are responsible for it forever."

Conclusion

I will conclude this chapter with the following observations about these "Chinese" gender identities of the protagonists. The *ruxia* persona of Scottie is shown to be unstable from the start whether it is in the prologue or in the following scene at Midge's apartment. The feminine or vulnerable side of *ru* tends to overwhelm the more conventional masculinity of the *xia* (the gallant, a word that also means chivalry), and this is thought to have been the case in China for well over 2,000 years since the establishment of the Confucian order over society. Scottie reminds me of the scholarly protagonist Gu Shengzhai in King Hu's *A Touch of Zen* (released in two installments, 1970–71), who stumbles into a political conspiracy but has no fighting skills with which to help the rebel side and instead lends his support by using his superior skills as a thinker and strategist. He finds a soul mate in the female *xia*, Yang Huizhen, who becomes his mate only out of pity for his status as an unmarried son. Scottie, like Gu Shengzhai, is unmarried, and his masculinity is a classic case of what Judith Butler says about masculinity—that it is "a fragile and fallible construct" because, in the first place, it "needs the social support of marriage and stable family life in order to find its right path."[64] Where Chinese melodramas are about marriage, they usually feature weak and effeminate sons who do not marry or end up in unhappy marriages. If we see Scottie as a Chinese character in a melodrama, he fits into the *wen* (literary and cultured) tradition in Confucian culture that effectively feminizes males (melodramas are known in Chinese as *wenyi pian*, films of the literary and artistic). Scottie is typically "weak" since he is given to morbidity if for no other cause.

We could say that Scottie is intrinsically bisexual, which crosses feminine and masculine sides as an attraction to the audience, the majority of which would be female. (A man who is "weak" and openly weeps is more attractive to women.) "Those crossings are as complex as anything that happens within heterosexuality or homosexuality," writes Judith Butler, and they "occur more often than is generally noted."[65] Scottie's position in the heteronormative patriarchal society of *Vertigo* is in any case highly problematic, already prefigured by his acrophobia, which makes him less masculine. He is undoubtedly a complex character, whether seen from a Western perspective or from a Chinese one. In at least one respect, he is very Chinese—the fact that he is not married, and therefore not a filial son. If Midge is the mother figure in *Vertigo*, her role is really to remind Scottie that he must get married, which is what all Chinese mothers do, remind their sons to get married. Thus, Scottie pursues Madeleine really "out of filial devotion," to use Jean Douchet's phrase (to describe an act by Norman Bates).[66] The courtship is tremendously complicated by factors outside and inside Scottie's character as well as in Madeleine/Judy's character. In this way, we can see how theirs was an impossible union. The green color of Scottie's personality is thence the ambiguous expression of his courtship: masculine in its angry responses to the unflattering connotations of cuckoldry (as, for example, in his outburst toward Judy in the last scene upon his discovery that Judy was Gavin Elster's accomplice and also, most probably, his lover and mistress) and gentle-feminine in its sensual responses to the seductive red of Madeleine. Green is ultimately the ambiguous expression of his bisexuality, the color of those "straight-coded Hitchcock protagonists" who "inhabit queer representational spaces."[67]

The green of Judy also marks her out in "queer" feminine and masculine aspects, for Judy too is "straight-coded" in her own way. Her feminine side is self-evident, and no further comment is necessary while the masculine side is shown in the sense of her gallantry, that is, a female gallant (*nüxia*). This *xia* nature comes through when she decides to stick it out with Scottie after their first meeting (she tears up the letter she writes confessing to being Madeleine and to being Gavin Elster's accomplice). That she goes through with all of Scottie's demands as he makes her over is as queer a representation as one can get in the Hollywood cinema of a gallant and sacrificial female. At the same time, it is very moving, with her feminine sensitivity always imminently putting her in harm's way and ultimately pushing her over the edge, literally. "You shouldn't have been that sentimental!" Scottie would cry, a desperate affirmation of Judy's gallant character but coming too late for him to get over the shame and humiliation of having been cuckolded (green is thus the color of this shame and humiliation). "What enrages him in the end is the revelation that the woman whom he has allowed to refashion him is actually a male construction," in other words, a construction of Gavin Elster's.[68] That green reinforces the feminine in Scottie is both a motif of his love for Madeleine and an enduring aftereffect of Elster's scheme, forever tagging him as cuckold.

Finally, this Chinese-identity gender aspect of Judy and Scottie subverts the general perception of *Vertigo* as a Western romantic text, turning the film into a Chinese ontological text instead. All that has been said above has been a process of queering Hitchcock from a cultural position, that is, looking at the Chinese design in *Vertigo* and analyzing it from a Chinese perspective. Such a theoretical position is inevitably outlying and subaltern, and as such it doubly reinforces the queering. This Chinese viewpoint adopts a stand of solidarity with other "queer" viewpoints. We might look at it as being part of the "queer Hitchcock" conundrum posed by Alexander Doty at the beginning of his essay of that title, but fundamentally it queers what I should call the "Anglo-America-normativity" of the critical literature on *Vertigo* (and indeed of film criticism in general). A Chinese Madeleine and a Chinese-feminine Scottie are queer embodiments of all the Eastern elements that make *Vertigo* Hitchcock's queerest and weirdest film in his Anglo-American canon. In the end, they project Hitchcock's theme that all desire is illusionary and only human suffering seems real. Thus, *Vertigo* attains its closure with a truly Daoist essence, following the teaching of the ancients to take life as a bereavement and death as a return (*yi sheng wei sang, yi si wei fan*).

Notes

1 See in particular chapter 2, "A User's Guide to Hitchcock's Signature Systems," in Cohen, *Hitchcock Cryptonymies, Volume 1: Secret Agents* (Minneapolis and London: University of Minnesota Press, 2005).
2 D. A. Miller, *Hidden Hitchcock* (Chicago, IL and London: The University of Chicago Press, 2016), p. 34.
3 Ibid., p. 43.
4 Ibid., p. 37.
5 Ibid., pp. 44–45.
6 In my discussion of Hitchcock's use of color, I am dealing with the symbolic meaning of color and do not wish to entangle myself in a complex discussion of how colors of the spectrum are classified and the naming of colors that physicists and linguists debate over. Color as an intellectual field of investigation and study can be approached from different angles. The field is open to both the arts and the sciences, as indicated by the collection of chapters in *Colour, Art and Science*, ed. Trevor Lamb and Janine Bourriau (Cambridge: Cambridge University Press, 1995). Some readers might want to argue whether the red that a Chinese person sees is the same red that a Westerner sees. I point them to the following comment from Linda Holtzschue's *Understanding Color: An Introduction for Designers* (Hoboken, NJ: John Wiley and Sons, 2011), p. 3: "Not only are colors themselves unstable, ideas about colors are unstable as well. The color that one person identifies as 'true red' will be a bit different from another's idea of 'true

red.' When colors are used as symbols, their meanings are equally mutable. A color used symbolically in one context may have another meaning entirely—and even be called by another name—when it appears in a different situation."

7   Richard Allen, *Hitchcock's Romantic Irony* (New York: Columbia University Press, 2007), p. 242.
8   Noël Carroll, "*Vertigo*, the Impossible Love," in K. Makkai (ed.), *Vertigo* (London and New York: Routledge, 2013), pp. 71–88.
9   Herbert Coleman, *The Man Who Knew Hitchcock: A Hollywood Memoir* (Lanham, MD: The Scarecrow Press, 2007), p. 245 and 248.
10 See Dan Auiler, *Vertigo, The Making of a Hitchcock Classic* (New York: St. Martin's Griffin, 2000), p. 99.
11 Tom Cohen, *Hitchcock's Cryptonymies*, Vol. 1, p. 37.
12 Katie Trumpener identifies the Chinese symbol but says merely that it is ironic. She does not go into any deep analysis of the Chinese meanings or ironic substance of the symbolism. See Katie Trumpener, "Fragments of the Mirror: Self-Reference, Mise-en-Abyme, *Vertigo*," in Walter Raubicheck and Walter Srebnick (eds.), *Hitchcock's Rereleased Films: From* Rope *to* Vertigo (Detroit, MI: Wayne State University Press, 1991), p. 182.
13 William Rothman, *The "I" of the Camera: Essays in Film Criticism, History, and Aesthetics* (Cambridge University Press, 2004), p. 231.
14 Richard Misek, *Chromatic Cinema: A History of Screen Color* (Chichester, West Sussex: Wiley-Blackwell, 2010), pp. 40–41.
15 Coleman, *The Man Who Knew Hitchcock*, p. 248.
16 The phrase comes from Stanley Cavell's essay on *North by Northwest*, analyzed as a comedy by Cavell. All the best comedies take as its goal the creation of "a new woman": "This takes the form . . . of something like the woman's death and revival, and it goes with the camera's insistence on the flesh-and-blood reality of the female actor. When this happens in Hitchcock, as it did in *Vertigo*, the Hitchcock film preceding *North by Northwest*, it is shown to produce catastrophe: the woman's falling to her death, precisely the fate averted in *North by Northwest*." See Stanley Cavell, "*North by Northwest*," in M. Deutelbaum and L. Poague (eds.), *A Hitchcock Reader* (Chichester, West Sussex: Wiley-Blackwell, 2009), p. 261.
17 The preproduction artwork of the apartment shows the mandala clearly evident in the same spot. See Auiler, *Vertigo, The Making of a Hitchcock Classic*, p. 100.
18 Robin Wood, *Hitchcock's Films Revisited* (New York: Columbia University Press, 2002), p. 385.

19 Ibid., see p. 384 and 386.
20 Charles Barr, *Vertigo* (London: Palgrave Macmillan, 2012), p. 74.
21 Brigitte Peucker, "Blood, Paint, or Red? The Color Bleed in Hitchcock," in J. Freedman (ed.), *The Cambridge Companion to Alfred Hitchcock* (Cambridge: Cambridge University Press, 2015), p. 198.
22 Ibid.
23 Ibid.
24 See the translation by John Minford of Pu Songling's stories in *Strange Tales from a Chinese Studio* (London: Penguin Books, 2006). "The Girl in Green" appears on pp. 356–59.
25 Cavell, "*North by Northwest*," p. 261.
26 Slavoj Žižek, "*Vertigo*: The Drama of a Deceived Platonist," *Hitchcock Annual*, 12, 2003/2004, p. 73. Elsewhere, Žižek refers to the "*allegorical* dimension" of Hitchcock by which his "diegetic content functions as the allegory of some transcendent entity (flesh-and-blood individuals personify transcendent principles: Love, Temptation, Betrayal, etc.; they procure external clothing for suprasensible ideas)." See Žižek, "In His Bold Gaze My Ruin is Writ Large," in S. Žižek (ed.), *Everything You Always Wanted to Know About Lacan. . . . But Were Afraid to Ask Hitchcock* (London: Verso, 1992), p. 218.
27 Fredric Jameson, "Spatial Systems in *North by Northwest*," in S. Žižek (ed.), *Everything You Always Wanted to Know About Lacan. . . . But Were Afraid to Ask Hitchcock* (London: Verso, 1992), p. 52.
28 See Paul Elliott for a discussion on the sensation of touch in Hitchcock's films, chapter 8 in *Hitchcock and the Cinema of Sensations: Embodied Film Theory and Cinematic Reception* (London and New York: I. B. Tauris, 2011). Elliott refers to Hitchcock films to exemplify touching as one of the vital sensations in his synaesthetic "embodiment" theory. He notes that Hitchcock plays up "images of distance and images of proximity and with the interchange between light and darkness" (p. 181) to achieve the result. Elliott does not mention the role of color as an ocular register that can increase our sense of touch. Rohmer and Chabrol put it very well when referring to the image in *To Catch a Thief* of a cigarette being stubbed out in an egg: "Here the presence of *color* strangely reinforces the strength of the impression" (emphasis theirs). See Éric Rohmer and Claude Chabrol, *Hitchcock: The First Forty-Four Films*, trans. Stanley Hochman (New York: Continuum, 1988), p. 131.
29 Allen, *Hitchcock's Romantic Irony*, p. 117.
30 Ibid., p. 220.
31 Ibid., p. 117.

32 Ibid.
33 Brigitte Peucker, "Aesthetic Space in Hitchcock," in T. Leitch and L. Poague (eds.), *A Companion to Alfred Hitchcock* (Chichester, West Sussex: Wiley-Blackwell, 2011), p. 211.
34 From Chen Hui's commentary on the *Yinchi rujing*, An Shigao's translation of the Skandadhatvayatana sutra into Chinese.
35 Wood, *Hitchcock's Films Revisited*, p. 115.
36 Carroll, "*Vertigo*, the Impossible Love," p. 72.
37 The translation is mine. For another translation into English of the preface to *Qingshi leilüe*, see Christoph Harbemeier, "Autochthonous Chinese Conceptual History in a Jocular Narrative Key: The Emotional Engagement *Qing*," in H. Joas and B. Klein (eds.), *The Benefit of Broad Horizons: Intellectual and Institutional Preconditions for a Global Social Science* (Leiden and Boston, MA: Brill, 2010), pp. 293–313.
38 Carroll, "*Vertigo*, the Impossible Love," p. 85.
39 Wai-yee Li, *Enchantment and Disenchantment: Love and Illusion in Chinese Literature* (Princeton, NJ: Princeton University Press, 1993), p. 92.
40 This is my own translation. The original tale is "Luoyang Wang mou" ("A Certain Mr. Wang of Luoyang"), available online (in Chinese), http://www.my285.com/gdwx/xs/bj/qs/217.htm (accessed November 30, 2016).
41 Elliott, *Hitchcock and the Cinema of Sensations*, p. 70.
42 Li, *Enchantment and Disenchantment*, p. 3.
43 Eske Møllgaard, *An Introduction to Daoist Thought: Action, Language, and Ethics in Zhuangzi* (London and New York: Routledge, 2007), p. 124.
44 According to Keiji Nishitani, the Buddhist sea of samsaric suffering likens the world "with all its six ways and its unending turnover from one form of existence to another, to an unfathomable sea and identifying the essential Form of beings made to roll with its restless motion as suffering." See Keiji Nishitani, *Religion and Nothingness*, trans. Jan Van Bragt (Berkeley, Los Angeles, and London: University of California Press, 1982), p. 169. The "six ways" (*liu dao*) are the heavenly, the human, the animal, the *asura* (demons), the hungry ghosts, and the hellish.
45 Barr, *Vertigo*, pp. 79–80.
46 See Rohmer and Chabrol, *Hitchcock: The First Forty-Four Films*, p. 113. Žižek's Lacanian interpretation is of a Jansenist bent in Hitchcock which allows for "the determinatedness of subjective destinies by the transsubjective blind automatism of the symbolic machinery" (see Žižek, "In His Bold Gaze My Ruin is Writ Large," p. 256).

47 Tom Gunning, "In and Out of the Frame: Paintings in Hitchcock," in W. Schmenner and C. Granof (eds.), *Casting a Shadow: Creating the Alfred Hitchcock Film* (Evanston, IL: Northwestern University, 2007), p. 31.
48 Ibid., p. 33.
49 Translation by John Minford, "The Painted Wall," *Strange Tales from a Chinese Studio* (London: Penguin Books, 2006), p. 23.
50 Quotations from Minford's translation, *Strange Tales from a Chinese Studio*, p. 25 and 27. For a commentary on this story, see Judith Zeitlin, *Historian of the Strange: Pu Songling and the Chinese Classical Tale* (Stanford, CA: Stanford University Press, 1993), pp. 183–99.
51 Zeitlin, *Historian of the Strange*, p. 187.
52 Friedlander writes, "Madeleine appears straight out of a painting (one might think here of Ingres's all too ideal, stony yet at the same time pliant women in their velvety interiors)." Eli Friedlander, "Being-in-(Techni)color," p. 176.
53 Wood, *Hitchcock's Films Revisited*, p. 385.
54 Ibid.
55 Tania Modleski, *The Women Who Knew Too Much: Hitchcock and Feminist Theory* (London: Routledge, 2005), p. 94.
56 Rothman, *The "I" of the Camera*, p. 236.
57 Jerome Silbergeld, *Hitchcock with a Chinese Face: Cinematic Doubles, Oedipal Triangles, and China's Moral Voice* (Seattle: University of Washington Press, 2004), p. 25.
58 Susan White, "A Surface Collaboration: Hitchcock and Performance," in T. Leitch and L. Poague (eds.), *A Companion to Alfred Hitchcock* (Chichester, West Sussex: Wiley-Blackwell, 2011), p. 192.
59 Coincidentally, *Rear Window* carries a brief reference to China during the conversation between Lisa Fremont and L. B. Jefferies in their first scene together early in the film: Lisa: "You know, this cigarette box has seen better days." Jefferies replies this: "I picked that up in Shanghai, which has also seen better days." This seems gratuitous until one realizes that it sets up the Cold War context and mood of the story. *Rear Window* is really a domestic spy movie wherein surveillance is modified into voyeurism. The Chinese element in *Vertigo* also turns it into a Cold War–type thriller although the motifs and themes are a shade more benign. Chinese red then becomes not the red of communism but the red of fortune and luck.
60 Modleski, *The Women Who Knew Too Much*, p. 92.
61 Ibid.
62 Susan White, "A Surface Collaboration: Hitchcock and Performance," p. 191.

63 Modleski, *The Women Who Knew Too Much*, p. 89.
64 Judith Butler, *Undoing Gender* (New York and London: Routledge, 2004), p. 90.
65 Ibid., p. 80.
66 Jean Douchet, "Hitch and His Public," trans. Verena Andermatt Conley, in M. Deutelbaum and L. Poague (eds.), *A Hitchcock Reader* (Chichester, West Sussex: Wiley-Blackwell, 2009), p. 21.
67 Alexander Doty, "Queer Hitchcock," in T. Leitch and L. Poague (eds.), *A Companion to Alfred Hitchcock* (Chichester, West Sussex: Wiley-Blackwell, 2011), p. 483.
68 Paula Marantz Cohen, "Hitchcock's Revised American Vision, *The Wrong Man* and *Vertigo*," in J. Freedman and R. Millington (eds.), *Hitchcock's America* (New York and Oxford: Oxford University Press, 1999), p. 168.

3

Orson Welles's *The Lady from Shanghai*

An Eastern exotic thriller

In Chapter 2, we examined Hitchcock's *Vertigo* as a model of a Hollywood thriller-melodrama containing Eastern motifs shaping and molding its themes and content. The motifs also helped to make the film an Eastern exotic thriller, a type of film that has antecedents in the Hollywood cinema. The best earlier prototype is Orson Welles's *The Lady from Shanghai*, released in 1948. Welles's film was cut by its studio, Columbia, from the original running time of 155 minutes to its current release version of 87 minutes. Due to this studio interference, the film suffers from certain lapses with the result that it is not as accomplished or well-made as Hitchcock's film. However, despite its slipshoddiness, it is highly original, with excellent if also very bizarre sequences, some of which have since become inspiring models of filmmaking (e.g., the Magic Mirror Maze sequence at the climax of the film). The plot is somewhat like *Vertigo*, which might be seen as a remake of Welles's film through its focus on a glamorous and exotic female protagonist and the spell she casts on the male protagonist. Michael O'Hara (played by Orson Welles) is an out-of-work sailor who meets the female protagonist Elsa Bannister (played by Rita Hayworth) in New York's Central Park and rescues her from a gang of thugs. Enchanted by her, he becomes irreversibly embroiled in intrigue and murder, later revealed to be her handiwork. The film's prototypical design is the femme fatale associated with the East, or indeed, originating from the East. Her Eastern character confers on the film the Eastern philosophical content which we will investigate below.

At their first meeting in Central Park, Elsa reveals that she is a White Russian born in Cheefoo, China (now Yantai, in Shandong province).

"The second wickedest city in the world," says Michael. "What's the first?" Elsa asks. "Macao," Michael replies (pronouncing it in the Portuguese style, "Ma-ca-yo"). "I worked there," Elsa says. "How do you rate Shanghai? I worked there too." "As a gambler? Hope you were luckier than tonight," Michael says. This section of dialogue establishes Elsa's and the film's unmistakable association with the East and evokes a vision of the East as sleazy and immoral. It also appears to denote that the title "The Lady from Shanghai" is something of a misnomer since it could be more rightfully titled "The Lady from Macao" or "The Lady from Chefoo." That Shanghai graces the title is probably because it is better known, and the other two cities are more obscure (if also more exotic sounding). However, all three cities appear to have no particular bearing on the plot, which otherwise takes place in New York, Mexico (Acapulco), and San Francisco. The Chinese cities are symbols of a past—Elsa's past, in terms of the plot, but also Welles's own past, in which Shanghai represented a formative part of Welles's life. There is also a wordplay in the name "Shanghai" in the femme fatale's virtual shanghaiing of the hero in the film's opening scenes. As André Bazin describes the plot in his book *Orson Welles*, Michael "is hired as a sailor on a millionaire's yacht, and thereby shanghaied, so to speak, into the dark and criminal ventures to which the beautiful Elsa Bannister . . . is but a partial stranger."[1] Or, as James Naremore writes in *The Magic World of Orson Welles*, "The lady of the title is of course a shanghaier of sailors, a Sternbergian Circe who lures an Irish Ulysses onto the rocks with her wet swimsuit, or who sings an incredibly bad song which turns O'Hara into a zombie."[2]

In his youth, Welles had travelled to the East twice, once when he was eight and the other time when he was fifteen. On his second trip, in the summer of 1930, Welles visited Japan and China. Various biographers have noted that his trip included visits to Beijing, Shanghai, and Hong Kong. It was Shanghai that seems to have exerted a lasting impact on Welles. In his book, *Young Orson*, Patrick McGilligan reported that Welles had wandered into a Chinese opera when he was alone one day in Shanghai and that he would recreate that same moment in *The Lady from Shanghai*.[3] Simon Callow notes that Welles had "written a vivid account of Chinese theatre in his local newspaper" and that "he had followed it knowledgeably" ever since his Shanghai experience.[4] There is another, more psychological, dimension to Shanghai for Welles. In their book *Noir Anxiety*, Kelly Oliver and Benigno Trigo claim that "the Far East in general and Shanghai in particular are sites that contain, preserve, but also repress the lost mother for Welles."[5] This claim is based on the information that Welles had embarked on his first trip to the East not long after his mother's death in 1923.

Thus, we may discern a biographical theme in the use of Shanghai in the title. Welles combines this biographical detail of his past with his status of being Rita Hayworth's husband by making his wife play a mysterious femme fatale from Shanghai (essentially, she is a Chinese refugee in America). Shanghai symbolically conveys a special meaning for the character, a sense of desperation, despondency, and loss that Macao or Cheefoo may not possess for her. It also enhances the mysterious femme fatale disposition of Elsa's character. The line "You need more than luck in Shanghai" confers the idea that she is gambling on her fate or destiny. This is probably the most symbolic theme that comes through from the title—Shanghai as an emblem of destiny. Welles might have felt this sense of destiny himself in real life when he visited the city; the incident at the Chinese opera foretelling his future in the theater. In terms of the characterization of Elsa, Shanghai is a metaphor of her identity, just as it is obviously a pre-sign of Welles's theatrical individuality. Shanghai uniquely distinguishes Elsa's identity in that "she is a femme fatale with a literally dark or non-white past."[6] Shanghai conjures up her racial identity and muddles it with her Western features. It also signifies the leading lady's character, effectively a prototype of the kind of femme fatale protagonist that would occupy Hollywood's noir cinema in the postwar period, as well as the Eastern qualities of the thriller. The "Eastern" branding of the female protagonist's identity is a trope of mystery, deceit, and evil, as well as the deeper layers of identity beyond the surface. In *Noir Anxiety*, Oliver and Trigo describe Elsa as "an Asian femme fatale" and such a depiction of Elsa was part of Welles's attempts "to produce a terrified shock in the audience," thus, "to escape clichés and even stereotypes."[7] Significantly, Welles, whose marriage with Hayworth was already breaking up at the time of the film's making, was deliberately undercutting Hayworth's image as a Hispanic exotic who had a "carefully balanced and highly popular nonwhite persona."[8] Jealously guarded by Harry Cohn, the chief of Columbia, which had produced her most famous star-making role, *Gilda* (1946), the persona came unhinged by Welles. He had set about to make her character a "'whiter than white' Asian femme fatale."[9]

Fans of Hayworth would most certainly have felt confused or have been shocked by this startling new image as "the domestic and treacherous Asian."[10] The gay Marxist critic Andrew Britton probably put it best in the title of his essay "Betrayed by Rita Hayworth: Misogyny in *The Lady from Shanghai*." Britton's essay essentially focused on attacking Welles for his misogyny, but to Britton, a fan of Hayworth, Welles had not only undermined the star's persona but also eliminated "its positive connotations": "The discarded Hayworth 'image' connotes vitality, exuberance, openness, and a carnality which, though self-conscious and sometimes deliberately provocative, also asserts its independence of male desire."[11]

> In *The Lady from Shanghai*, Hayworth's iconic lucidity is redefined as Machiavellian cunning, and her erotic energy is confined and immobilized in a succession of sculptured poses which transform her face into a mask of sphinxlike inscrutability. This radical reconception of the very nature of Hayworth's beauty obviously coincides with the film's view of Elsa's character. The beauty is entirely a matter of surface, and its function is to conceal the essential nature of the woman who manufactured it.[12]

Britton undertakes a defense of Hayworth's studio-created persona from a subjective gender perspective, but it seems somewhat credulous, in my opinion, particularly in his belief that it asserts "its independence of male desire." Britton then reminds me of Michael O'Hara in the opening scenes and his gullibility over Elsa's beauty, which is, of course, a mistake. Michael's naiveté extends to his creating his own image of Elsa, that of the princess Rosalie. Clearly, Britton, like O'Hara, does not grasp the illusionary nature of appearances, a basic Eastern theme introduced by these opening scenes. The article reveals Britton's antipathy toward Welles and his redefinition of the Hayworth image into an Asian or Oriental femme fatale. Britton shows his dislike of this new image, and he therefore sees nothing in it, no innovative conceptions of gender or identity, certainly. For us, Welles's redefined image is crucial in suggesting how an important Western filmmaker had infused Eastern philosophy into a Hollywood thriller, as I will try to demonstrate below. I will show that Rita Hayworth's image in *The Lady from Shanghai* is a kind of breakthrough in the construction of the Western femme fatale in Hollywood cinema. Welles challenged the ethnicity of the role and invested the character with an Eastern identity.

From our perspective, if one were to adopt Britton's stance and uncritically accept Hayworth's studio-constructed persona, this would at worst foreclose any reading of the Eastern identity and characteristics of the star part in *The Lady from Shanghai*. At best, it would deem any such reading to be a perverse outflow of Welles's egregious creativity. Welles has certainly created a character that transcends whiteness, or Western identity, by emphasizing Eastern or Asian qualities and essence rather than physical features. The character speaks Chinese (or rather, Cantonese) and is on familiar ground in Chinatown (San Francisco's). That she is evil is incidental to the provocativeness of the prototype, and I would venture to say that such a prototype is not without positive connotations. Through this character, Welles would invoke Chinese thought to infuse a stream of otherworldliness into the narrative, exploring the theme of the nature of character (*ben xing*, in Chinese).

Character and nature

Welles's films mostly revolve around a central character whose role is deterministic. We think of Kane in *Citizen Kane*, Hank Quinlan in *Touch of Evil*, Arkadin in *Mr. Arkadin*, Falstaff in *Chimes at Midnight*, and Mr. Clay in *The Immortal Story*. It is not for nothing, therefore, that the actor Micheál MacLíammóir (who played Iago in Welles's *Othello*) once described Welles as a "Philosopher of determination."[13] It is fair to say that Welles steeped himself in such philosophy of determination, which we can surmise through a reading of his central characters and the way they shape his films. *The Lady from Shanghai* is the only film directed by Welles in which such a character is female. Thus, Elsa Bannister determines the events of the narrative of *The Lady from Shanghai*. As George M. Wilson has argued, there is an "attribution of strange causal powers to the woman (which) is systematically integrated with her peculiar role in the surrealistic context of this unusual film."[14] What is it about Elsa that makes her have "strange causal powers"? Is it her beauty, which is the most immediately obvious feature of her personality? Obviously, there is something more than her beauty. There is something in her character, "some peculiar moral or metaphysical status she seems to occupy," as Wilson has put it.[15] The attribution of strange causal powers to her character "is consonant with a number of other features and devices of the film which indicate that the unfolding of the narrative action is, in other ways, nonstandard." The first device that ensures that the narrative action unfolds in the most nonstandard way is Welles's molding of Elsa as a highly unorthodox character in the Western cinema although she may not be the first instance of such a type. Elsa, after all, is an *Asian* femme fatale with white Western features, and her character exudes not merely sexuality but a far more complex suite of subjectivity that twists one's notion of identity.

To investigate character, one must begin with identity, which is how Welles proceeds. Interestingly, Oliver and Trigo aver that the film "is determined by a logic of identity," by which they mean the logic of the identity of Elsa.[16] On the face of it, her identity is a Western identity. Welles's subversiveness overturns this impression in its peculiar way of integrating Hayworth's star image constructed by her Hollywood studio and Welles's own reconstruction of that image. *The Lady from Shanghai* is a process of subject formation, as analyzed by Oliver and Trigo, a process which produces "normative difference," alluding to Homi Bhabha's analysis of colonial discourse, here resting on the awareness of the subject as an Asian, albeit a white one.[17] This produces a sense of dislocation in the audience (assumed predominantly white). "The audience searches in vain for the stereotypical phenotype of the Oriental in her face. It looks closely at her makeup, unsuccessfully seeking traces that hint at her Chinese background."[18] Welles has undoubtedly created a transgressive and ambiguous prototype—ambiguous in East-West terms and transgressive in its muddling of both Eastern and Western consciousness of identity.

In the political and historical context of the period in which the film is set, Elsa is a subject that stems from the consciousness of the colonial era of Western encroachments into China. She is a white woman born in China and apparently brought up in Chinese ways. Now in America, her desire is to mimic the West, to evoke Homi Bhabha's notion of colonial mimicry. From this perspective, Elsa is "a recognizable Other, *as a subject of a difference that is almost the same, but not quite*" (italics Bhabha's).[19] Insofar as it pertains to our discussion of the character and her nature as well as her past—the past surfacing in the shape of her personality, to follow Deleuze[20]—Elsa as Other displays an ambivalence of East and West, pulled by the East and pulled by the West as if simultaneously. Is Elsa an "Other" of the East or of the West? Her ambivalence means that she can function as both.

Oliver and Trigo note that "Elsa Bannister's alien femme fatale made audiences see Rita Hayworth differently by flaunting the artificial markers of her sexual and racial difference."[21] "Through the manipulation and recombination of enhanced racial and sexual markers, Welles not only sought mastery and authority as a filmmaker"—his real purpose "was to show an alternative reality that both shocked the audience into interrupting a natural identification with Elsa and left her image open to interpretation and criticism."[22] Britton's criticism of that image is an example of how a critic sympathetic to Hayworth's conventional star persona rather than to Welles's destruction of it had reacted in the literature. Britton reproaches Welles for constructing a narrative "that leaves no ideological problems to be solved and no subversive criticisms of our culture's sexual values to be recuperated."[23] Britton is no doubt influenced by both his Marxist and gay viewpoints but he zones in on Welles's perceived misogyny in the film, attributing the defects of the female character to the director personally and not to generic determinants of the noir thriller genre into which category the film falls. Neither does Britton provide any historical social background that might explain Welles's misogyny as being more a standard practice of the era. Bazin, who wrote about Welles at an earlier period, had pointed out that Welles's kind of misogyny was par for the course in the American cinema and that it had already become a "commonplace of intellectual criticism."[24] Bazin was more generous to Welles, stating that Rita Hayworth was one of the first victims of this misogyny, "and remains, through Welles' genius, its most glorious martyr."[25] On the other hand, other critics in the Anglo-American sphere were less generous. James Naremore sees a satire emerging from Welles's approach while recognizing that Welles was "a major contributor to the misogynistic tone of forties melodrama."[26] At least Naremore is more open to the idea of Welles's purpose of creating "an alternative reality." *The Lady from Shanghai* is Welles's "most misanthropic treatment of American life":

> In a sense, it is a dream about typical movie dreams, and can almost be read as an allegory about Welles's adventures in Hollywood, showing his simultaneous fascination with and nausea over the movie industry. Hiding

behind a phony Irish brogue instead of the putty nose he would later adopt, Welles enters the film as a wanderer from another country . . . and finds himself in a world of shark-eat-shark individualism.[27]

Naremore catches the gist of Welles's treatment of an alternative reality by suggesting that the director was reacting against Hollywood itself and its "typical movie dreams." He draws his conclusion from Welles's style, "with its fantastic distortions, its complex play of light and shadow, its many levels of activity" which "had always been suited to the depiction of corruption and madness."[28] This Wellesian style, with its own brand of extremes, merged "out of sheer necessity" with "the extremes of Hollywood convention."[29] In this way, *The Lady from Shanghai* is essentially a metafilm, a critique on Hollywood morality. Naremore's take is reasonable and credible but this kind of critical stance would probably infuriate Britton. To Britton, the attack on Hollywood morality is nothing but a form of "sententious homily" that covers up the deeper misogyny of Welles. The critical question, then, of this chapter is whether Welles's incorporation of Eastern philosophy and his redefinition of the femme fatale as Eastern vamp is an integral part of his idiosyncratic style or a sign of his personal misogyny (his bitterness toward Hayworth as his real-life spouse at the time). We will address this question through a greater interpretation of the film as Eastern thriller, a highly unusual form given its credentials as a work produced in Hollywood under the studio system, albeit under the artistic supervision of a maverick director.

To begin with, one should recognize the film's major function as a fable about the nature of character, where one's character tends toward the vulgar and the bad, and the social world around it is that of "shark-eat-shark individualism." This gels with the "essential obsessions of Wellesian ethics," to quote Bazin, who says that there is present in the film "an eminently contemporary awareness of the freedom of choice between good or evil, together with the feeling that this freedom of choice doesn't depend exclusively on the will of man, but is inscribed within a modern form of destiny."[30] This description by Bazin encapsulates what would be the Eastern point of view of Welles's moral philosophy. Fate or an eternal essence of nature rules our lives and submitting to nature is to know one's limits and to act within it. This is a viewpoint that Welles had inscribed into his film. Such an inscription comes a bit later in the film, during the Caribbean cruise, in a scene on the yacht Circe at the steering wheel where Michael and Elsa talk of love.

> Michael: Do you believe in love at all, Mrs. Bannister?
> Elsa (after a pause): Give me the wheel. (She goes to the wheel and after a further pause) I was taught to think about love in Chinese.
> Michael: The way a Frenchman thinks about laughter in French?
> Elsa: The Chinese say: It is difficult for love to last long. Therefore, one who loves passionately is cured of love in the end.
> Michael: That's a hard way of thinking.
> Elsa: There's more to the proverb. Human nature is eternal. Therefore, one who follows his nature keeps his original nature in the end.

This dialogue sharpens and deepens the Eastern tone of the thriller. It is an inscription of Eastern philosophy by Welles at an appropriate moment of some repose in the narrative. (It follows the torch song sequence where Elsa sings the signature tune "Please Don't Kiss Me.") Her taking the wheel is a sign of her determinative role *within* the narrative of the film, as if she is trying to steer events (this contrasts with Michael's voiceover, the self-exculpatory tone of which denotes that he is merely a participant of events steered by Elsa). Robert Pippin, in his essay "Agency and Fate in Orson Welles's *The Lady from Shanghai*," alludes to this steering as a language of agency and determination from both the perspectives of Michael and Elsa, she *"being the one who steers"* (italics Pippin's) and Michael intervening and counter-turning the wheel, "presumably to keep her on course"[31] (see Figure 3.1).

Michael may or may not be going against Elsa. There is just as much room to say that he is supporting or complementing Elsa. In any case, his and Elsa's steering illustrates the theme of fatalism that marks the lovers, a theme deriving from the Chinese proverb that Elsa articulates. The Chinese proverb then is a key marker of the film's conception as an Eastern thriller. The scene on the boat postmarks an inscription of Eastern philosophy that Welles would have anticipated as a crucial point in the narrative, which it is. This scene is like the one in Hitchcock's *Vertigo* in which Scottie tells Madeleine about the Chinese saying that "once you've saved a person's life, you're responsible for it forever." As with Welles in *The Lady from Shanghai*, Hitchcock carefully inscribes a Chinese saying some way into the story to develop the Eastern

Figure 3.1 Michael and Elsa steering the wheel.
The Lady from Shanghai, Producer: Orson Welles.

tone of his thriller more extensively (see my analysis in Chapter 2). Previously in the narrative he had dabbled in Chinese motifs to build up to this more philosophical moment.

It is possible that Hitchcock was really following Welles's narrative prototype of the Eastern thriller, right down to the association of the femme fatale with Chinese themes or designs. In *The Lady from Shanghai*, we have a femme fatale tutored in Eastern philosophy. She gives the keynote speech of the film, as it were. This is where Hitchcock's film differs from Welles's in that his femme fatale is not as conspicuously Eastern and not as knowledgeable of the East, although both are platinum blondes. While Madeleine's blondeness in *Vertigo* is a synthetic marking of white identity, Elsa's blonde hair can stand as a sign of her *Eastern* identity. At any rate, the similarities of the two films are unmistakable. Their use of "Chinese" sayings bound them together even more strongly. This is interesting since I suspect that the sayings in both films are not actually Chinese as such but are Western literary adaptations of Chinese thought with an emphasis on fate. In fact, the Chinese proverb in *The Lady from Shanghai* sounds very much like Welles could have made it up, although when asked by Peter Bogdanovich about it, Welles said it was Chinese.[32] It is difficult to trace both sayings in the Hitchcock and Welles films in their original Chinese if they do exist, but their implications in the themes of love, fate, destiny, character, and nature are certainly resonant of Chinese—or Eastern—thinking.

In Welles's case, the proverbs touch on love and nature. There is, in fact, a common Chinese saying, *ai ji sheng hen* (love in the extreme will breed hate). Welles might have adapted this proverb to fit into his own view and experience of love, deemphasizing hatred. Thus, one is cured of love who loves passionately. (This may be how he felt in real life toward Rita Hayworth.) The other part of the proverb recalls the Daoist notion of following one's natural instincts. This Daoist concept agrees with the philosophy of determination in Welles's cinema. Evil nature invariably predestines one to be evil. There is indeed a Chinese saying that it is difficult to change one's nature, *ben xing nan yi*. This may be the source of the Wellesian idea that one who follows his nature keeps his original nature in the end, a saying which rhymes with the fable of the scorpion and the frog told in *Mr. Arkadin* as well as the story that Michael tells about the sharks feeding on one another.

Thus, the idea of *ben xing* (original human nature, or simply, original nature) is very much at the heart of Welles's philosophy, and his films are examinations of one's original nature. In *The Lady from Shanghai*, what seems startling and provocative in our more politically correct times is that it is an examination of a woman's original nature. Elsa, in giving voice to her philosophy of human nature, therefore changes the tone of the narrative from one of glib observations about characters to a more reflective concern about character and their nature. Robert Pippin makes the point that "the sweeping philosophical themes introduced explicitly in the dialogue—the nature of love, the eternality of one's nature, following one's nature or searching for something 'better,' compromise or struggle with evil" elevate the film, which would otherwise be "some kind of case study of a group of near-psychotic, perverse individuals."[33]

Pippin is preoccupied with the question of agency and fate, questioning whether the characters have any control over events while believing they are exercising some control over events. While Elsa exerts a deterministic role in the story and in her active manipulation of events, she has no control over her own fate. Her evil or maleficent nature finally determines her fate, as Pippin concludes "Heraclitus is right: *ethos anthropoid daimon*, character is destiny."[34] This is also the Chinese moral of the story. Heraclitus is close to Chinese thinking on the issue, but the Chinese believe that character is destiny because it is hard to change one's character or identity. According to the Chinese saying, it is easy to change the rivers and the mountains, but not one's nature (*jiangshan yi gai, ben xing nan yi*). Character is fated since life and death are determined by fate, a saying in the Confucian Analects (chapter 12, verse 5), which also declares that rank and riches are decreed by heaven (*si sheng you ming, fugui zai tian*), and in the *Zhuang Zi* (chapter 6), it is stated, "Life and death are destined. Their constant alternation, like that of day and night, is due to heaven. What men are unable to interfere with are the attributes of all things."[35] Elsa is the embodiment of the human preoccupation with life and death, rank and riches. Her fault is not to know the actions of Heaven:

> She who knows the actions of heaven will live in accordance with heaven. She who knows the actions of men can nourish what is unknown to her intellect with what is known to her intellect. Thus she can live out the years allotted to her by heaven and not die midway.[36]

The trouble with Elsa, then, is that she devotes her intellect completely to "the actions of men," that is, to secular real-world problems. Her philosophy is not to fight a bad world (one dominated by bad men) but to get along with it, deal with it, and make terms. We might recognize this as something of a cliché, part of the philosophy of wicked femme fatales, but this is reasonable to her intellect, given that she is a Chinese refugee or immigrant, Xinlin Zhang (the name that she gives in her phone call at the theater). She must live by her wits, essentially in exile from home, seeking only to survive. The Chinatown theater sequence supports this thesis, as I see it, and more. Elsa is entirely at home here. She is familiar with the Opera troupe, and the actors pass her knowing glances. Barbara Leaming calls this whole sequence a Brechtian demonstration of alienation effect by Welles.[37] However, the sequence is determined by Elsa and her desperate plight, a point not analyzed by Leaming, who tends to view the opera sequence as a self-contained exotic moment in the narrative, which is, by definition, how an alienation effect is supposed to function. The overall effect, in my view, is quite superficial. (Heavily truncated by the studio, we do not know how the sequence plays out in its original cut and will never know unless it is possible to restore all the missing parts into the sequence.[38]) The sequence, as it plays out now, has a narrative consistency with plot and character, placing Elsa in a domestic, interior space where she easily captures Michael, with help from her Chinese friends. If it was somewhere else, she probably could not have done it. The contrast between the home and

Figure 3.2 Elsa at the opera theater.
The Lady from Shanghai, Producer: Orson Welles.

the world, as it were, could not be clearer. The Chinatown sequence may be alienating and strange to a Western audience, but it functions to naturalize Elsa in a "home" setting, largely without resorting to negative stereotyping. Here, Elsa becomes Xinlin Zhang, able to express herself without readapting to another language and culture (Figure 3.2).

While Elsa's "world is bad" philosophy is interpreted negatively by Welles through his alter ego, Michael, a "foolish knight-errant," as Elsa calls him, whose worldview is much more naïvely idealistic, there is some latitude to view Elsa sympathetically despite Michael's (and thus Welles's) stand on the matter. Since Elsa/Xinlin Zhang is a refugee, it is possible to see the film as commenting on the nature of this Asian female refugee who integrates herself into a Western materialistic lifestyle, entailing a necessary change of point of view.[39] She largely succeeds but does not know her limits, and her relationship with Michael is an appeal for help. Her pragmatism and natural knack for manipulation conflict with Michael's romantic notions of chivalry. A self-confessed fool, Michael can only rekindle her dilemma of being a torn personality. If the film is about her nature, we might ask, which nature does she follow? Is it that of the West or of the East? Since she is in the West, she must get along with it on the principle of colonial mimicry. She follows the nature of the West, which Welles shows is a world of sharks, and she appears to assimilate into it perfectly. However, her Western nature does not efface her Eastern character. Her nature cannot change all that easily, following the principle of *ben xing nan yi*.

Thus, one of the more interesting ways in which to interpret the axiom that character is destiny is as an East-West dilemma in Elsa's character. In this way, agency and fate, which Pippin discusses as standard noir themes, are at the core of this dilemma. We may think of agency, the belief that individuals control their own fate, as a Western tendency. Fate is the Eastern belief that one's life is predestined. Elsa tries to change her fate (her steering of events), her Western character coming to the fore, but her Eastern character preordains that her fate cannot be changed no matter how hard she tries. "The idea of humanity taking charge of its destiny makes sense only if we ascribe consciousness and purpose to the species," writes John Gray.[40] Here, the female of the species in the person of Elsa is torn between her Eastern destiny and her Western consciousness. It is this dilemma that makes her very vulnerable, perhaps the most vulnerable of femmes fatales in all of noir cinema (Figure 3.3).

Therefore, Elsa should arouse sympathy, but most Western viewers and critics would likely not feel in any way her kind of East-West dilemma. To them, Elsa comes across essentially as a negative, amoral prototype. Yet, the film does pose this dilemma in a transcendent way, the Eastern

Figure 3.3 Elsa, the vulnerable femme fatale.
The Lady from Shanghai, Producer: Orson Welles.

and the Western opposed to each other but ineradicably entwined. Elsa of course embodies this opposition and entwinement, but so does Michael's personality, whose experience of the East comes through his occupation as a sailor. Michael possesses an Eastern immanence while being outwardly a typical Westerner.

We can fathom this immanence by considering the film's point of view. Though she graces the title, it is not her perspective that drives the film. As Pippin says, "We see almost nothing from her point of view."[41] The point of view is that of Michael, and it is a complex process of reflection as well as refraction, like the images seen in the Magic Mirror Maze sequence. If we see Michael as the hero, his point of view immediately refracts this image. "I start out in this story a little bit like a hero, which I most certainly am not," he says. There is a yin and yang aspect here. A yin characteristic is already evident in the way that Michael is a passive hero for the most part, taking in and being swayed by the events put in place by Elsa, Arthur Bannister (Everett Sloane), and George Grisby (Glenn Anders). There is something consumptive about Michael, a condition essentially driven by desire, following J. P. Telotte. He is a consumer of tall tales, swallowing whole all the stories set up by Elsa and George Grisby, and coming across as "the observer caught up in that which he observes, trapped by his own fascinations within a consumptive whirl."[42] His desire for Elsa is the heart of the matter, but he "lacks the money to take her away from Arthur, then, Michael readily listens to Grisby's proposition about feigning his murder so that he might go off to the South Seas unmolested."[43] Michael appears very gullible and innocent, of course, which is how Welles prepares us for the last scene where Michael leaves Elsa dying outside the Magic Mirror Maze.

So far, we have largely concentrated on analyzing the character of Elsa, that is, her moral character as well as what she is in terms of her identity. However, the film does not proceed from her perspective. For this reason, Elsa's "wicked" moral character becomes the endpoint of the film. Michael's own moral character is not in question, which is to say that other characters do not question his moral temperament. He confesses to having killed someone in Spain (which is his yang side) but all who are involved with him (Elsa, George Grisby, Arthur Bannister) see nothing wrong with it. What we know about Michael comes through his own capacity for self-analysis, which we hear in his narration. Such a capacity seems infinite and we might think of Michael as a wise narrator. (Of course, his character grows wise after the fact, but Michael does aspire to be a novelist, and as such is a philosopher.) More significantly, Michael appears in his own story in near total dreamlike fashion (more on this later). Though the effect is vigilambulistic, it is also self-referential.

Michael's self-referentiality is Welles's manner of being both subjective and objective about his character Elsa. At the ending, Welles affects a transcendent attitude, rooted in Eastern philosophy. His attitude is that of the Daoist sage who is not benevolent, the kind of sage who deals with the world as nonhuman, viewing the multitudes as straw dogs (*chugou*, sacrificial offerings that are trampled upon and discarded after the sacrifices are done).[44] This non-benevolence of the sage is that of a man who assumes human form "but is without human emotions," as Zhuang Zi has defined it, a man who does not "inwardly harm his person with 'good and bad' but rather [accords] with the spontaneous and not add to life."[45] Such a man can easily be misconstrued and his attitude misinterpreted. Thus, Britton charges Welles with misogyny and writes that Welles "hardly bothers to conceal his satisfaction that O'Hara is at last in a position to put Elsa firmly in her place."[46] Actually, Michael leaves Elsa to die, and therein lies the rub. Bazin perfectly describes this astounding moment. Welles, he writes, "let her die like a bitch on the floor of a hellish chamber while he walked out indifferently, eager to have things over and done with, without even obeying the elementary rule that the heroine should be paid the courtesy of dying in the arms of the rugged sailor."[47] Politically incorrect, even shocking and unconscionable from the Western liberal standpoint, this ending (which Britton calls "indisputably, one of the cinema's most disgraceful endings"[48]) is in keeping with Welles's character as an irreverent and anarchistic artist.[49] In *The Lady from Shanghai*, Welles delights in subverting Western behavior and thinking. However, he is far from being a simple *provocateur*. Welles poses a philosophical question, which is that of original nature, and it is more than plausible to see the film as an attack on the Western mind and character, from a Western insider's perspective, which is why, in my opinion, Welles is a major Western artist (Figure 3.4).

If we see Welles as the non-benevolent Daoist sage, he regards Elsa as a straw bitch, so to speak, reflecting on how the West has corrupted her. But character is destiny, in the final analysis. ("You said the world is bad, we can't

Figure 3.4 Michael leaves Elsa to die.
The Lady from Shanghai, Producer: Orson Welles.

run away from the badness, you're right there, but you said we can't fight it, we must deal with the badness, make terms, and didn't the badness deal with you, and made its own terms in the end, surely?") Welles's transcendent attitude on character, nature, and fatalism reaches its apotheosis here. One cannot save Elsa if her original nature is that of evil, and one cannot save her if she is fated to die. (Her exhortation, "I don't want to die!" is her final attempt to change her fate.) Nature can only take its course and it is not up to Michael to save her. What about love, since this was the subject of conversation between Michael and Elsa? "It is difficult for love to last long," Elsa says, but the ultimate principle of love, in the Eastern philosophical sense, is that it is entwined with fate. As much subjected to the element of fate, Michael cannot love her just as she cannot love him. Welles then considers death to be "incidental."[50]

There is a Daoist attitude of death in *The Lady from Shanghai*, which is very personal in the fact that Welles is really mourning his own wife, metaphorically speaking. This recalls the *Zhuang Zi*, chapter 18, entitled "Ultimate Joy," where Zhuang Zi mourned his own wife by beating the basin and singing, appalling Master Hui who went to offer his condolences. When asked about it, Zhuang Zi says, "How could I of all people not be melancholy?" and he goes on to explain the cycle of life and death, "like the progression of the four seasons." "There she sleeps blissfully in an enormous chamber. If I were to have followed her weeping and wailing, I think it would be out of keeping with destiny, so I stopped."[51] Zhuang Zi asks,

> Is there ultimate joy anywhere under heaven? Is there a method for keeping the person alive? Now if there is, what would one do and what should one rely upon? What should one avoid and what should one dwell in? What should one resort to and what should one leave behind? What should one enjoy and what should one detest?[52]

Michael's Eastern dream

In this concluding section, we summarize Michael's point of view by examining its foundation in dreams and illusions. We begin with the point, made above, about Michael being a consumptive character. He swallows whole the tall tales and events in the story but in a telling scene at the Crazy House, the Chinese amusement park where he comes to after falling down unconscious at the opera theater, he is himself swallowed up by a dragon, the symbol of the East. The Chinese motif in the Crazy House sequence suggests that Michael does not swallow the illusions; they swallow him up. This sensation of being swallowed up makes the film work like a dream—and more like an Eastern dream with its basis in *Zhuang Zi*. Michael wakes up in the Crazy House and his narration states, "For a while there, I thought it was me that was crazy. After what I'd been through, anything crazy at all seemed natural." Michael is transparently the alter ego of Orson Welles who seizes on the role to become an incarnated Zhuang Zi dreaming that he was a butterfly. When Zhuang Zi woke up, he did not know whether he had dreamed of a butterfly or a butterfly dreaming that he was Zhuang Zi. Michael's narration after waking up in the Crazy House reminds one of the story of Zhuang Zi's dream, and the idea of moving between the dreaming and the waking world manifests itself throughout the film. The film itself takes on the quality of the Crazy House. Because told from Michael's point of view, it is as if it is a projection of Michael's mind. Yet there are moments that make it *seem* as if he is an active protagonist in the real world, like in a daydream. The characters he meets manipulate events in which he becomes a patsy. This slippage between dream and reality anchors itself in Michael's narration (or his mind), which is the film's basis for further perpetuating events in a dreamlike manner.

The film moves in and out of several settings that function more like sultry illusionary spaces—from New York City to South America, from the luxury yacht to the jungle picnic, from the courtroom to the Chinese theater, and from the Chinese theater to the Crazy House—each space increasing in intensity of delirium. Inside the Crazy House, we end up in the Magic Mirror Maze, which further confuses our sense of reality and illusion by its frenzied duplications of one's image. The shootout shatters the mirrors (and thus the duplicated images) but it does not really offer any consolation to the mind because the dream has already transformed our impressions of things. Michael's dream mind is the center of the web-like maze of the narrative, the "single narrating consciousness out of which the film tale emerges, thereby suggesting that the ultimate source of this propensity lies within the self."[53]

The dreamlike narrative represents Michael's version of events. Michael as narrator renders the story inaccessible and ungraspable, as Mark Graham asserts. Much of the film's elusiveness results "from the treatment of narrative point of view": "Michael O'Hara is both voiceover narrator and a major participant in the action"; "he is both observer and observed, subject and object, as well as the only character in this director's work who is centrally engaged in commenting upon his own visually rendered past."[54] Graham effectively alludes to Zhuang Zi's butterfly dream without making the connection, and this is an intriguing convergence. How does Zhuang Zi's dream help us to access or grasp the nature of dreams or the nature of the self when one finds oneself right at the center of the dream phenomenon? The events of *The Lady from Shanghai*, as Graham says, "represent not physical but mental phenomena—that is, the manifestations of the narrator's memory."[55] Memory is another way of saying that we are in Michael's state of mind where, as the incarnation of Zhuang Zi, he does not know whether he is the butterfly or the butterfly is he. "Now there must be a difference," Zhuang Zi says. "This is called the transformation of things."[56] Michael's dual role as narrator and participant, observer and observed, causes a transformation of his own self into the Other. The narrator dreams of himself as the Other and the dream transforms into a full-fledged narrative, a story featuring his Other as protagonist. There is a constant need for the narrator to project himself into the narrative and for the participant to project out of the narrative. One moment he is rather lucid in announcing that he is a fool, aware that he shouldn't be a fool, the next moment, he deliberately does foolish things because he cannot help it. "Is Michael to be regarded as the film's protagonist and a major initiator of the action or merely as a rather passive victim, an incidental and convenient patsy?" writes Graham.[57]

No doubt, Michael has a stake in his own role within the story. He *must* be the patsy of the story. On the other hand, he is the narrator, fully cognizant that he is the patsy only against his own best interests. Is Michael the patsy or the patsy Michael? The patsy is the character Michael in the story. Michael is the narrator outside of the story. The transformation of things is the transformation of Michael into the narrator. The patsy is still Michael in the story, and as such, subjected to the element of fate as much as is Elsa in *his* story (Elsa sets him up as patsy). Michael is self-conscious about this fatalism and it is due to his transformation of himself as narrator. Transformation explains why Michael is such a passive character, the residue of his role as narrator. Finally, Michael the narrator is really the transformation of Orson Welles. *The Lady from Shanghai* is essentially a story told by Welles where he deliberately muddies our sense of objectivity and subjectivity and executes visual styles to challenge our perceptions of characters. An example is the feverish close-ups of George Grisby and Elsa, which "causes the two characters, their faces, and the shots themselves to seem even more inaccessible, because abstract and fantastic, transcending the dimensions of both realism and the merely human."[58]

Then there is the plot, which "in no way 'explains' the essential mystery of this world of stunning, inscrutable surfaces," instead there is a "welter of plotful incidents" that finally conveys "not the meaning but the incomprehensibility of a world whose parts refuse to add up, to make sense."[59] All of this sums up the role of Orson Welles as the center of the dream world created by him, and like a magician, executes the transformation of things. Welles is the incarnation of the Daoist sage, waking up to the world in which he is still dreaming. As the dreamer, he is the center that holds. In waking reality, he is off-center in the Hollywood system, but his film still bears his mark of the dreamer. Hence, Welles is the self and the Other, the narrator and the participant, the pivot of the dream world and the waking world. "Only when the pivot is located at the center of the circle of things can we respond to their infinite transformations," says Zhuang Zi.[60] We can only be grateful that Welles is the pivot at the center of *The Lady from Shanghai*. As a result, it remains a fascinating film, timeless almost, for we continue to respond to its infinite transformations through Welles's magic, not least the transformation of a Western narrative into an Eastern thriller.

Notes

1. André Bazin, *Orson Welles: A Critical View* (Los Angeles, CA: Acrobat Books, 1991), p. 93.
2. James Naremore, *The Magic World of Orson Welles* (New York: Oxford University Press, 1978), p. 160.
3. Patrick McGilligan, *Young Orson: The Years of Luck and Genius on the Path to Citizen Kane* (New York: HarperCollins, 2015), p. 172.
4. See Simon Callow, *Orson Welles, Volume 2: Hello Americans* (New York: Viking, 2006), p. 375.
5. Kelly Oliver and Benigno Trigo, *Noir Anxiety* (Minneapolis and London: University of Minnesota Press, 2003), p. 62.
6. Ibid., p. 51.
7. Oliver and Trigo, *Noir Anxiety*, pp. 53–54.
8. Ibid., p. 52.
9. Ibid., p. 63.
10. Ibid., p. 52.
11. Andrew Britton, "Betrayed by Rita Hayworth: Misogyny in *The Lady from Shanghai*," in B. K. Grant and R. Wood (eds.), *Britton on Film: The Complete Film Criticism of Andrew Britton* (Detroit, MI: Wayne State University Press, 2008), p. 239.
12. Ibid.
13. Peter Conrad, *Orson Welles: The Stories of His Life* (New York: Faber and Faber, 2003), p. 5.
14. George M. Wilson, *Narration in Light: Studies in Cinematic Point of View* (Baltimore, MD and London: The Johns Hopkins University Press), 1986, p. 203. For his example of the attribution of "strange causal powers" to the Elsa character, Wilson refers to a series of sequences and shots that occur after George Grisby has shot the butler ("I was just doing a little target practice"). Grisby gets into a car, with Michael driving. As the car speeds into the night, a truck

pulls up suddenly in front of them and the car crashes into the back of the truck. Intercut between the shots of the truck and the car's collision is a series of quick shots of Elsa pressing a button (summoning the butler in the kitchen). Cut in such a way, the shots suggest that Elsa causes the crash. See Wilson, pp. 1–3.

15 Wilson, *Narration in Light*, p. 3.
16 Oliver and Trigo, *Noir Anxiety*, p. 50.
17 Ibid., p. 51.
18 Ibid., p. 64.
19 Bhabha, *The Location of Culture*, p. 122.
20 See Gilles Deleuze, *Cinema 2: The Time-Image*, trans. Hugh Tomlinson and Robert Galeta (Minneapolis: University of Minnesota Press, 1989), p. 113.
21 Oliver and Trigo, *Noir Anxiety*, p. 53.
22 Ibid.
23 Britton, "Betrayed by Rita Hayworth," p. 240.
24 Bazin, *Orson Welles*, p. 94.
25 Ibid.
26 Naremore, *The Magic World of Orson Welles*, p. 162.
27 Ibid., p. 161.
28 Ibid.
29 Ibid.
30 Bazin, *Orson Welles*, p. 94.
31 Robert Pippin, "Agency and Fate in Orson Welles's *The Lady from Shanghai*," *Critical Inquiry*, 37 (2), 2011, p. 232 and 234.
32 Orson Welles and Peter Bogdanovich, *This is Orson Welles* (New York: Da Capo Press, 1998), p. 196.
33 Pippin, "Agency and Fate," pp. 227–28.
34 Ibid., p. 244.
35 Mair, *Wandering on the Way* (Honolulu: University of Hawai'i Press, 1994), p. 53.
36 Ibid., p. 51.
37 See Barbara Leaming, *Orson Welles, A Biography* (New York: Limelight Editions, 1995), pp. 336–37.
38 This is only speculation, but I would think that the original sequence would have more of the Opera, to show it as an alternate world and to counterpoint the Western trial process (a trial scene is being performed on the opera stage). As it is now, we see only very rough snippets of the Opera being performed (a Cantonese opera) and somewhat more of a scene showing a woman on trial in a Chinese court. This may have been quite an extraordinary way for Welles to contrast the farcical court scene undergone by Michael in the previous scenes

with the theatrical court scene performed on the Chinese stage he is watching. The implication is that the "Western" court scene is as operatic as the Eastern one. Welles already signals this by including in the public gallery two Chinese girls, commenting on the trial and the proceedings as Arthur Bannister takes the witness stand: "Why is he doing this?" "Maybe the man is in the wrong?" "Don't tell me he wants to kill him" "You ain't kidding" (the last line spoken in English).

39 Welles puts the excesses of Western materialism on satirical display in *The Lady from Shanghai* and hints at an equal form of Eastern materialism through the biographical information of Elsa's background in Macao and Shanghai (her life as a gambler, for instance). It was not until *The Immortal Story* (1968), set in Macao, that Welles shows an impressive parade of Eastern mercantilism. The character of the Jewish clerk walks through a market square bestridden with money shops and financial houses, the streets festooned with banners hung vertically announcing the names of companies, with words indicating prosperity and wealth written in Chinese and hung upside down to signify fortune falling onto the businesses' laps. This kind of detail proves that Welles possessed a near nativist knowledge of the East.

40 Gray, *Straw Dogs, Thoughts on Humans and Other Animals*, pp. 5–6.
41 Pippin, "Agency and Fate," p. 234.
42 J. P. Telotte, "Narration, Desire, and a Lady from Shanghai," *South Atlantic Review*, 49 (1), 1984, p. 65.
43 Ibid.
44 From the *Daodejing*, chapter 5.
45 Mair, *Wandering on the Way*, p. 49.
46 Britton, "Betrayed by Rita Hayworth," p. 238.
47 See Bazin, *Orson Welles*, p. 94.
48 Britton, "Betrayed by Rita Hayworth," p. 238.
49 When asked about his political leanings, Welles described himself as a "liberal leftist" in his interview with Kenneth Tynan, 1967. See Mark W. Estrin (ed.), *Orson Welles Interviews* (Jackson: University Press of Mississippi, 2002), p. 139.
50 In one of his lunch conversations with Henry Jaglom, Welles remarked that in some ancient religions, "death is incidental," and he named Judaism, Confucianism, Daoism, Shintoism. See Peter Biskind (ed.), *My Lunches with Orson Welles* (New York: Metropolitan Books, 2013), p. 125.
51 Mair, *Wandering on the Way*, p. 169.
52 Ibid., p. 166.
53 Telotte, "Narration, Desire, and a Lady from Shanghai," p. 59.

54 Mark Graham, "The Inaccessibility of 'The Lady from Shanghai,'" *Film Criticism*, 5 (3), 1981, p. 21.
55 Ibid., p. 23.
56 Mair, *Wandering on the Way*, p. 24.
57 Graham, "The Inaccessibility of 'The Lady from Shanghai,'" p. 27.
58 Ibid., p. 28.
59 Ibid., p. 34.
60 Mair, *Wandering on the Way*, p. 15.

4

Le Samouraï, Eastern Action in the *Milieu*

Melville's Eastern tendency

Jean-Pierre Melville's *Le Samouraï* (1967) is possibly the most influential French crime thriller ever made, a mixture of a police procedural (*le film policier*) and a suspenseful action thriller concentrated on a professional hit man, Jef (spelled with one "f") Costello, played by Alain Delon, giving the definitive performance of his career. The film is a "Polar" (the term for a police-cum-gangster thriller in French cinema) with an Eastern sensibility. Mainly, the film incorporates certain tenets of Bushido philosophy as propounded in ancient texts like Miyamoto Musashi's manual of martial arts *Go Rin No Sho* (*The Book of Five Rings*), Daidoji Yuzan's *Budo Shoshinshu* (*The Primer of Bushido*), and Yamamoto Tsunetomo's *Hagakure* (*In The Shadow of Leaves*), a series of injunctions for "the Way of the Warrior" (the translation of Bushido) which is possibly the one most relevant to Melville's film.[1] In more modern times, *Bushido, The Soul of Japan*, written in English by the Japanese Christian Inazo Nitobe and published at around the turn of the twentieth century, is the most renowned.[2] Melville's film is only superficially influenced by all these Japanese texts although it is perhaps more indebted to the *Hagakure* than has been acknowledged thus far.[3] In a deeper sense, what is Eastern about it is that it seeks to impart a Transcendental style through its invocation of Bushido and its central principle of a hero who is like a samurai on a trajectory toward death and/or nihilism. The film seems to echo the first injunction of the *Hagakure*, "The Way of the warrior (bushido) is to be found in dying. If one is faced with two options of life or death, simply settle for death."[4] The whole film testifies to Jef's Way of Bushido, carrying out his mission with an unyielding "pure will" (*ichinen*)—"a will of no specific good, in fact a will of nothing or nothingness, that is, of death."[5] Throughout the film, Jef's composure is as if he is already dead. "Only when you constantly live as though already a corpse . . . will you be able to find freedom in the Way, and fulfill your duties without fault throughout your life."[6]

Thus, we see in the film a transcendentalism that may be thought of either as Zen or as Daoist in essence, reflecting the hero's desire to achieve quietude and meditative stillness in preparation of his death.[7] The sense of quietude is also striking because of its apparent contrast to the hubbub of French underworld society, which includes the police. Jef interacts with both the police and the *milieu* (the French term for the criminal underworld). Melville is a specialist in the French underworld, and *Le Samouraï* is his most accomplished film set in the *milieu*. It "is the purest and most intense of his crime films," writes Peter Hogue.[8] For our purposes, it is the most successful of Melville's films in its portrayal of a hero (the samurai of the title) in such a way that makes it an Eastern transcendental thriller with an emphasis on repose or calmness and the dialectical movement that it inspires. The Daoist qualities of *xujing* (void and quietude) are embodied in the hero empowering him to move outwardly in his aggressive mode as a killer-assassin. In the terms of Bushido philosophy, the hero embodies the quality of calmness as a prerequisite for death. (Another injunction in the *Hagakure* puts it this way: "Begin each day pondering death as its climax. Each morning, with a calm mind, conjure images in your head of your last moments."[9]) In terms of Daoist philosophy, it is the interspersing of yin and yang—the yin of stillness and the yang of the mental agitation of the death wish, soon to be translated into physical action. Melville realizes this idea through the popular form of the French Polar, not the kind of genre that one would usually associate with an Eastern sense of transcendentalism.

While I account for the film's debt to Bushido principles, I will also use Daoist philosophical ideas to interpret the film's Eastern connotations, mainly conveyed by and concentrated on the lone figure of the hit man. This chapter will then offer an analysis and interpretation of *Le Samouraï* from a broad Eastern perspective, invoking Bushido philosophy, Chinese Daoist philosophy, and Japanese Zen philosophy. Clearly, by invoking Daoist thought and ideas, I do not wish to limit Melville's film purely to its Japanese sources of inspiration and my reading runs the risk of being too eclectic. However, what is fascinating about the film (and its hero) is the abstraction of its

Eastern allusions, and its scope seems much broader than the reference to Japanese Bushido might imply. Such a reading is without precedence since the literature on Melville has almost nothing to say on the director's Eastern tendency or influences. Melville himself is not forthcoming on this subject, as, for example, in Rui Noguiera's interview book, which is generally considered to be the most authoritative of literary texts on Melville's work. In general, the literature has neglected the Eastern aspect of Melville, perhaps sensing in it an Orientalism that is far too frivolous for comment. Instead, Melville's indebtedness to Hollywood cinema (the American tradition of the gangster genre or the American strain of film noir) has been emphasized (perhaps overemphasized). Melville himself affected an Americanophilia, publicly wearing Stetsons and Ray-Bans, driving American cars, and listening to American jazz on the American Forces Network radio. So preeminent is this image of Melville that Ginette Vincendeau's English-language book on Melville is subtitled "An American in Paris" and it seems entirely befitting. (Even the surname "Melville" was taken from the author Herman Melville whom the director admired; Melville's own real surname was Grumbach.) Yet, his Orientophilia (or some might say, his Orientalist tendency) is probably just as significant and just as structurally embedded in his films. There may be in fact a kind of overlapping of Western and Eastern sensibilities in Melville. His affinity for an individualistic hero against the system of the law is very American but it can just as well be Eastern in both a Japanese and Chinese sense—as a Japanese *kusemono*, a type of warrior that flouts conventions (the kind of hero model behind the *Hagakure*), or as a Daoist nonconformist warrior with an active contempt for the Confucian state.

The American sensibility of Melville is something of a paradox, in fact. His films today, if it were not very obvious at the time (Melville's fame reached its peak in the 1960s up until 1973 when he died at the age of fifty-five), stand in even starker contrast to Hollywood action thrillers: far too slow, too meditative, and preoccupied with details that Hollywood filmmakers would consider superfluous and dragging. It would be truer to say now that Melville's films are actually more Eastern than American, or that he was offering Eastern variations of Hollywood thrillers—and *Le Samouraï* is his most Eastern of all his films. Eastern in the spiritual sense or, if one prefers, in the Bressonian sense of transcendentalism. (Bresson's films are of course entirely incompatible with

Hollywood.) Like Bresson, Melville is something of an oddball who prized his independence from the system, and though Melville's path takes a different trajectory from that of Bresson's, he partakes of the sort of transcendentalism that Bresson offers, one based on fatalism, destiny, and sublimity of style. There has been no real effort to analyze Melville's films from this perspective, which would entail analysis and recognition of his Eastern influences.

The lack of recognition of Melville's brand of transcendentalism (his Eastern sensibility) is probably due to the feeling that Melville's films are, despite even the American influences, very French. Melville is very rooted in modern French social, cultural, and political history. Overall, his films can be summarized as following two lines of development, one line devoted to the depiction of French underworld society and the other to the history of the Resistance during the Second World War. In the Resistance vein are films such as his debut feature film *La silence de la mer* (1947), *Leon Morin, Prêtre* (1961), and *L'Armee des ombres* (1969). His underworld films include *Bob le flambeur* (1955), *Le Doulos* (1962), *Le Deuxième souffle* (1966), *Le Samouraï*, *Le Cercle rouge* (1970), and *Un flic* (1972). The *policiers*, in the strict sense of the police procedural (which constitute Melville's best work), are ironic testaments to French police methods. The feeling is that they have not much to do with Eastern culture or philosophy despite references to Eastern sayings and the insertions of Eastern decorative motifs in some if not all of these films.[10] *Le Samouraï* is clearly the most indebted to Eastern philosophy but even here, the case for analyzing the film from the Eastern point of view may be considered weak, mainly due to the sense that Melville is only superficially engaged with Eastern ideas or philosophy. However, the lack of special interest in Melville's obvious taste for the East, in turn, engenders the sense of superficiality. Since his films have never really been analyzed for their Eastern content, it can only be perceived as superficial.

Most critics generally skim over the Eastern aspect implicit in Melville's films. When they touch on it, they succeed only in pointing out its cosmetic value. Roland Carrée, writing about the recurrence of snow in Melville's films, recognizes it as an Eastern motif of death and mourning but does not go into any depth, which thus leaves us with only an impression of snow as mere "Eastern" decoration.[11] Ginette Vincendeau suggested that Melville's "extensive use of orientalism in his décors" was part of "fascination with the exotic," which had "permeated French culture in the 1960s, culminating in Roland Barthes' book, *L'Empire des signes* (1970)."[12] All this, again, give the impression that Melville's Eastern sensibility is more of a decorative Orientalist instinct, an aesthetic rather than intellectual interest with a tendency toward the exotic. At worst, one might argue that Melville shows a low-grade Orientalism in his films. However, I will demonstrate, below, that a film like *Le Samouraï* shows Melville to have more than cosmetic or aesthetic interest in the East. The film carries significance as a structural signifier of the Eastern in the French cinema. Melville has inscribed an Eastern poetic sensibility and ethical manner into the action and behavior of his chief protagonist, Jef Costello, which permeates through to the rest of the film since Costello is the driving force of the narrative.

A samurai in Paris

For starters, we might do well to contrast the beginning of *Le Samouraï* with its original inspiration, the Hollywood production of *This Gun for Hire* (1942), based on a novel by Graham Greene. (Melville's film is commonly thought to be a remake of this film.) Raven, the hired killer (played by Alan Ladd) of *This Gun for Hire* is lying on the bed in his apartment when the narrative fades in after the credits. An alarm bell rings and he gets up, checks out the address where he is to make the hit, reaches for his gun which he puts into a valise, puts on his jacket, and feeds his cat. After a scene in which the female cleaner who comes in and abuses the cat, inviting Raven's violent reaction toward her (he slaps her and orders her to get out), Raven leaves his apartment to carry out his mission. The killing accomplished (Raven is also forced to kill a female witness); there is another brief scene showing Raven interacting coldly with a little handicapped girl who asks him to retrieve her ball. (He is about to kill her but decides not to.)

In Melville's film, Jef Costello lies on his bed in his apartment, as Raven does at the beginning of *This Gun for Hire*, but here the similarities end. Melville focuses on the starkly decorated apartment in a long shot. It appears like a theatrical tableau which, after the title credits and an epigraph, "there is no greater solitude than that of the samurai, unless it is that of the tiger in the jungle, perhaps," gives a sensation of suddenly floating before our very eyes, a sensation achieved by a simultaneous track and zoom. The epigraph may be mistaken for an aphorism from the *Hagakure*, but it is Melville's own invention.[13] As a pure invention, it suggests a highly abstract theme for the film which has the effect of setting an Eastern tone right away. The effect of the scene as a floating tableau conveys the idea of the illusionary world in which the protagonist will wander through with his mission of death. In his interview with Noguiera, Melville explained that the protagonist, being a hired killer, was "by definition a schizophrenic."[14] The track and zoom effect was meant to depict "the mental disorder of a man who unmistakably had a tendency to schizophrenia."[15] This does not tell us anything at all about Melville's Eastern sensibility and his intentions in depicting a hero he dubbed "Le Samouraï." Melville sheds no further light on this subject in other writings or interviews nor has any critic or scholar, to my knowledge. Hence, we cannot depend on Melville's words or utterances to comprehend the Eastern characteristics of his film. What follows is my own free interpretation of Melville's mise-en-scène, which lacks obvious inscriptions of Eastern characteristics except for the title and the epigrammatic reference to Bushido. Why did Melville choose to call his film *Le Samouraï* in the first place? Most Western critics do not really answer this question and address its implications. My analysis below is an attempt to set things right. Melville's intention in so naming the film is to establish a cardinal association of his hit man with the Eastern samurai warrior. The mind or the spirit of the samurai is the crux of the film. In a sense, the sensation of schizophrenia that the floating tableau conveys is the perverted effect of the samurai intruding into a Western environment. More than that, it is an Eastern mind inserting its presence into a Western mentality: perhaps Melville's professed Eastern sensibility has something of this effect and the scene is a metaphor of his own mind. Alain Delon, a classic dandy-Frenchman portraying an Eastern samurai immediately conveys this schizophrenia. The cultural underlining of the Eastern allusion to the samurai then demands a substantive interpretation than has ever been given in the literature (predisposed to entirely neglect the Eastern allusions and forgo any Eastern readings).

Following the "floating tableau" scene, we see a plume of smoke rising out of the bed. Only then do we sense a figure lying on the bed (Jef smoking his cigarette). The smoke and the floating sensation can be seen as a metaphor of the "floating cloud" (*fuyun*), a reference to a xia (knight-errant swordsman) with magical powers in Chinese mythology (the xia with such powers has the ability to hide in a floating cloud, hence the allusion), who, however, will eventually come to a bad end.[16] The floating cloud, in Chinese literature, also refers to a wanderer who leads a nocturnal existence, as in a line from Li Bai's poem, "Farewell to a Friend" ("Song youren"): "Wandering like a floating cloud, as the sun sets, my emotions rise" (*fuyun youzi yi, luo ri gu renqing*, English translation mine). These metaphors paint a picture of Jef Costello as a solitary figure and a nocturnal wanderer, a knight-errant (or in fact, an assassin: *cike*), primed or trained to be fatalistic and nihilistic in order to carry out his mission. The floating cloud of Li Bai's poem also points to the fact that Jef is not friendless or entirely without emotion; that in fact, he owes emotional debts (*renqing*, or *ninjo* in Japanese) to the women who have helped him, as I will go on to discuss (Figure 4.1).

The opening scene therefore suggests all the Eastern conceptual elements (asceticism, solitude, stillness, death, and meditative silence, as well as mysticism and aloofness from worldly affairs) connected to the character of Jef Costello, the samurai of the title. These conceptual elements can be summarized in one word—Zen. The relationship between Zen and Bushido is longstanding, with past samurai theorists representing Zen as "the true spirit of the samurai": "Zen was credited with providing the oft-heralded Stoic or

Figure 4.1 The "floating cloud" scene.
Le Samouraï, Producers: Raymond Borderie, Eugène Lépicier.

even welcoming attitude towards death and killing that was believed to define Japanese warriors," as Oleg Benesch informs us.[17] One influential writer, D. T. Suzuki, saw Bushido "as a vehicle for promoting Zen" and he was "one of the most significant disseminators of a Zen-based *bushido*."[18] In his book *Zen and Japanese Culture*, Suzuki wrote that Zen "was intimately related from the beginning of its history to the life of the samurai," Zen having sustained the samurai in two ways: "Morally, because Zen is a religion which teaches us not to look backward once the course is decided upon; philosophically, because it treats life and death indifferently."[19] Jef exhibits the Zen discipline of the single-minded fighter: "Zen discipline is simple, direct, self-reliant, self-denying; its ascetic tendency goes well with the fighting spirit."[20] The only thing missing in the scene is the sword, or rather the gun (in *This Gun for Hire*, one of the first things that Raven reaches out for after rising from the bed is his gun). The absence of the sword (gun) in this whole scene in the apartment, however, does contribute to a spiritual or psychic sense of Jef's warrior determination, his apparent quietude belying a sense of internal disquiet. Zen teaches the samurai essentially "to be always ready to face death, that is, to sacrifice oneself unhesitatingly when occasion arises."[21]

Thus, the Zen-like quality of Jef's death composure is only to be expected since in philosophical terms, Zen "treats life and death indifferently." Suzuki points out further that Zen has no special doctrine or philosophy except that "it tries to release one from the bondage of birth and death."[22] Here, then, lies the Eastern transcendental tendency in *Le Samouraï*, which is probably the first action feature film of this kind in the West. The French film scholar Nicole Brenez has argued that "cinema surely can never show Martial Art, because it is a spiritual movement" (the inherent Daoist kind of yin stillness and yang determination) but that, on the other hand, "cinema can always develop many and more ways to describe the non-figurative phenomenon of psychic energy."[23] Melville has done precisely this with his characterization of Jef Costello as virtually a psychic samurai, weaponless, alone (though he has the company of the bullfinch). The gun will come later. (He buys a gun from a provider who also changes the license plates of his stolen cars.) Melville shows us Jef's total preparedness for death in line with the first injunction of the *Hagakure*: Jef's body lying in bed is practically a prefiguration of his corpse, as Philippe Rouyer has pointed out.[24]

The Eastern preoccupation with death infusing the opening scene makes it somewhat different from its Hollywood inspiration, *This Gun for Hire*, although to be fair, Alan Ladd's performance as Raven does contain some inkling of this theme. Ladd's customary coolness in his acting marks his portrayal of Raven. It easily conveys the character's death symbolism, which was to define Ladd's star persona (arguably seen to better effect in his Western, *Shane*, where he was the gun slinging cowboy-angel of death). However, the Hollywood film is not content to simply show Raven's coolness and placid character as a sign of his sublime nature. He has to get down to business and exhibit the toughness and ruthlessness of his killer personality. For example, his slapping of the house cleaner, his killing of the female witness in his victim's apartment, and even his reaching into his valise where his gun is hidden when the little girl asks him to retrieve her ball (although he spares the girl) are actions which mark him out fully as a killer. All of these are typically Hollywoodish embellishments of character, which Melville dispenses with entirely. Instead, Melville is completely devoted to showing the interior side of his character, something that Hollywood would find antithetical to the tone and rhythm of the action thriller. Hence, the visual impact of Jef's apartment is crucial right from the very beginning. The abstract quality of the "floating" effect complements Jef's interior attribute as a hollowed-out character along the Daoist line of *xujing* (void and quietude), a concept mentioned in the *Daodejing*, chapter 16. Jef is a man who has attained "complete vacuity" and maintains "steadfast quietude."[25] He is, in other words, completely impassive, a kind of hero who needs no recourse to toughness or violence to show his killer side. Therefore, he does not slap a girl in his apartment (there is no girl to slap), and he does not kill the female witness.

Delon more than matches Ladd's natural coolness. Melville gives him a lot of room to instill this coolness into the viewer, such as when he steals the Citroen DS and when a pretty woman drives up to the red light and looks at him seductively. Jef looks away and shows no interest in her, a sure sign that we are watching a very un-French hero, a kind of hero more appropriate to an Eastern genre whose rejection of a woman is a sign of his celibate nature as a killer samurai or a xia. Jef's turning away from the woman's look is probably a pivotal point in the film, about which, I will have more to say. At this stage, we should observe that it signposts Melville's orientation toward the Eastern with certain ramifications for gender analysis. This is an important aspect of the film since Ginette Vincendeau, whose book on Melville is the only major book in the English language on the director, has brought attention to the idea of Delon's masculine persona as being problematic and has restated the claim that the women in the film are "tragically useless."[26]

First, the significance of why Jef looks away from the woman in the car is to denote the Eastern, as opposed to Western, attribute of Alain Delon's masculinity. He is a samurai, bound by the warrior's code to keep "warily aloof from sexual feelings, the foremost confusion of humankind"—an injunction from Daidoji Yuzan's *Budo Shoshinshu*.[27] The Eastern sense of masculinity, inherent in the title itself, is behind Delon's acceptance to do the film. According to Melville in his interview with Rui Noguiera, Delon, when told the title of the film immediately got up and asked Melville to follow him to his bedroom, which was decorated with a samurai lance, sword, and dagger.[28] Delon probably has also read the *Hagakure* and had modeled his performance on some of the descriptions of samurai in the book. Delon earned his fame and status through a narcissistic display of his erotic features, a conscious part of the actor's appeal, but according to Darren Waldron, there were "frequent obvious signs of vulnerability and self-doubt that traverse Delon's career and image."[29] His role as Jef in *Le Samouraï* is probably the most important "sign" of this vulnerability and self-doubt in his entire career. Delon showed an introspective side that seemed to fit naturally with the Eastern characteristic of the character, and Melville filled in the rest (the stillness, the silences, the death symbolism, etc.). Second, in Delon's "Eastern" character, we will see a different type of relationship with women in the French thriller setting. Though Jef ignores the woman in the car, the film goes on to show him owing certain emotional debts to women, compelling him to meet his fate on the battleground, as it were. Thus, Jef's relationships with these women manifest the characteristic of obligation or duty (*giri*), one of the highest precepts of Bushido that a samurai is supposed to observe.

Vincendeau, writing from a Western feminist perspective, has pointed out that the women in Jef's life, Jane Lagrange (Nathalie Delon) and Valerie, the pianist (Caty Rosier), are marginal characters in the film and neither one "has any impact on Jef's fate."[30] The women, moreover, attest to Jef's problematic masculinity, "so self-enclosed that it becomes 'autistic.'"[31] From Vincendeau's

Western perspective, Jef is an *autistic* personality showing a detachment from women, unable to communicate with them, and is unable to show emotion. However, from the Eastern perspective, it is not an accurate description of Jef's character at all. If one relates it to Bushido, a trait of nihilism naturally emerges from Jef's preparedness for death. Such nihilism, despite its trappings with death, "can only be known existentially."[32] Keiji Nishitani speaks of nihilism as "a solitariness absolutely shut up within itself" and "a state of absolute self-enclosure": "in human awareness, this solitariness is expressed as being suspended, all alone, over a limitless void."[33] This suspension over a limitless void rhymes with my earlier description of Jef as the floating cloud. Jef's nihilism is therefore an existentialist standpoint and an Eastern character orientation which is blanked out by the charge of autism. Such a charge is also inappropriate in the mythical context of Jef's *milieu*. After all, Jef is a "samurai" in Paris and is by Zen training a solitary and celibate figure. Under Zen discipline, Jef would not wish to have any emotional encumbrances. However, the film does show Jef saddled with some of these encumbrances despite himself. The women, far from being "useless," have a role to play in support of Jef's occupation as a killer. Vincendeau betrays a lack of feeling for Jef (she takes Jef's coolness too literally, perhaps) as well as for the women's emotions toward Jef. It is simply not true to suggest that the women are "marginal." Jane is crucial for Jef as his alibi, and the pianist is similarly crucial in not identifying him as the killer. Similarly, it is untrue that Jef does not communicate with the women, or vice versa. The women communicate with Jef in his own taciturn manner, communicating through actions, gestures, looks, or smiles, which are all in tune with Jef's Eastern sensibility. Their form of communicating with Jef is as sublime as Jef's is with them.

Thus, when the pianist looks at Jef in their final encounter at the nightclub, he seemingly about to shoot her (fulfilling his last contract), she smiles in response, continuing to play at the piano, with no words exchanged between them because words would be superfluous. The meaning is quite clear to both. I referred earlier to *renqing/ninjo*, human emotion or sentiment (literally the quality of being human), which is what passes between Jef and the pianist through their looks, as well as the pianist's smile. As for Jane, she shows by her action unremitting support for Jef. She lies for him and stands up to the *commissaire*'s harassment by refusing his offer to protect her from the vice department. Jane is as bound to the underworld code of behavior (loyalty, friendship, righteousness) as Jef is and they maintain an almost wordless reciprocity and harmony in their relationship. This interaction between them refutes the idea that Jef is "self-enclosed," used somewhat misleadingly by Vincendeau to suggest Jef's total break from the social world. While Jef might not really belong to the world at large, he is not unsocial within the *milieu*, otherwise he would not have been able to establish his alibi (an important theme driving the narrative in the first twenty minutes or so of the film). This *milieu* in Chinese would be called the *jianghu* (rivers and lakes), referring to secret societies and the Chinese underworld in general (also used in an imaginary sense to refer to the world of xia).

The *jianghu* in Paris

I invoke the concept of the *jianghu* to denote an Eastern demarcation in Melville's abstract world of the samurai-hit man from the normal Parisian society. It emphasizes Melville's break with the reality of Paris or French society. Philippe Rouyer writes that critics had reproached Melville "for his taste in abstraction" but that in fact the filmmaker had "broken off all links with realism" and that one would search in vain in his films "for a sectional portrait of French society."[34] Rouyer points out that Jef as well as other lead characters in Melville's polars exist in their own universe, one "reduced to vacant apartments without soul, to improbable nightclubs that they only frequent for business, and to a labyrinth of streets, which they cross alone in the pale day or at nightfall."[35] All of this constitutes "a closed world meticulously reconstructed by the director in his own studios, in rue Jenner," writes Rouyer.[36] While all that Rouyer says is true, he does not provide any more definition of the kind of world or universe that Melville creates, being content with it purely as an abstraction. In commenting about *Le Samouraï*, Peter Hogue points to "an imaginary figure (trench-coated gunman) in a real landscape (modern Paris) and a recognizable personality (isolation by choice) in a fantasy construct (crime story)," which suggests a bit more definition of Melville's abstract world.[37] Jef "is at once a unique individual and a figment of fantasy who has no existence apart from his basic role in cinematic myth."[38]

The problem for us is to denote the cinematic myth that gives Jef his role. Hogue may be referring to the cinematic myth of the American gangster film, but Melville is constructing an entirely new cinematic myth—the myth of the Eastern warrior manifesting as a Western European killer and moving around in an Eastern universe though it appears situated in France. I have called it the *jianghu* to denote a total imaginarity. Rouyer quotes Melville as having said that the *milieu* in his polars was "not the real underworld but one that is as transposed as the European courts or the bourgeois settings that Shakespeare used to tell his stories."[39] This point then doubly underscores the *jianghu* concept applied to *Le Samouraï*. Transposed to France, it is the underworld of the medieval knights-errant or *ronin* of Eastern folklore. Melville creates a mythical world of the Eastern warrior in which he locates Jef. (The apartment is the microcosm of this world and its "floating" nature is instructive as a sign of its dreamlike countenance.)

We can already sense the *jianghu* through the abstraction of the opening scene, but the scene of the woman in the car focuses our mind on the abstraction of Melville's mise-en-scène rather beautifully. The woman drives up alongside Jef, and Jef looks at her; she looks at him (the camera zooming in on a closer shot as she looks), then Jef turns his face back to the front. She drives off, and he drives off. They go into their separate realms. One might see this as the perfect illustration of Jef's schizophrenia if we go by Melville's explanation of the scene. "A normal man would have followed the girl, or at least smiled at her," Melville says.[40] First, it would be important to note that Jef, of course, is not a normal man. Second, Jef is (Figure 4.2) a samurai in Paris. Somehow, he must keep faith with his Eastern mind—the state of mind of the martial arts, as Miyamoto Musashi expounds it in *The Book of Five Rings* ("Pay attention to the mind, not the body")[41]—while existing in a Western environment. I have described this schizophrenia as that of an East-West split in personality. Jef keeps aloof from the woman who undoubtedly represents the West and the temptation to be completely overwhelmed by it. Jef steers clear of this temptation and drives into the bleak milieu of the French *jianghu* (the East), which is what we see in the next shot (Jef meeting his underworld provider to buy a gun and have the license plates to his stolen car changed). The beautiful woman drives into her own realm, which is as far away as is possible from Jef's *jianghu*. Everything else that unfolds in the film from then

Figure 4.2 The woman in the car.
Le Samouraï, Producers: Raymond Borderie, Eugène Lépicier.

on takes place in the *jianghu*. It is where Jef arranges an alibi with his lover Jane, kills Martey (the nightclub owner), meets the pianist as he comes out from Martey's office, and where, after his arrest, is exposed to the police and subjected to their methods in trying to establish his guilt (including bugging his apartment).

Jef is, of course, not the sole *personnage* of this *jianghu*, which we might easily think is the case from the opening scene emphasizing his solitude. Everyone he encounters, including the police, are the subjects of the *jianghu*. The point that the police is just as implicated in the *jianghu* as the criminal is not as clearly enunciated as it should be in *Le Samouraï*, but Melville goes on to make this clear in his subsequent policiers, *Le Cercle rouge* and *Un Flic*. The inspector general in *Le Cercle rouge* tells the commissaire (André Bourvil) that "everyone is guilty" (including the police). This makes sense only if we understand the notion of the *jianghu*, which Melville conceives as a red circle, attributed to the thoughts of Shakyamuni Gautama Buddha: "When men, even unknowingly, are to meet one day, whatever may befall each, whatever their diverging paths, on the said day, they will inevitably come together in the red circle." The saying, also apparently made up by Melville, is the epigraph that opens the film. Melville's theme, associating the police and the criminal as doubles inhabiting a common milieu (call it the red circle or the *jianghu*), is taken up in John Woo's *The Killer* (1989), a remake of *Le Samouraï*, and in the films of the Hong Kong action director Johnnie To, particularly

The Longest Nite (1998) and *Running out of Time* (1999).[42] These Hong Kong directors are admirers of Melville, whose policiers are clearly the forerunners of their equivalent films. The Hong Kong *jianghu* is an expanded form of the Melvillian red circle (itself influenced by Eastern concepts), which contains its own rules. Fate or destiny determines relationships, a more pronounced theme in the films of the Hong Kong directors but one already well manifest in Melville's cinema. All are guilty in the *jianghu* because fate implicates them all.

Thus, with the mythic scene of the *jianghu* jungle (Jef is characterized as the "tiger of the jungle"), fate is the invisible player that pulls Jef to his inevitable meetings with the key characters of the film, the pianist, the commissaire (François Périer), Olivier Rey. The coincidence of his meeting with the pianist in the nightclub after he kills Martey is of course a fateful moment. Melville indulges in such coincidences to show the element of fate-destiny at work: in *Le Cercle rouge*, the meeting of Corey and Vogel is of this category. (Melville seems to have taken to heart the ancient Chinese saying that there are no stories without coincidences *wuqiao bu cheng shu*.) Why does Jef not kill the pianist right there, as Raven does the female witness in *This Gun for Hire*? The answer is that Jef is not a typical killer like Raven. He is the samurai who follows an ancient code of behavior. Why does the pianist not cry out? The answer is that she is as immersed in the world of the *jianghu* and its codes as Jef is. This code binds her during the identity parade at the police station where she holds fast against identifying Jef as the killer. Melville in responding to the question of why she is unafraid gives an answer that stresses a certain mysticism. Jef "has the hypnotic power of the serpent which just stares at its prey until it can no longer move" and in this way, "he prevents her from crying out just by looking at her."[43] Since Jef possesses a certain animal magnetism and hypnotic power (part of Alain Delon's persona), I can see Melville's point, and it leads us to comprehend Jef as a warrior-mystic with magical powers, thus validating in another way the metaphor of the "floating cloud" as a symbol for a xia with magical powers. One sign of his powers is his ability to "communicate" with the bird, for example.

More importantly, Melville declares that the pianist personifies death and that Jef falls in love with death.[44] This corresponds with the notion of fate. Jef and the pianist are fated to meet and Jef will die. He does not kill the pianist because, on the one hand, he cannot kill death, and on the other hand, he is fated not to kill her. The pianist's apparent betrayal of Jef (a subtle plot twist that reveals her relationship to Rey as well as Rey's ultimate treachery) is an operation of fate, and that is why Jef ultimately does not kill her. (He kills Rey, whose treachery already condemns him.) Melville also appears to suggest that Jef has agency over his own death when responding to the question of Jef's statement "I never lose, not really." (Melville: "These words reveal his lucid grasp of his own destiny.")[45] This reading may be an example of what Colin McArthur calls "Americanophile existentialism," a trend marrying American-style individualism with the personal choice of whether to live or die.[46] This being the case, another kind of existentialism is also possible, though hardly broached at all. I would rather suggest, in keeping with the theme of schizophrenia defining his identity, that Jef is an Eastern existentialist, one who recognizes that the events put into play by destiny will result in his death. Jef owes a debt to the pianist for not informing on him at the police identification and is obliged then to repay this debt by not killing her. This entails in turn his own death since he fails, deliberately, to carry out a professional contract. The fateful coincidence of his meeting the pianist in the first instance overrides any notion of Jef's agency over his own destiny. What then does Jef's statement mean? It means that in life or in death, Jef will follow the path meted out to him by destiny. The theme of fatalism or death is so generic in all of Melville's films that it does not seem to stand out as being particularly "Eastern" but in *Le Samouraï*, it is quite distinctively Eastern given the association of the traditional samurai figure with death and with the practice of *seppuku* (the ritualized disembowelment death by suicide of samurai warriors). Again, here, the title is crucial in signifying the Eastern, manifested as the film's death theme.

Death and the dandy

Apart from the fatalism of Jef, there is the romantic aspect to his character. This is another dimension of the *fuyun* (floating cloud) metaphor which portents a wanderer taking leave of a friend for whom a depth of emotion cannot be expressed simply. Jef is the wanderer taking leave of the pianist, whom he loves, as Melville tells us. (Melville, in fact, is following the plotline of *This Gun for Hire* where Raven saves the life of the Veronica Lake character and then falls in love with her.) He then wanders off into the heavens, so to speak. This xia-like romanticism is fatalistic in spirit and therefore very much engaged with death. If we follow this *fuyun* metaphor, friendship is the paramount value of the xia. Jef's friendship with the pianist begins, as fated, when she lies for him by not identifying him as the killer. This demands a reciprocal engagement of friendship on Jef's part, a friendship of equal depth or sublimity, and what greater show of friendship than to die for a friend? Jef's relationships with the two women (the pianist and Jane) fully demonstrate his romantic side, but there is a corresponding narcissistic aspect to Jef's romanticism, also related to death. This is his image of the dandy. As incarnated by Alain Delon, Jef is a Baudelairean dandy, one whose characteristic beauty "consists, above all, in his air of reserve, which in turn arises from his unshakeable resolve not to feel any emotion."[47] Not feeling any emotion is consistent with the Zen training of the samurai to exist as if already dead. Jef's narcissism (his constant looking at himself in the mirror) then seems to reaffirm the dandy characteristic of not feeling any emotion. "Be sure to look at yourself in the mirror when fixing your appearance," so it is said in the *Hagakure*.[48] Thus, Jef is a samurai dandy to whom appearance is crucial. "Without composure and resolve you will appear to lack grace. Ideally, one should be reverent, refined, and poised."[49]

As part of his dandy image in the Western sense, Jef wears a trench coat (he actually has two trench coats, one white and one black, the latter he wears after he is injured). This trench coat is not so much a sign of the American detective (or gangster) but a death sign of Jef's samurai heritage. The trench coat approximates the *hukama* and *kimono* of the samurai. It should be noted that this is not the armor of the samurai but rather the normal wear of the samurai in peace time. (Since he lives in a time of peace, there is no need to put on armor.) Yet, even wearing a coat demands a whole ritual of dressing up, and these ritualistic scenes of Jef reminds me of the tale of Zhuang Zi dressing up in formal regalia as the xia swordsman supreme when he goes to meet the king of Zhao (described in chapter 30 of the *Zhuang Zi*, "Discoursing on Swords"). In Zhuang Zi's case, he dresses up to meet the king whose fondness for swords has resulted in his employment of thousands of low-class, excessively violent swordsmen who have "disheveled hair, locks that bulge out from their temples, drooping caps with plain throatbands, coats that are short in back, glaring eyes, and combative speech."[50] Through his superior logic, Zhuang Zi persuades the king to stop using the swordsmen. They all commit suicide in their rooms.

Jef's dressing up follows the tradition of the philosopher-xia in the Zhuang Zi sense rather than that of the bedraggled *ronin*, which may be more in the line of Jef's occupation as an assassin and a masterless samurai. However, even if he is a *ronin*, he is clearly one who pays attention to his daily appearance, as instructed in the *Hagakure*. Melville has chosen to depict him as a Baudelairean dandy perhaps in line with the tradition of French gangster films in which such an image was earlier incarnated by Jean Gabin. Gabin clearly personifies the European dandy for whom personal appearance and material elegance "are symbols of the aristocratic superiority of his personality."[51] I would contend, however, that Delon's dandyism as exhibited in *Le Samouraï* is of a different order: Delon does not strike me as obviously imitating Gabin. Despite his Baudelairean air, Delon's dandy is infused with the elegance of samurai grace and the calmness or purity of mind necessary to carry out his mission with a readiness to die. "Although paying so much attention to personal appearance may seem vain, it is because of the samurai's resolve to die at any moment that he makes preparations so meticulously. If slain with an unkempt appearance, it shows a lack of forethought regarding his fate, and he will be scorned by his enemy as being unclean."[52]

Jef's style of wearing a hat and running two fingers on the brim ensures that he is not of the class of the swordsmen with disheveled hair, locks bulging out from the temples, drooping caps with plain throatbands. His trench coat is certainly not the coat that is short in back. The trench coat "becomes a mantle of death," as Susan Hayward tells us.[53] It assumes a nuance of ritualized death, namely the samurai form of suicide. Jef puts on the trench coat for his last mission (to kill Olivier Rey) and then takes it off, as well as his hat, in the nightclub as if readying himself to commit *seppuku* in his final encounter with the pianist—and he dies "like a true samurai."[54] Dandyism, narcissism, all point to a mind-preparation to die and this is the most profound variation of the Baudelairean tradition evoked in Melville's film. Stanley Cavell writes about the dandy as someone who "does not *know* he will succeed; what he knows is himself, his readiness" (italics Cavell's).[55] Jef, the Eastern dandy, says, "I never lose, not really," and, as I have interpreted it above, this statement means that he knows he will die. The dandy as samurai *knows* he will succeed.

Jef prepares himself to die through the exercise of stillness (*jing*), the Daoist idea that finally distinguishes the film as an exceptional action thriller. The opening scene of Jef on the bed conveys stillness, and one might take this as a metaphor of death. Once Jef gets up and dresses himself, Jef already acquires a sage-like countenance of stillness in his bearing, and he goes on to define this quality of stillness in the rest of the film. "The stillness of the sage is not because stillness is said to be good and therefore he is still. It is because the myriad things are unable to disturb his mind that he is still."[56] This philosophy is at the heart of Jef's outwardly cool character, and it ensures his survival when the police is on his heels and when his employer dispatches another gunman to kill him. In these moments, we see the ideal quality of the samurai-swordsman in action—the ideal quality of stillness, that is, which can easily be misunderstood. "He is all technique and not much affect," as Peter Hogue describes him.[57] Indeed, there is not much affect because he has emptied his mind such that the myriad things are unable to disturb him, and so it plays out through his reactions to subsequent events (evading the cops on his trail and turning the tables on the gunman who intrudes into his apartment, forcing him to divulge the name of his employer).

To round off the matter of death, I come to the item that I have saved for last, which is Jef's distinct way with the gun as he carries out the assassinations of his victims. First, he exposes both hands (in white gloves) giving the impression that he has no gun, and when the enemy takes advantage and tries to shoot him, he shoots them first. Hogue has described this idiosyncratic form of Melvillian action as "abrupt, absurd, and a little fantastical."[58] Vincendeau writes that Melville emphasizes "the icon of the gun and the white gloves, and shows the shots, in effect as 'impossible', since Jef's hands are out of his pockets as his adversary draws his gun; yet he still fires first."[59] The "fantastical" and "impossible" effects are, on the face of it, the results of the découpage techniques deployed by Melville, but I believe Melville's techniques are attempts to transpose a sword action in the French *milieu* of the hired killer, who naturally uses a gun. Melville is effectively trying to show how Jef uses the gun as a samurai uses a sword, based on certain principles in the *Zhuang Zi*. Zhuang Zi, in his meeting with King Zhao, tells the king that one who wields a sword "reveals his emptiness to his opponent, gives him an advantageous opening, makes his move after him, arrives before he does."[60] This is the ethical way of swordsmanship. When Jef kills Martey and Rey, he follows Zhuang Zi's instructions to the letter (Figure 4.3).

Melville does not show us how the gun gets to be in Jef's hand. His cutting avoids this detail, an ellipsis prompting the descriptions by Hogue and

Figure 4.3 Jef uses a gun as a samurai uses a sword.
Le Samouraï, Producers: Raymond Borderie, Eugène Lépicier.

Vincendeau, to the effect of "abrupt," "fantastical," and "impossible." Such words actually stress the magic of the xia swordsman (Jef's own magical powers, referred to earlier), or in Zen swordsmanship the mysterious quality of *myoyu* (in Chinese, *miaoyong*), indicating an effect of the marvelous.[61] Melville's ellipsis then becomes the magic of the gunman (swordsman). On the other hand, it is obviously a gamble with death. Jef exposes himself to the enemy's sword stroke (in a manner of speaking), a crucial concept in Zen swordsmanship showing the swordsman's transcendence of birth and death. Jef's superior skill in "arriving before the enemy does" ensures his survival. This unique technique illustrates Jef's readiness to die. The style is a remarkable interpretation, in Melville's idiosyncratic manner, of Daoist thinking in the use of swords, translated into guns in the context of the modern thriller. Though it makes up only a minimal part of the film, it is nevertheless an utterly distinctive action style marking Melville out as a neo-experimental action director. (Being an Eastern thriller, his whole film is, of course, an experiment in the genre.)

Conclusion

Melville's film finally offers a challenge in viewing the French polar in Eastern perspective. The title *Le Samouraï* is a notification of the challenge—a challenge, one might note, not usually taken up by Western commentators.

I have attempted to read the film as a generic Eastern adventure thriller where the central protagonist is interchangeable as a xia hero as well as a samurai. Jef is like one of those heroes featured in the classic novel *The Water Margin* who possesses magical powers as a xia swordsman. (The character he most reminds me of is Dai Zong, the "magic traveler.") He takes on the whole system of the law, easily evading the legions of police on the streets and in the Métro, and fights for justice as he sees it in his own way. If he survives, the system might even accept and incorporate him (in which case, the system has become righteous), and that is what happens to the heroes of *The Water Margin* in the end.

However, it is his destiny not to survive. Jef then becomes the kind of fatalistic hero portrayed by Jimmy Wang Yu in Zhang Che's wuxia films such as *The Golden Swallow* (1968) and *The Assassin* (1967). His dandy image also fits into the kind of hero played by Jimmy Wang Yu in these two films. In the Japanese tradition, Jef is a *kusemono* for whom death is the path to honor. When we see Jef lying on his bed in his threadbare apartment at the film's beginning, he may well be contemplating the words of Daidoji Yuzan in *Budo Shoshinshu*, quoted by D. T. Suzuki:

> Think what a frail thing life is, especially that of a samurai. This being so, you will come to consider every day of your life your last and dedicate it to the fulfilment of your obligations. Never let the thought of a long life seize upon you, for then you are apt to indulge in all kinds of dissipation, and end your days in dire disgrace.[62]

Jef dies neither in dissipation nor in disgrace. By the terms of the samurai code, he dies an honorable death. With his samurai death, Melville sums up the film as the most Eastern of French action thrillers, and in Jef, he has succeeded in portraying the most Eastern of French assassins.

Notes

1 All three ancient texts have been translated into English. See *The Book of Five Rings*, trans. Thomas Cleary (Boston, MA and London: Shambhala, 1993; this book also includes Yagyu Munenori's *Heiho Kadensho* [*The Book of Family Traditions on the Art of War*], *Budo Shoshinshu*, translated as *Code of The Samurai* by Thomas Cleary (Boston, MA: Tuttle Publishing, 1999), and

Hagakure: The Secret Wisdom of the Samurai, trans. Alexander Bennett (Tokyo: Tuttle Publishing, 2014).

2 See Inazo Nitobe, *Bushido, The Soul of Japan* (Tokyo: Tuttle Publishing, 1969).

3 The *Hagakure* is extensively quoted in Jim Jarmusch's *Ghost Dog: The Way of the Samurai* (1999), which is partly a reworking of *Le Samouraï*. As such, it is the one prominent work of reference that acknowledges Melville's film to be influenced by *Hagakure*.

4 *Hagakure*, p. 42. The *Budo Shoshinshu* also propagates much the same injunction in its very first chapter: see *Code of the Samurai*, p. 3.

5 See Olivier Ansart, "Embracing Death: Pure Will in *Hagakure*," *Early Modern Japan*, 18, 2010, p. 57. According to Ansart, the focus of *Hagakure* is on "the will of death" and that its author, "convinced that the class of the samurai was on the verge of extinction, was imagining a desperate 'identitary quest' organized around the flaunting of the core item of the cultural capital of the *bushi*—the act of death" (p. 57).

6 *Hagakure*, p. 43.

7 Though his work is different in substance to that of Robert Bresson (the subject of Chapter 5), both directors engage in a Transcendental style. In fact, Melville claimed to have influenced Robert Bresson, whose *Diary of a Country Priest* (1950) showed some stylistic similarities with Melville's first film *Le Silence de la mer* (1949). See Richard Neupert, *A History of the French New Wave Cinema*, Second Edition (Madison: University of Wisconsin Press, 2007), p. 66.

8 Peter Hogue, "Melville: The Elective Affinities," *Film Comment*, November–December 1996, p. 21.

9 *Hagakure*, p. 237.

10 There is a Chinese restaurant in *Bob le flambeur*, a Chinese painting in *Le Deuxième souffle* (in Jo Ricci's office), a Buddha statue and other Oriental artifacts in *Le Samouraï* (in Olivier Rey's apartment), and a screen with Eastern motifs in *Le Cercle rouge* (in Corey's apartment, shared with his ex-mistress).

11 Roland Carrée, "Il neige chez Melville," *Positif*, February 2011, p. 72.

12 Ginette Vincendeau, *Jean-Pierre Melville: An American in Paris* (London: British Film Institute, 2003), p. 182.

13 See Rui Noguiera (ed.), *Melville on Melville* (London: Secker and Warburg, 1971), p. 129.

14 Ibid., p. 126.

15 Ibid., p. 130.

16 In the tale of Nie Yinniang (the original inspiration of Hou's *The Assassin*), the character of the sorcerer monk has the ability to hide himself in a floating cloud,

from a later iteration of the story in *Taiping guangji* (*The Extensive Records of the Taiping Era*), volume 195.

17 Oleg Benesch, *Inventing the Way of the Samurai: Nationalism, Internationalism, and Bushido in Modern Japan* (Oxford: Oxford University Press, 2014), pp. 137–38. Zen's connection with militarism was already established in China from at least the time of the Song Dynasty (960–1280) if not earlier. See Hirata Seiko, "Zen Buddhist Attitudes to War," in James W. Heisig and John C. Maraldo (eds.), *Rude Awakenings: Zen, the Kyoto School, & the Question of Nationalism* (Honolulu: University of Hawai'i Press, 1994), pp. 3–15.

18 Benesch, *Inventing the Way of the Samurai*, p. 139.

19 D. T. Suzuki, *Zen and Japanese Culture* (London: Routledge and Kegan Paul, 1959), p. 61.

20 Ibid., p. 62.

21 Ibid., p. 70.

22 Ibid., p. 63. Suzuki relates some striking anecdotes about Zen's influence on Bushido in regard to the samurai's attitude toward death on pp. 83–84.

23 Nicole Brenez, "The Secrets of Movement: The Influence of Hong Kong Action Cinema upon the Contemporary French Avant-garde," in M. Morris, S. L. Li, and S. Chan Ching-Kiu (eds.), *Hong Kong Connections: Transnational Imagination in Action Cinema* (Hong Kong: Hong Kong University Press, 2005), p. 169.

24 Philippe Rouyer, "Le petit théâtre de Jean-Pierre Melville," *Positif*, December 1995, p. 101.

25 See Wing-tsit Chan, *The Way of Lao Tzu* (New Jersey: Prentice Hall, 1963), p. 128.

26 Vincendau, *Jean-Pierre Melville: An American in Paris*, p. 181.

27 See *Code of the Warrior*, p. 23.

28 Noguiera, *Melville on Melville*, p. 129.

29 Darren Waldron, "On the Limits of Narcissism: Alain Delon, Masculinity, and the Delusion of Agency," in N. Rees-Roberts and D. Waldron (eds.), *Alain Delon* (London: Bloomsbury, 2015), p. 15.

30 Vincendeau, *Jean-Pierre Melville: An American in Paris*, p. 181.

31 Ibid., p. 182.

32 Keiji Nishitani, *Religion and Nothingness*, trans. Jan Van Bragt (Berkeley, Los Angeles, and London: University of California Press, 1982), p. 174.

33 Ibid., p. 145.

34 Rouyer, "Le petit théâtre de Jean-Pierre Melville," p. 101.

35 Ibid.

36 Ibid.

37 Hogue, "Melville: The Elective Affinities," p. 21.

38 Ibid.
39 Rouyer, "Le petit théâtre de Jean-Pierre Melville," p. 101.
40 Noguiera, *Melville on Melville*, p. 132.
41 *The Book of Five Rings*, p. 18.
42 Susan Hayward writes that there is "a curious reverse mirroring" in several of Melville's films. "Inspector Blot (Meurisse) is the cerebral player who slowly undermines Gu's physical game (*Deuxième souffle*); Inspector Coleman (Delon) the cool voyeur who slowly unravels his opponent, action man Simon (*Un flic*). The inscrutable Inspector Mattei (Bourvil) eventually corners the overly transparent Corey (*Cercle rouge*)." See Susan Hayward, "French Noir 1947-79: From Grunge-Noir to Noir-hilism," in H. B. Pettey and R. B. Palmer (eds.), *International Noir* (Edinburgh: Edinburgh University Press, 2014), p. 56. I would note that there is also an interesting cross-referencing in Melville's films in expressing this doubling theme. Alain Delon virtually repeats his cool performance as the killer of *Le Samouraï* in *Un flic*, where he portrays a police officer, thus illustrating a doubling or "reverse mirroring" in these two characters as portrayed by Delon. It is as if the killer in *Le Samouraï*, if he had lived, had reformed and was then co-opted and reintegrated into the police force in *Un flic*. In the Hong Kong action thriller, Woo's *The Killer* best exemplifies the double theme, with Chow Yun-fat's killer and Danny Lee's cop as the mirror images of each other (and Lee at the end practically becoming the killer as Chow expires).
43 Noguiera, *Melville on Melville*, p. 134.
44 Ibid., p. 130.
45 Ibid., p. 134.
46 See Colin McArthur, "*Mise-en-Scène* Degree Zero: Jean-Pierre Melville's *Le Samouraï*," in S. Hayward and G. Vincendeau (eds.), *French Film: Texts and Contexts* (London and New York: Routledge, 2000), p. 190.
47 Quoted in Stanley Cavell, "The Dandy," in Cavell, *The World Viewed: Reflections on the Ontology of Film* (Cambridge, MA, and London: Harvard University Press), 1979, p. 55.
48 *Hagakure*, p. 87.
49 Ibid., p. 94.
50 Victor Mair, *Wandering on the Way: Early Taoist Tales and Parables of Chuang Tzu* (Honolulu: University of Hawai'i Press, 1994), p. 313.
51 Cavell, "The Dandy," p. 55.
52 *Hagakure*, p. 77.
53 Hayward, "French Noir 1947-79," p. 57.
54 Ibid.

55 Cavell, "The Dandy," p. 56.
56 Mair, *Wandering on the Way*, p. 119.
57 Hogue, "Melville: The Elective Affinities," p. 21.
58 Ibid., p. 17.
59 Vincendeau, *Jean-Pierre Melville: An American in Paris*, p. 184.
60 Mair, *Wandering on the Way*, p. 314.
61 On the concept of *myoyu*, see Suzuki, *Zen and Japanese Culture*, p. 142.
62 Suzuki, *Zen and Japanese Culture*, p. 72.

5

Robert Bresson, French or Daoist?[1]

The Transcendental in the material

In his book *Transcendental Style in Film*, Paul Schrader notes a similarity of the style that he calls "Transcendental" between the Japanese director Ozu Yasujiro and the French director Robert Bresson. In Bresson's case, the style "is as much influenced by Bresson's cultural traditions as it is by Zen culture," and Schrader goes on to say that "it is easier for a Western viewer to recognize Bresson's *use of culture* than Ozu's" (italics mine).[2] In this chapter, I will examine Bresson's style from my perspective as an Eastern viewer. I will analyze Bresson's film *Au hasard Balthazar* (1966) as a manifestation of Daoist principles. Mindful of Schrader's caveat about culture, I should say right off that I make no pretense of knowing French culture, or indeed, European culture from which Bresson hails. Nevertheless, Bresson's style smacks highly of Eastern (Daoist) essence despite the cultural pretexts of Bresson's personality and background. It is a style not just reminiscent of an Eastern quality but practically invites an Eastern interpretation. Transcendental style to Schrader is a universal form of representation. It has a unique power to "transcend culture and personality,"[3] and it is this power that compels my application of the Eastern approach to Bresson's work.

Schrader investigates Transcendental style in the works of Bresson and the Danish director Carl Dreyer, two Western directors using the style to represent the way, "a *tao*, in the broadest sense of the term," as Schrader says—and Schrader refers to "the 'spiritual universality' of transcendental style" which may be variously interpreted by critics.[4] My particular thesis here is the Daoist spirit of Transcendental style. I will undertake a reexamination of Transcendental style from the Eastern perspective focusing on Bresson's film in this chapter and on Dreyer's *Vampyr* in Chapter 6 (Schrader essentially giving his own Eurocentric approach to the styles of these two directors). In beginning my discussion on Bresson, my point of departure is that the Eastern functions as a universalizing force streaming through the cultural pretexts of Bresson's French background and his adherence to French religious traditions and culture, filtering, clarifying, and purifying the style itself. This may be an esoteric style because of the force of Eastern universality, but even if one's tendency is to appreciate Bresson purely from his own cultural and religious tradition, the style that he evolved from at least *Pickpocket* (1959) onward was highly distinctive, unique even to Bresson himself and specific to his own manner and form, not prototypical of his culture at all.[5] There is a need to further define this personal specificity and since Western analysis is taken as a given, almost reaching a state of saturation, an Eastern approach would seem necessary in assessing Bresson's Transcendental style.

Bresson is therefore inimitable, and he seems to me quite detached from the rest of French culture. Probably his most distinctive trademark was his actors whom he called "models," instructed not to act, to drain themselves of emotions, and to be like automatons, which is symbolic of Bresson's stance. Schrader asserts that Bresson was a "consummate oddball," "a cultural reactionary and an artistic revolutionary" who was "alienated from his contemporary culture."[6] From the evidence of Bresson's work, his writings, and his appearances in filmed interviews, it is hard to disagree with this observation by Schrader. Bresson's films are ultimately "estranged from their culture and are financially unsuccessful," but it might also be true to say that they are estranged from the medium itself. As Schrader comments, "In a medium which has been primarily intuitive, individualized and humanistic, Bresson's work is anachronistically nonintuitive, impersonal, and iconographic."[7] This estrangement from culture is an abstraction of culture, and the estrangement from the medium is an abstraction of form, but is Bresson's style truly Transcendental? To address this question, we must first recognize that the most important element in style is that of technical skill and that to achieve the Transcendent one must merge one's skill with the Dao and move with the spirit. The parable of the Dexterous Butcher in the *Zhuang Zi*, chapter 3, underscores this principle. A lord sees his cook carving up an ox and is amazed by his skills. "What your servant loves is the Way, which goes beyond mere skill," the cook says.[8] Bresson undoubtedly displays technical mastery in his films and like all directors worthy of being called masters, he seeks to transcend skill and convey knowledge and wisdom. Our aim is to discover and identify the Eastern transcendental matter in Bresson's knowledge and wisdom and which transcends his *use of culture*.

Hence, to understand Bresson as a Daoist artist, let us begin with the eternal puzzle of whether there is a Transcendent. Schrader states that "if there really is a Transcendent, then the critic can never fully comprehend how it operates in art."[9] If there really is a Transcendent, it is not a thing one could name. One could never know what it is, like the Dao, that which is nameless and eternal. "The Dao that can be told is not the eternal Dao. The name that can be named is not the eternal name. The Nameless is the origin of Heaven and Earth."[10] Thus, if we name Bresson's style "Transcendental," it is not the eternal Transcendent. If we refer to an event that is yet ethereal, then the event "is not namable according to any species," to quote Roland Barthes from his *Empire of Signs*.[11] Effectively, Transcendental style can only take a form in a material way. Bresson's style is therefore materialistic instead of transcendental, a point already noted by several scholars.[12] However, his materialistic style contains the Transcendental. Bresson reaches for the Transcendental but it is not enough to call his style "Transcendental" to make it so. Thus, Bresson's style is no simple matter, whether defined as transcendental or materialistic.

A film like *Au hasard Balthazar* (hereafter referred to as *Balthazar*) is exemplary in showing both aspects, as I will demonstrate. It features a donkey, a down to earth kind of animal, as chief protagonist. In doing so, Bresson signals his adherence to matter and form. In fact, Bresson depicts the vicissitudes and hardships of life and shows little if any interest in transcendental retreat. The donkey itself suffers through these hardships and Bresson shows it as indomitable spirit, suffering to the very end. While the donkey Balthazar is the perfect manifestation of materialism, it is also a manifestation of a nonhuman view of the world, seen from the donkey's perspective.[13] All the human characters revolve around this donkey and their experience of the world is really an observation from the donkey's point of view. This nonhuman perspective is quite startling, given Bresson's background and his perceived tendency to reaffirm Catholic or Christian faith (though many critics have noted the peculiarities of Bresson's dedication to faith, labeling his treatment as "Jansenist"). At the same time, the film is also disconcerting for its elemental view of human materialism, thus, Bresson's materialism

> radiates from all embodied forms—the human and the animal—revealing a similitude so unthinkable (so appalling to think) that resistance to the identification of human and animal bodies provokes cruelty to the animal, even as its beauty at other moments fascinates with an allure apparently devoid of human counterpart.[14]

For its revelatory view of materialism in a social human and animal context, *Balthazar* is Bresson's most singular work in his entire oeuvre. It is a work where he appears to condense all his obsessions in a most original way. From our Eastern perspective, it is certainly his most important film because it resounds his Other side—his Daoism—which has lain hidden, or, in fact, not so hidden, only not widely recognized and discussed. From a philosophical point of view, it shows his broad outlook of the world, though, superficially, the French or Western cultural and religious context tightly bounds the film together. This context invites Christian interpretations of its content. In interviews, Bresson himself indulges in these interpretations but the Christian viewpoint is already evident in the title where the donkey's name Balthazar, one of the Three Wise Men, immediately evokes Christian readings.[15]

Despite its apparently Christian name, Bresson's donkey can be thought of as a symbol of all faiths. The donkey is also associated with Eastern religions. The founder of Daoism, Lao Zi, is often shown in popular art riding on a donkey. One of the Daoist immortals, Zhang Guo, is associated with a white donkey, which he rides back to front, and legend has it that he can transform the donkey into a paper clipping, storing it away inside his pocket, and changes it back to real when he needs to ride on it. The symbolism of the donkey stands for *you* or wandering, a key concept in Daoism, which enjoins all practitioners to wander in the Way (*dao*) in order to find their true selves or to be one with nature. In Buddhism, there is a short sutra devoted to the donkey, the Gadrabha Sutra. This exhorts monks to train themselves in virtue, mind, and discernment, all of which are symbolized by the donkey. In the sutra, the donkey follows a herd of cows saying that it is a cow. Its color is not that of a cow, and neither is its voice and hoof. Yet, it keeps following the herd insisting it is a cow. The sutra is a parable for monks (or disciples and devotees) lacking resolve and training but who follow a community of monks, saying, "I am a monk!" The donkey has an illusionary view of itself, but it is necessary for it to step off the path of delusion to be truly noble, like a monk, or like the Buddha.

Balthazar might be a tale of this donkey, which steps off the path of delusion and treads the path of the material world, subjected to a tough regimen of training to be noble. It is exposed to punishment and bad treatment by humans. The donkey surpasses all expectations. "He's a saint," says a character, toward the end of the film. The material world is yet the world in which to achieve spiritualism and deliverance. It is the dharma realm. One must dutifully live one's life to realize one's dharma—and the donkey of Bresson's film does all its given duties unflinchingly. In Daoism, one must wander through the *dao* (the Way), and the donkey is the Daoist mascot that, again unflinchingly, indeed valiantly, undergoes all kinds of trials and tribulations in its wandering. The element of destiny or fate is also part of it. As written in the *Zhuang Zi*,

> Life and death, preservation and loss, failure and success, poverty and wealth, worthiness and unworthiness, slander and praise, hunger and thirst, cold and heat—these are all the transformations of affairs and the operation of destiny.[16]

Balthazar depicts all the above conditions word for word. They somehow summarize the plot of the film, what Balthazar and the human characters go through in the material world, or that part of provincial France in which they find themselves. Bresson expresses the material world indubitably, which seems to be a stark contradiction of the oft-stated claim that he is a "spiritual" filmmaker.

To some critics, spiritualism in Bresson is associated with his style and form. According to Susan Sontag, Bresson's use of form as anti-dramatic, his use of words and non-expressiveness of performance create a "spiritual style."[17] However, in *Balthazar*, it just as well creates a material style. This is important to consider when we later ponder on Bresson's "transcendentalism" ("spiritual style" is more or less the same as "Transcendental style"). What is transcendental in *Balthazar* is the concentration on the donkey, its total experience. This experience is material and yet infinite. Thus, the donkey stands for both materialism and transcendentalism, which in Daoist thought, is the difference between the realm of man and the realm of Heaven. In Daoism, under the aegis of Zhuang Zi, this is the difference "which is the prerequisite for being a true human being" and empowers one "to transcend the self and plunge into the infinite."[18] To the extent that Bresson is concerned with the spiritual, he is concerned with how to be a true human being. This would be the theme of his films, perhaps best exemplified by a film like *Pickpocket*. *Balthazar* is revolutionary among Bresson's films in that he shows the spiritual through an animal and his human models are manifestly materialistic, driven by desire, fame, and money. The problem posed by the film is how to view the spiritual and the materialistic as being one. Do we become animal to be more spiritual? Or is Bresson viewing the animal in strictly metaphoric terms? On the other hand, Bresson's rigor in presenting a nonhuman perspective seems to cut off the allegorical. The donkey's presence is not justifiable as representing anybody or anything. William Johnson points out that "the donkey's importance in the film, and his place of honor in the title, do not depend on symbolism" and that Bresson is "as direct as ever." Any signs of "humanity or divinity in the donkey are as illusory as the arithmetical ability he displays at the circus."[19]

In his attentiveness to the donkey, Bresson treats all things as equal, and this is tantamount to a cosmic point of view. It is the closest that Bresson gets to be a Daoist sage, the kind who looks at the world in all its disparities and sees oneness. "Disparity is the paradox of the spiritual existing within the physical, and it cannot be 'resolved' by any earthly logic or human emotions," writes Schrader.[20] From the Daoist point of view, a sage who eschews human emotions and adopts a nonhuman perspective can live with disparity, seeing its potential for the spiritual. In his other films, Bresson was perhaps a closeted Daoist, particularly in the manner of his models who appear as if to exist in a world regardless of themselves, speaking dialogue "as if he were listening to his own words reported by someone else," the automaton, or "the authentic Vigilambulist," as Deleuze puts it.[21] They are models for the sake of appearance, yet pointing to another state of existence within—the pure appearance. For these models, the world is an illusion. In *Balthazar*, the world is all too real even when the models follow the rule of automatism, because an animal embodies the spiritual dimension (Marie chides Jacques for being unrealistic as he continues to harp on loving her and wanting to marry, which no longer corresponds with Marie's view of the world). This is the most striking disparity between Balthazar and the human models who occupy the film. It is also the most striking disparity between this film and Bresson's other films.

Au hasard Zhuang Zi

If we see Bresson as the Daoist he is, his film assumes the point of view of a Daoist sage. In the film itself, within its narrative, the sage is none other than the donkey. In the Eastern tradition, reincarnation is a fundamental belief. The *Zhuang Zi* recounts a tale of a sage-like luminary who is dying. His friend comes, sees the family weeping, and shoos them away. "Do not disturb transformation!" he says, and then turns to his dying friend: "Great is the transforming creator! What next will he make of you? Where will he send you? Will he turn you into a rat's liver? Will he turn you into a bug's leg?" In reply, the dying sage says, "If I, who have chanced to take on human form, were to say, 'Man! I must remain a man!' the great Transforming Creator would certainly think that I am an inauspicious man. Now, once I accept heaven and earth as the Great Forge, and the Transforming Creator as the Great Smelter, I'm willing to go wherever they send me."[22] Balthazar the donkey may by chance be the Daoist sage. Let us say that he is Zhuang Zi and recall the dream of Zhuang Zi in which he dreams of being a butterfly or is it the butterfly dreaming that it was Zhuang Zi. In another famous instance, Zhuang Zi claims to know the joy of fishes as though he were a fish, earning the excoriation of his friend who asks, "You are not a fish, how do you know what the joy of fishes is?"[23] In these parables, Zhuang Zi suggests he may be a butterfly or a fish. It is the natural transformation of things. Au hasard Balthazar, au hasard Zhuang Zi? Since chance (*hasard*) is key to transformation, the donkey may just as well be Zhuang Zi (Figure 5.1).

The donkey as Zhuang Zi presents some possibilities for East-West civilizational observations. Indeed, we can say that Bresson adopts an outsider's perspective to view his human beings in a French provincial setting. This is the donkey's perspective. Bresson acutely observes the degeneration of Western civilization through a narrative of his human characters entangled in all too human vices: lust, fame, pride, money, and drunkenness. The donkey observes all that goes on. The narrative "is generated by iniquitous character behaviour, or, in theological terms, by sin," as Tony Pipolo puts it.[24] Iniquity and sin is at the heart of civilization, part of a discourse about the value of civilization itself, its rise and fall. The donkey's name being Balthazar already presents a civilizational discourse since it carries a symbolic value through

Figure 5.1 The donkey Balthazar and Zhuang Zi.
Au hasard Balthazar, Producer: Mag Bodard.

its ties to ancient history, literature, and religion, as Pipolo has explained.[25] Pipolo, however, points out the Christian and Western aspects of the donkey, totally neglecting its Eastern or Other-religious constituent. Pipolo, of course, is in good company in showing this neglect. As far as I know, no Western critic has analyzed Bresson or his films from the Eastern side of things. However, the donkey as Balthazar, even if he belongs more to the Christian discourse, incorporates the Eastern hemisphere and its civilizational dimensions. The original Balthazar is said to have come from Arabia and usually depicted as dark-skinned.

The donkey's braying that interrupts Schubert's Sonata No. 20 on the soundtrack over the credits is a rude interruption of Eastern civilization into Western civilization. One can see this as a touch of humor and irony in Bresson, which might seem at odds with the general view of Bresson as a heavily serious filmmaker. The French critic Jean Sémolué has written precisely on this subject.[26] Bresson structures irony into the narrative, which works as direct contradictions, one scene contradicted by another. Sémolué gives several examples: The opening scene of the father who says "impossible" to his children when they want to have the donkey only to be contradicted in the next image showing the father and his children walking away with the donkey; Arnold swearing that he will not touch another drop of drink contradicted by the next image showing him picking up a glass of drink; and the teacher refusing the grain merchant's offer to receive the donkey as payment of a debt only to walk the donkey back to his house in the next image. We should consider the interruption of the Sonata with the braying as one of such "inconsistencies" (*inconséquences*), as Sémolué calls it. In this way, "the film highlights the inconsistencies of men and the 'irony of fate' with a relentlessness that only ceases with the calm death of Balthazar in the mountain."[27]

Since the irony is structural and it engenders the kind of ellipses habitually employed by Bresson in his narrative style, there is more to a given fact than what we might suppose. "It leads us to suppose that facts may be more perverse than what have occurred," as Sémolué says.[28] Thus with the momentary interruption of the braying and the resumption of the Sonata, Bresson sets up the intervention of a strange Other civilizational force into a given culture (in this instance, Western culture). The music proceeds again with transformed circumstances that the culture must adjust to, with all its adverse or perverse effects affecting the protagonists as the narrative unfolds. At the same time, the donkey is a symbol of the Other, which functions as the basis of its Eastern perspective that opposes the Western viewpoint and its actions. It silently observes the West, occasionally rebels, but mainly receives all that is meted out to it with resignation. Inscribed and hidden within the form of the donkey, this Other perspective (the Eastern perspective) is primed to be neglected. In some way, Bresson ensures its neglect. Perhaps this is what Schrader means when he writes, "Form is the operative element in Bresson's films but it operates through personality and culture and is necessarily influenced by them."[29] Fortunately, Bresson invites open interpretations of his donkey, a living ellipsis itself because we can never know what the animal thinks, just as he invites open interpretations on what happened in certain scenes of the protagonists (Did Arnold commit a murder? Did Marie sleep with the miser? Was she gang-raped? Did she die, or did she just leave?).

Because the Eastern is inherent in the donkey, it would not be too fanciful then to see the donkey as Zhuang Zi. It is in the spirit of the donkey being sage-like as well as in the spirit of Bresson's humor. In addition, Zhuang Zi is a kindred spirit to Bresson. With the donkey as Zhuang Zi, the film naturally takes on a more Daoist shade of meaning. First, let us consider nature. The braying is the voice of nature interrupting Schubert. Nature is probably Bresson's central obsession, which then converges with Daoism. His rationale for filmmaking is to realize novelty and nature. "Not the natural, nature," he emphasizes. "I want moments like that to create something within me and what is created is what I want to commit to film." "Basically, my film is a product of chance."[30] Chance is something that occurs in nature. The donkey encapsulates both chance and nature.

One may misunderstand chance as accident, but it is the chance that is immanent in things. When placed within nature, there is yet an element of predestiny and its occurrence is spontaneous. Bresson hopes to capture this spontaneity above all else and assiduously works at it (stories of him shooting many takes of his models are legend) so that a being emerges. Kent Jones refers to a "strange mixture of careful planning with the spontaneous shock of perception that gives Bresson's cinema its special brand of vertiginousness."[31] This still implies a certain precariousness in chance, but Bresson's work is a sure and stable configuration of chance. Chance, therefore, does not preclude order. Bresson liked to call himself a *metteur en ordre* (one who imposes order) as opposed to a *metteur en scène*. However, it begs the question of what kind of order he seeks to impose for it is not just a lack of chaos and a neatness of hierarchy in the scene's proceedings. It is an order of nature he imposes. This order of nature determines a certain style to his films. There is the structural trait of contradiction and paradox, as discussed above, "which are perfectly natural phenomena," as Charles Barr points out.[32] There is also the deployment of a certain rhythm in his scenes, of which more shortly.

Another style resulting from the imposition of order is his peculiar mode of performance by models. This merits a bit more discussion here for his obsession with the automatism of his models converges with an element of Daoist thought. According to Bresson, automatism approximates chance and nature. In his *Notes of the Cinematographer*, Bresson explains, "Nine tenths of our movements obey habit and automatism. It is anti-nature to subordinate them to will and to thought."[33] His instructions to his models are as follows: "'Don't think what you're saying, don't think what you're doing.' And also: 'Don't think *about* what you say, don't think *about* what you do.'"[34] "Models mechanized externally, internally free. On their faces nothing wilful. 'The constant, the eternal beneath the accidental.'"[35] Bresson's thoughts could just as well have come from the Daoist idea of the fasting of the mind.

Maintaining the unity of your will, listen not with your ears but with your mind. Listen not with your mind but with your primal breath. The ears are limited to listening, the mind is limited to tallying. The primal breath, however, awaits things emptily. It is only through the Way that one can gather emptiness, and emptiness is the fasting of the mind.[36]

Thus, with fasting of the mind, one loses one's identity, and this can be called emptiness: the emptiness of feeling in one's mind and being one with nature. "If you are impelled by human feelings, it is easy to be false, if you are impelled by nature, it is hard to be false."[37] "One who attends to one's own mind and who is not easily diverted by sorrow and joy, realizing their inevitability and accepting them as if they were destiny, has attained the ultimate integrity."[38] This principle of the fasting of the mind was probably an influence on later Zen (in Chinese, Chan) thinking, as propounded by the Chan patriarch Shen Xiu in his famous poem: "The body is like the Bodhi tree, the mind a bright mirror, polish it at all times, do not let the dust taint it" (translation mine). Dust, for our purposes, is the metaphor of will and thought, the illusionary world projected by acting, and the mind as a bright mirror is precisely the world of pure nature.

Bresson's models may have more in common with Stanley Cavell's musings on automatism being an avenue of modernist art in redefining all kinds of media to generate new instances.[39] In Bresson's case, his insistence on the automatism of his models redefines the medium of film. Bresson calls his kind of filmmaking *cinematographe*, as opposed to *cinéma*, which he considers merely filmed theater. *Cinematographe* is a kind of writing, *écriture*, as well as a photographic style emphasizing a flat natural look. The models cinematographically transform film from theater into nature, effectively a new instance of art. Bresson strives to capture nature on film but his models have mostly been human. Only in *Balthazar* does Bresson concentrate on an animal as model, an even more revolutionary instance of his art. The animal mirrors nature completely, and it is perhaps Bresson's ironical intent to show nature at its best or most benevolent, playing off against his human models, shown as being mostly venal, cruel, and foolish, "evidence of the flawed human condition and the fall from grace."[40] Here, nature clearly is the transcendent, felt and seen through the donkey. The donkey represents the Way, the path, le chemin (all abstract thoughts), but Bresson depicts the original nature of the donkey every step of the way as it treads the path, walks the Way. In this natural manner of showing the transcendent, Bresson preaches that humans must shed off the way of man and follow the Way, which is the way of Heaven. This moral is quite translucent in *Balthazar*, and as such, it is a very Daoist work. Bresson's Way is a strange one. Michel in *Pickpocket* refers to "quel drôle de chemin il m'a fallu prendre." Le chemin is far stranger in *Balthazar* than in *Pickpocket*. It is strange for its abstruseness in an Eastern way (the Eastern already signified by the name "Balthazar"), and strange too because the path is taken by a donkey.

The Way is genuinely strange in *Balthazar*, therefore, since it is tread upon by the donkey, and its point of view reflects its strange destiny and its interlocking relationships with the human characters. In *Pickpocket*, Michel's way is still marked with human obsessions and emotions, and the film appears to prod our conscience, but the donkey's way in *Balthazar* tells us that "the world is wider than our conscience," as Jean Collet makes clear.[41] "He bravely exchanges his ass wisdom against our madness of men."[42] Yet the donkey's wisdom remains ungraspable, because language "is no longer current" in its domain, as Collet explains.[43] Some characters are more cognizant of the inner beauty of the beast; others simply mistrust it: communication between the humans and the donkey being a very indeterminate factor. In any case, as Collet says, "Communication between Bressonian protagonists through the usual means is a very awkward thing."[44] The strangeness inherent in this incongruence between the donkey and the humans is of the level of the Zen utterance: "Walk while riding on a donkey."[45] D. T. Suzuki explains that a nonsensical statement like this is designed to "break up the intellectual aporia" (of those who think too much) "by means of the '*Mu!*' (emptiness, italics in the original) in which there is no trace of intellection but only of the sheer will overriding the intellect."[46]

As it happens, in another touch of Bressonian humor, we see intellectuals riding on Arnold's donkeys (including Balthazar) pontificating on topics such as art (action painting) and on whether one can be held responsible for a crime committed involuntarily and forgets out of nervous shock ("the criminal may awaken unaware that he is a criminal"). The intellectuals pontificate on the Way but do not walk it. Their knowledge is academic, and they lack the will of true action. The moral is that one must walk the Way as a measure of self-worth, training oneself in the rigors of the Way. It is not enough to ride the donkey since it could lose its way. Yet the donkey represents the Way itself. Balthazar walks the Way. Marie and Gerard, creatures of instinct, do not walk and do not ride the donkey. Their will is weak, distracted by life's vicissitudes and its vices. (Gerard is practically evil, but he naturally puts into practice the concept of action painting.[47]) Arnold rides the donkey but is too drunk to walk. He falls off the donkey, hits his head, and dies. The Way of the donkey is strange, but it is nevertheless the Way of nature. Bresson portrays a distinction between the Way of nature and the way of man. While the way of man is precisely the vices indulged by humans, the donkey also bears the mark of the way of man: harnessed, reined, shoehorned, and whipped[48] (Figure 5.2).

On another level, nature works for Bresson as pure rhythm, which might be an extension of automatism. He frames and constructs his sequences on rhythm not on the logic of the scenes, which explains why some scenes are often incomprehensible. The images "are independent to some degree from the demands of the story," as Nick Browne explains it,[49] but not of the rhythmic form that Bresson imposes. I said before that Bresson invites open interpretations on some sequences. If we fall into the rhythm of the scenes and their natural sense of events, there may not be any need to interpret. More importantly, we need to capture the rhythm of nature. Thus, on the question of whether Marie died at the end, or whether she just left home to go to Paris, as some have hypothesized, our subjectivity determines the need for interpretation, prejudged by our feeling toward death. A character in *L'Argent* (1983) says, "We fear death because we love life." Bresson proposes that the

Figure 5.2 Gerard and his "action painting."
Au hasard Balthazar, Producer: Mag Bodard.

idea of death should be considered upfront as a natural rhythm of life and that death should not be feared (the widow in *L'Argent* personifies this non-fear and indeed, prepares for its inevitability, perhaps Bresson's best model expressing this theme). Daoist sages say that "whoever knows the oneness of life and death, of existence and nonexistence" shall be our friends.[50] "Life and death are destined. Their constant alternation, like that of day and night, is due to heaven. What men are unable to interfere with are the attributes of all things."[51] Balthazar the donkey performs the natural sequence of life and death throughout his film. It is an incarnation of a Daoist sage.

Death recurs so much in Bresson's films that we cannot escape the truism of life and death as destined. It is part of nature's rhythm in his films. *Balthazar* gains a further distinction as a film of mourning—the mourning of a donkey through its braying on the soundtrack.[52] The donkey's bray was a sign of mourning in medieval China. An anecdote in the fifth-century collection, *Shishuo xinyu* (*Recent Anecdotes and the Talk of the Age*) relates how the friends of the poet Wang Can mourned him on his death. Because Wang loved the sound of the donkey's bray, they mourned him by braying. Another anecdote tells of a similar case where a writer mourned his patron by braying, incurring the laughter of the assembled mourners.[53] If we interpret the donkey's bray in *Balthazar* as mourning, this is in keeping with the death theme in Bresson, perhaps the most solemn of Bresson's themes (often accompanied with depictions of violence). However, the donkey's bray might be mistaken for sweet music on the soundtrack of the film, in which case, it should incur laughter. I had earlier suggested it as the sound of nature, and mourning would clearly be a natural sound to suggest the film's view of the world, and the donkey mourning its own existence in the world of suffering. If the donkey is Zhuang Zi, this kind of mourning is more than likely. Since Zhuang Zi claims to know the joy of fishes, he would know the mourning of donkeys.[54] Some have interpreted the donkey's bray as that of a birth bray at the point when it is born, if so, this could be the bray of Zhuang Zi on his reincarnation as a donkey.

The donkey as a model is Bresson's most revolutionary variation of his method. We might ask why Bresson has resorted to the use of a donkey as model. It would be facetious to claim that the donkey is the best performer of the fasting of the mind principle, but there is no doubt that we do see a perfect manifestation of nature in it. It is nature animafied, so to speak, and this allows Bresson to state his philosophy of nature in a single stroke. The donkey stands for a particular style of living, and dying, which contrasts with the style of living and dying of the humans. Does the donkey represent any single character in the film in its saintliness and way of life? There is perhaps a case to say that Marie is the closest to the donkey in terms of character. She is certainly close to the donkey in a physical way—recall the scene where Gerard spies on her with the donkey at night and we see that she has placed a crown of flowers on the donkey's head. Gerard says to one of his gang that she may really love the donkey and the donkey loves her back. "In mythology . . . ," but then he stops. Bresson does not follow through, in an obvious break with his literary tendency. Why did Bresson stop there?[55] Perhaps it is because Marie, after all, is not a mythological character and the film's content is far from mythological. In the next section, we will consider why Bresson subtly brings up the mythological while suggesting certain sexual imputations (through Gerard) in Marie's character in her relationship with the donkey.

Marie and Balthazar

Marie, Balthazar, and Gerard obviously constitute a love triangle. (Balthazar, in fact, is the constant third party in Marie's relationships with either Gerard or Jacques.) When Marie appears like a child of nature, gathering flowers to put as a crown on Balthazar's head, she kisses the donkey. Gerard interprets it as love, and it is apparent that Gerard desires Marie (he later beats the donkey as if out of jealousy). Bresson brings up the reference to mythology almost as if he wanted to introduce it as an element in respect to Balthazar, and at the same time, denies it to Marie. It is not out of the bounds of possibility even for Bresson to suggest that the donkey may have magical powers. It could transform into a human being and reciprocate Marie's kiss, as in the donkey tales of the Brothers Grimm and Apuleius's *The Golden Ass*, cited as an influence on Bresson.[56] Early in the film, in the scene where Balthazar seemingly topples the cart with the farmer on it, we see a human hand reaching out as if to dismantle the cart from the donkey as it picks up speed, and then, shortly afterward, the cart topples. The farmer, shaken, gathers a group of other farmers and chases after Balthazar, to punish it. Bresson cuts the scene in such a way as to suggest that the hand has caused the accident, but whose hand is it?[57] Here, there is a sense that the donkey, in touch with providence, could be responsible. We get the first hint of the donkey as a mythological animal. The second hint of the mythological is Marie's love for the donkey.

From our Eastern perspective, since we have identified the donkey with Zhuang Zi, it is pertinent to bring up the myth of the *xia*, the ancient knights-errant in Chinese culture, and in particular, the *xianü*, the female knight-errant. Zhuang Zi's time was in fact the era of the *xia* at its peak. There is a chapter in the *Zhuang Zi* entitled "Discoursing on Swords," in which Zhuang Zi, an accomplished swordsman, explains to a despotic king the right, ethical way to use a sword. One who wields a sword "reveals his emptiness to his opponent, gives him an advantageous opening, makes his move after him, arrives before he does."[58] The Daoist tradition of *xia* may therefore have been established by Zhuang Zi from his time onward. The tale of the *xianü*, Nie Yinniang, first published in the era of the Tang Dynasty as a *chuanqi* (a literary form),[59] filmed by Hou Hsiao-hsien as *The Assassin* (2015), is precisely a tale of a Daoist knight. She classically expresses "emptiness," gives opponents advantageous openings, makes her move after them, and arrives before they do. (This is most evident in the film version, in the few scenes showing her in action.) I bring all this up to suggest a mythological context that is absent in Bresson's film so that we may better understand Marie and her relationship with the donkey. Nie Yinniang rides a white donkey. In the original story, there is also a black donkey, ridden by her husband, a mirror polisher. The story was adapted into a drama during the Qing dynasty re-titled *The Black and White Donkeys* (*Heibai wei*), which Hou would surely have researched into. Hou's opening scene in *The Assassin* is a shot of the two donkeys, which seems to me an allusion to *Balthazar*, although, superficially, there is no correlation with the film at all. However, *The Assassin* has very much a Bressonian feel, almost the same rhythm of a Bresson film and there are distinct parallels with *Balthazar*.

The tale of Nie Yinniang, as told in Hou's film, is a transposition and inversion of Marie's tale in *Balthazar*. (Hou, it should be noted, had made his own changes to the original *chuanqi*, but it is not known whether he is influenced by Bresson's film.) Marie now becomes the mythological Nie Yinniang, the female assassin. Jacques, her childhood lover, is the lord of Weibo (played in Hou's film by Chang Chen), and Gerard is the mirror polisher in Hou's film, a benevolent version of Gerard (we may recall that in Bresson's film, Gerard breaks a mirror). Arnold is a kind of usurper, like the usurpers who seek to subvert and topple the lord of Weibo, including the sorcerer monk who practices black magic. (Arnold, constantly intoxicated, appears to possess magical powers that allow him to cure Balthazar and own it.) Nie Yinniang's parents, like Marie's, thanklessly serve another lord, and Yinniang's father nearly loses his life (Marie's father dies). At the end, Yinniang leaves, happily, with the mirror polisher, together with their donkeys. Marie, on the other hand, also leaves but is rejected and abused by Gerard, the mirror breaker (her mother says she has gone and will never come back). Balthazar, appropriated by Gerard, is left to die in the mountain. Hou, in his scenario, has thoroughly mythologized Marie, as it were. He puts Marie (transformed as Nie Yinniang) in a mythological context whereas Bresson deliberately cuts her off from this context.

Of course, if Bresson had wanted to, he could have placed Marie in a European medieval setting and told a myth about Marie and the donkey. Bresson is not averse to mythology, as demonstrated by his version of the Arthurian legend, *Lancelot du Lac* (1974). To some extent, *Trial of Joan of Arc* (1962) partakes of the kind of historical myth evoked by the tale of Nie Yinniang. Jeanne is like a female knight-errant, particularly when asked by her inquisitors to put on a dress instead of the manlier apparel she wears. Marie is like Jeanne in that she has fighting spirit, but she lives in the twentieth century and instead incarnates the rebellious spirit of the times, which explains why she chooses Gerard rather than Jacques. Marie is the out-of-place female knight, misplaced into a different era and into another reality that is intensely un-mythological, "la réalité c'est autre chose," says Marie, referring to this reality. In fact, Bresson demythologizes Marie and the donkey and emphasizes how they are in the wrong place, in the wrong time, hence, Gerard's sarcasm about the donkey being "modern" and the father's remark about the donkey being "antiquated," making them look ridiculous; and Marie saying to Jacques that "our vows of love, our childhood promises were in a world of make-believe, not reality." Balthazar represents a mythological past, and for Marie it points to a past life of pure myth. Marie appears conscious of this in her remarks about reality, said to Jacques (in this scene, Balthazar is present, reminding Marie of a past that conflicts with reality).

Marie's fate is of course predestined. That she cannot love Jacques is also predestined, in the Chinese sense of *yuanfen*, romantic destiny (in the same spirit, her affair with Gerard is also destined to fail). The mythological context of *The Assassin* would place Marie quite appropriately into her past life, almost as if she had left twentieth-century France to go back into her past, into another reality, to realize all that she cannot realize in *Balthazar*. Thus, Marie ends up in the ancient East, as the original knight-errant that she is, her emptiness manifested as the training of the knight-errant, her rebelliousness the urge of the righteous. Here, her fate is to marry the one she loves, the polisher of mirrors not the breaker of mirrors (see Figure 5.2). The mirror polisher will keep the mirror mind clean and pure. She rides her donkey, and the husband his. The donkey is then quite content, knowing that the fate of its keeper will be secure. In Hou's film, there is no need to focus on the donkey because the Marie figure, Nie Yinniang, is in her reality. In Bresson's film, the focus on the donkey reminds us that present reality is different, and that Marie will be a tragic victim of the times. In this way, the donkey is an allegory of time and reality (the present and the past), always perceived as tragic if we do not live by the precepts of the Way. This is the reason why Bresson steadfastly denies Marie her status (or her place) in mythology (Figure 5.3).

Figure 5.3 Nie Yinniang and her donkey.
The Assassin, Producer: Wen-Ying Huang.

Conclusion

I have tried to show that *Au hasard Balthazar* is a singular work in Bresson's oeuvre, his most Eastern film, the one film of all his works that is the most resonant of Daoist philosophy. It is singular in Bresson's handling of themes of inner spirituality, predestiny, and nature as the Way. The Way, or the Dao, is the universal idea guiding Bresson's idiosyncratic treatment of his themes, leading him to a radical, non-anthropocentric vision of the transcendental. Here, the donkey carries the weight of transcendentalism. How strange we may feel is the Way treaded by the donkey to reach its apotheosis of "calm death in the mountain," as Sémulué puts it, is a matter of one's subjectivity but it is inescapably profound. It draws us into a vision of oneness with nature, of being into nonbeing, and of being and nonbeing. The originality of the film lies in its signification of a core of abstraction represented by the donkey and its "interior movement."[60] Its outer reality is that of the rural French provincial township that Bresson depicts. The culture is clearly French, and the language is French. But the donkey, is it French or Daoist? This is the mystery of the eye of the donkey (see Figure 5.1), which Bresson regularly draws our attention to, an enigma within the riddle of the narrative—in the circus scene, we also see the eyes of the tiger, the polar bear, the orangutan, the elephant, as if to reemphasize the enigma. Sharon Cameron observes that Balthazar's eye "becomes a figure for a sentience that is illegible." "Balthazar's eye is like a Buddha eye, or like a neutral camera eye, or, in being just the donkey's eye, like any enigmatic animal eye. We can't penetrate that eye."[61]

Finally, is Bresson French or Daoist? *Au hasard Balthazar* seems to me to be his one film where he tries to transcend his French identity, doing so through his use of the donkey. Bresson's *use of culture* (to refer to Schrader's statement again) makes him culturally French, to be sure, but the core abstraction of the donkey is the very substance of Bresson's Transcendental style. His style therefore works best when the core is abstract. My analysis above has set out to demonstrate the donkey as incarnation of Daoist thought and beliefs, a Zhuang Zi avatar. We may say therefore that Bresson is finally Daoist by association. The donkey stands for wandering in the Way but as a living thing subjected to the natural laws of existence and nonexistence; it is both physical and metaphysical, abstract and material. Chance, Bresson's great theme, remains the key to grasping the experience that Bresson seeks to impart through the donkey. Chance is ultimately the chance of transcendence that seems even to transcend itself in its focus on the animal rather than the human.

Notes

1. This question was posed by Bernardo Bertolucci in an article included in the anthology *Robert Bresson*, ed. James Quandt (Toronto: Toronto International Film Festival Group, 1998): see p. 529.
2. Paul Schrader, *Transcendental Style in Film: Ozu, Bresson, Dreyer* (New York: Da Capo Press, 1972), p. 86.
3. Ibid., p. 9.
4. Ibid., p. 3.
5. The latest book on Bresson, Colin Burnett's *The Invention of Robert Bresson: The Auteur and His Market* (Bloomington and Indianapolis: Indiana University Press, 2017) locates Bresson within the locus of French culture and its avant-garde. The book, semi-biographical, draws general conclusions about Bresson's highly idiosyncratic style by linking it to the early Parisian avant-garde and Bresson's associations with members of that group. It also claims that Bresson was responding to demands of the market as far as he could. Bresson's first four films do not strike me as very avant-garde, and those works beginning from *Pickpocket* onward are quite singular (some more so than others), certainly unconventional but in an individualistic and deliberately mysterious way that they all seem undefinable. However, Burnett's main thesis is that Bresson's achievements in the avant-garde was in the field of adaptation, which might ring true for most of Bresson's films, but not so *Au hasard Balthazar*. This film seems to fall outside of Bresson's established pattern of adapting stories from other sources (despite claims by some people that it is drawn from Dostoevsky's *The Idiot*, the film's connection with that novel is far too tenuous for it to be called an adaptation), and even further apart from anything that had been done up to that time in French cinema and since.
6. Schrader, *Transcendental Style*, p. 87.
7. Ibid., p. 59.
8. Mair, *Wandering on the Way*, p. 26.
9. Schrader, *Transcendental Style*, p. 85.
10. From the *Daodejing*. The translation is Wing-tsit Chan's. See Chan, *The Way of Lao Tzu (Tao-te ching)*, p. 97.

11 Roland Barthes, *Empire of Signs*, trans. Richard Howard (New York: Hill and Wang, 1982), p. 83.
12 See Steven Shaviro, "A Note on Bresson," in *The Cinematic Body* (Minneapolis and London: University of Minnesota Press, 1993), pp. 241–52. Shaviro exclaims Bresson to be "a powerfully materialist filmmaker" (p. 252), due, basically, to the director's "intense and precise attention to the body" (p. 243). Brian Price shows a similar obsession with materiality and declares Bresson to be a radical political instead of a transcendental filmmaker in his book *Neither God nor Master: Robert Bresson and Radical Politics* (Minneapolis and London: University of Minnesota Press, 2011). See also Shmuel Ben-gad, "To See the World Profoundly: The Films of Robert Bresson," *Cross-Currents*, 47 (2), 1997, pp. 230–35. "Bresson's art," Ben-gad writes, "is rooted in the material" because it "lucidly recognizes the importance of [the] 'surface' of reality"; "it does not offer meanings, explanations, or answers but rather lucidity, reality, and profound mystery" (p. 235).
13 The best study of the donkey's point of view is Nick Browne, "Narrative Point of View: The Rhetoric of Au Hasard, Balthazar," *Film Quarterly*, 31 (1), 1977, pp. 19–31. See also Rochelle Rives, "'The Voice of an Animal': Robert Bresson and Narrative Form," *symplokē*, 24 (1–2), 2016, pp. 345–70.
14 Sharon Cameron, "Animal Sentience: Robert Bresson's *Au hasard Balthazar*," *Representations*, 114 (1), 2011, p. 3.
15 See the supplements in the Criterion Collection disc of the film, published in 2005, which includes a filmed TV interview, broadcast in 1966, where Bresson also explains that "Au Hasard Balthazar" was the motto of the Lords of Baux, a feudal house in southern France, who claimed to be descendants of Balthazar.
16 Mair, *Wandering on the Way*, p. 47.
17 See Susan Sontag, "Spiritual Style in the Films of Robert Bresson," in *A Susan Sontag Reader* (New York: Farrar, Strauss, and Giroux, 1982), pp. 121–36.
18 Eske Møllgaard, *An Introduction to Daoist Thought: Action, Language, and Ethics in Zhuangzi* (London and New York: Routledge, 2007), pp. 7–8.
19 See William Johnson, "Balthazar," *Film Quarterly*, 20 (3), 1967, p. 27.
20 Schrader, *Transcendental Style*, p. 82.
21 Gilles Deleuze, *Cinema 2, The Time-Image*, trans. Hugh Tomlinson and Robert Galeta (Minneapolis: University of Minnesota Press, 1989), p. 178 and 242.
22 See Mair, *Wandering on the Way*, p. 59.
23 There is a collection of essays on this episode in the *Zhuang Zi*, edited by R. T. Ames and T. Nakajima, *Zhuangzi and the Happy Fish* (Honolulu: University of Hawai'i Press, 2015).

24 Tony Pipolo, *Robert Bresson: A Passion for Film* (New York: Oxford University Press, 2010), p. 183.
25 See Ibid., pp. 184–85.
26 See Jean Sémolué, "Humour et ironie dans les films de Robert Bresson," *Positif*, February 2004, pp. 48–52.
27 Ibid., p. 51.
28 Ibid., p. 52.
29 Schrader, *Transcendental Style*, p. 86.
30 See the TV interview shown on Swiss television TSR in 1983, part of the supplements in the *L'Argent* DVD published by New Yorker Video, 2005. Though Bresson's remarks refer to *L'Argent*, it could just as well refer to *Au hasard Balthazar*.
31 Kent Jones, *L'Argent* (London: British Film Institute, 1999), pp. 18–19.
32 Charles Barr, "Au Hasard, Balthazar," in I. Cameron (ed.), *The Films of Robert Bresson* (London: Studio Vista, 1969), p. 114.
33 Robert Bresson, *Notes on the Cinematographer*, trans. Jonathan Griffin (Copenhagen: Green Integer, 1997), p. 32.
34 Ibid., p. 25.
35 Ibid., p. 56.
36 Mair, *Wandering on the Way*, p. 32.
37 Ibid., p. 33.
38 Ibid., p. 34.
39 See Stanley Cavell, "Automatism," in *The World Viewed: Reflections on the Ontology of Film* (Cambridge, MA, and London: Harvard University Press, 1979), pp. 101–08.
40 Pipolo, *Robert Bresson, A Passion for Film*, p. 5.
41 See Jean Collet, "Le drôle de chemin de Bresson à Balthazar," *Études*, July–August, 1966, p. 90.
42 Ibid., p. 91.
43 Ibid., p. 87.
44 Ibid.
45 See D. T. Suzuki, *Selected Works of D. T. Suzuki, Volume 1: Zen* (Oakland: University of California Press, 2015), p. 169.
46 Ibid.
47 See Raymond Watkins, "Robert Bresson's Modernist Canvas: The Gesture toward Painting in *Au hasard Balthazar*," *Cinema Journal*, 51 (2), 2012, particularly the section entitled "Gerard as Action Painter," pp. 4–11.

48 The *Zhuang Zi* defines what is heavenly and what is human thus: "Oxen and horses having four feet is what is meant by 'heavenly'. Putting a halter over a horse's head and piercing an ox's nose is what is meant by 'human.'" See Mair, *Wandering on the Way*, p. 159.
49 Browne, "Narrative Point of View," p. 26.
50 Mair, *Wandering on the Way*, p. 58.
51 Ibid., p. 53.
52 Matthew McDonald argues that Schubert's music expresses a theme of death. See McDonald, "Death and the Donkey: Schubert at Random in *Au Hasard, Balthazar*," *The Musical Quarterly*, 90 (3/4), 2007, pp. 446–68.
53 Both anecdotes are recounted in Jack W. Chen, "On Hearing the Donkey's Bray: Friendship, Ritual, and Social Convention in Medieval China," *Chinese Literature: Essays, Articles, Reviews*, 33, 2011, pp. 1–13.
54 From a Daoist perspective, mourning is relative to the idea of death as emancipation, part of the transformation of things. Accordingly, sadness is a burden that one should shed. Schubert's music that accompanies Balthazar's death scene, inspiring sadness in the viewer, is not the kind of mourning that Daoism would favor, and Bresson himself did not seek to instill sadness in the viewer. According to James Quandt, Bresson "later regretted the rather programmatic and sentimental use of the Schubert in *Balthazar*." See Quandt, "Au Hasard Balthazar and Le Diable Probablement (The Devil Probably)," in M. L. Bandy and A. Monda (eds.), *The Hidden God: Film and Faith* (New York: Museum of Modern Art, 2003), p. 18.
55 In his abstruse manner, Bresson may be disclosing his indebtedness to Dostoevsky, one of his major literary influences. Here he is alluding to *The Idiot* in which a line about falling in love with the donkey occurring in mythology is spoken by Mrs. Epanchin in response to Prince Myshkin's recounting of being aroused one evening by the bray of a donkey during his stay in Basel, Switzerland. The prince is telling stories of his Swiss sojourn to Mrs. Epanchin and her three daughters. The stories include the episode of his time as a teacher in a village where he befriends Marie, a peasant girl. These stories of the donkey and of Marie (both not related at all in the novel) are the film's most direct links with the novel. (Otherwise, it has no connection with the main plot.) Obviously, Bresson was inspired by these minor episodes to concoct an entirely original story of his own, so the film can hardly be said to be an adaptation of the novel, as I have noted before (see Endnote 5).
56 See Pipolo, *Robert Bresson, A Passion for Film*, p. 185.

57 The découpage of this scene is reminiscent of that in *The Lady from Shanghai* where Elsa seemingly "causes" an accident. See my discussion in the Welles chapter in this volume.
58 Mair, *Wandering on the Way*, p. 314.
59 For an English translation, see Karl S. Y. Kao (ed.), *Classical Chinese Tales of the Supernatural and the Fantastic: Selections from the Third to the Tenth Century* (Bloomington: Indiana University Press, 1985), pp. 357–62.
60 From Bresson's remark, "'le cinema est movement intérieur.'" See the article, "'Plongée dans le cinémacinema,'" in *Séquences*, 16, January 16, 1959, p. 24.
61 See Cameron, "Animal Sentience," p. 21.

6

Dreyer's *Vampyr*: Wandering in the West

Transcendentalism and the vampire film

Carl Theodor Dreyer is the quintessential European director. Born in Denmark, he started his professional life as a journalist and became a filmmaker in his own country, making his debut as director with *The President* in 1919. He went on to direct films in Norway, Sweden, Germany, and France for some of the most prestigious production companies in the continent. Most critics and scholars venerate Dreyer not only for his spiritual and psychological content but also for his cultural knowledge and resonances with historical and contemporary European art and letters. Well steeped in European culture and history with a special affinity for religion, Dreyer's content is inseparable from its European roots. I think it would be safe to say that this is generally acknowledged. Boerge Trolle made the point that Dreyer's important works "appear solidly based on a common foundation, rooted psychologically in the late Middle Ages and in the Calvinism and Anglo-Saxon Puritanism that were the extreme religious consequences of this epoch."[1]

Dreyer, indeed, seems to me to exhibit a typically European sense of aesthetics and love of form but as a non-European, I find many of his films, particularly the late works, which includes *Ordet* (1955) and *Gertrud* (1964), culturally and emotionally distant. To my mind, Dreyer has made only three films that I would consider transcendent of "European" sensibilities, even though they are clearly European on the face of it: *Michael* (1924), *The Passion of Joan of Arc* (1928), and *Vampyr* (1932). These films are outliers in terms of subject matter, styles, and obsessions, somehow not fitting completely into Dreyer's main body of work along the line of Boerge Trolle's description above (although *Passion* would be the best fit with the late masterpieces). *Michael* is a gay film; *Passion*, a morbidly intense psychological study of a young woman driven into martyrdom; and *Vampyr*, a modern vampire film. While these simple descriptions may not do the films justice, they do point to Dreyer being more diversified, less aloof, and somewhat unpredictable than his image of a serious, solemn, and austere filmmaker would suggest.

Of the three films, *Vampyr* stands out even more than the others do, quite literally for its out-of-this-world quality. It is the focus of this chapter. I consider it the weirdest and most numinous of those of Dreyer's works tending toward matters of the spiritual, frequently dealing with witchcraft and the occult (or suspicions of these). As well, for our purposes, it successfully integrates Eastern motifs and concepts into its structure or narrative, and I will lay out the Eastern ingredients below. Dreyer utilizes these materials in such a way that they spring organically out of Western culture and folklore (the folklore, specifically, of the vampire, dating back to the nineteenth century, the era of Dreyer's source materials of his film, Sheridan Le Fanu's *In a Glass Darkly*, published in 1872). This achievement of natural integration and evocation of the Eastern may have resulted in the film's unique solitariness among his works and departure from them.

In his book *Transcendental Style in Film*, Schrader praises the singularity of *Vampyr* as demonstrating Dreyer's versatility and "his intuitive cinematic genius for varying types of film style."[2] However, Schrader does not really address the film in his analysis of Dreyer, perhaps because he considers it less transcendental stylistically speaking than it is just "transcendent" in a spiritually infusive way. Schrader sees it as an expressionistic work functioning within the Kammerspiel (the chamber form) that is ultimately antipathetic to transcendental style. In truth, the film, more so than Dreyer's other films, has generated misgivings or misperceptions about its style, bathed in an engulfing vagueness, a work of indeterminacy and penumbra (one major sequence gives full vent to a stylization of animated shadows of dancing phantoms on a wall, like an Eastern shadow play—more on that later). Kirk Bond asserts that it "might well be the most confusing of all films" and that in his opinion it is not really "a major film."[3] Robin Wood states that it is "a peculiarly difficult film to write about,"[4] while David Bordwell confirms its difficultness in his usual exercise of formalist analysis, linking this to the absence of cause in a narrative structure built "so as to make the following of story events exceptionally difficult."[5] The confusion and the difficultness of *Vampyr* is the entry point into our Eastern interpretation of it.

Alison Peirse consigns the film to the ranks of the European avant-garde. She claims that Dreyer had absorbed influences from such movements as surrealism and Bauhaus as well as the works of Swedish director Victor Sjöström (*The Phantom Carriage*): "Its myriad of avant-garde and artistic European influences create a spectacularly dense and haunting text, with staring characters, oblique narratives and a languid, almost somnambulant tone."[6] I argue that this apparently European tone and substance of *Vampyr* is something of an illusion, a trompe l'oeil. While I do not deny its reception of European avant-garde influences (there are other influences too, including German Expressionism and Murnau, as well as literary influences such as Kafka[7]), the idea of its European provenance simply reflects the overwhelming dominance of Western or European commentators on the discourse of the film, and the cinema in general. The film's ambiguity and vagueness is a sign of its transcendentalism. The ambiguity overrides the Western essentialism that decorates the film's structure or the behavior of the characters. While it appears Western, these features are illusory. Dreyer's concern, after all, is with the inner, a notion inevitably entangled with the transcendental.

Schrader includes Dreyer among transcendental filmmakers but states that his works show ambiguity about the nature of the Transcendent circling around the questions of "whether art should express the Transcendent or the person (fictional character or film-maker) who experiences the Transcendent; whether the Transcendent is an outer reality or an inner reality."[8] Such ambiguity is a sign of the dualism in Dreyer which Schrader claims Dreyer never forsook—and it is possible to see this dualism in East-West terms, a stance I will employ as a recurrent rhetorical device as I move along. Thus, the outer European world of Dreyer's film is his Western essence and that of the Eastern stems from the inner transcendentalism inherent in the film— the East intimating the transcendent while the West is a transparent outer manifestation of the physical experience (what we are watching). Of course, it seems indisputable to me that Dreyer was more involved with the inner. He himself had declared that the artist "must describe inner, not outer life" and that he should "abstract himself from reality in order to strengthen the spiritual content of his work": abstraction is a chance "of replacing objective reality with his own subjective interpretation."[9]

The literature on Dreyer, all written by Western scholars and critics, generally indicates that Dreyer is more Western than Eastern in terms of both content and form. Even Schrader essentially affirms this placement by questioning whether Dreyer is a transcendental filmmaker, doubting that his style is transcendental because of "his failure to achieve stasis."[10] But style is not a reliable indicator of the transcendental. Other major studies of Dreyer and of *Vampyr* have dealt primarily with formal and structural issues in Dreyer's art, raising questions of some incongruity that suggest at the very least Dreyer's unorthodox approach toward formalism. Bordwell's study of the film in his book on Dreyer is the classic of this kind. We have already noted that his take on *Vampyr* is the absent cause, or the film's failure to account formally for causality. This indicates to me that there is something about Dreyer's art that is fundamentally transcendental, which by definition cannot be formally discerned. Prior to Bordwell, Mark Nash's essay, "*Vampyr* and the Fantastic," published in 1976, is a linguistic-structural analysis of Dreyer's work, its general thesis being that Dreyer contravenes codes of film and genre through his own peculiar use of "pronoun functions" and their displacement by "'false' pronouns" in formulating point of view in the context of the fantastic.[11] This creates a disruption of "subject continuity," "eyeline mismatching," "uncertain spatio-temporal relationships"—all terms used by Nash to denote Dreyer's structuring of the fantastic.[12] Nash bases his linguistic case analysis of Dreyer's style on Tzevetan Todorov's studies of the literary fantastic (primarily his book *The Fantastic: A Structural Approach to a Literary Genre*, published in an English translation in 1975). Simply put, the obsessions with the formal and the stylistic, and the structural, revolve around the idea of hesitation in the context of the fantastic, as articulated by Todorov. Hesitation points to the protagonist of the tale as he ponders on whether what is happening to him is real and "whether what surrounds him is indeed reality" or a dream, an illusion.[13] The protagonist mirrors our hesitation in approaching the world depicted on screen. Thus, the question of style and structure accounts for hesitation in that the real world naturally and prejudicially structures the protagonist's and the viewer's responses to the fantastic. Noël Carroll believes there is no hesitation at all in *Vampyr*, which is closer to our Eastern understanding of the film.

Carroll does not offer any Eastern interpretation of non-hesitation. Rather, he sees the film as an example of generic horror, which "requires a positive commitment to the supernatural of the sort that we find in *Vampyr*."[14]

> There is really no possibility at virtually any point in the film that the events portrayed are anything but supernatural. And surely by the end of the film, there are no grounds for the least suspicion that there could be a naturalistic account of what has happened.[15]

In the world of its fiction, "it becomes rational to accept the existence of supernatural phenomena."[16] Although Carroll does not really address how Dreyer constructs his fiction to make it rational for us to accept the existence of supernatural phenomena, we may take it as given that Dreyer transports us into the abstract world of our inner imagination, which is the state of the transcendental (or the metaphysical, if one prefers). What is not given is how this inner world is associated with the Eastern and how we may interpret it as Eastern. This will now be our task.

Dreyer's approach to his Gothic material is to explore the spiritual and the psychological, and it is in this exploration that the film attains transcendental heights. *Vampyr* is part of a modern movement in analytical psychology that has absorbed much Eastern concepts into its system, through the pioneering efforts of Carl Jung. "I know that our unconscious is full of Eastern symbolism," Jung had declared.[17] *Vampyr* is an expressionistic work of this unconscious, and it is particularly rich with Eastern symbolism, as I will demonstrate. Robin Wood had stated that *Vampyr* was not amenable to psychoanalytical interpretation "because there is no defined character to be psychoanalyzed."[18] "Rather, one must relate it to Jung's theory of the 'collective unconscious', and see its dream imagery as rooted in universal archetypes and race memory."[19] How Dreyer's film relates to the collective unconscious and its archetypes is often an exercise in Western perspective as the universal standard. No one, as far as I know, has yet accounted for all its rife Eastern symbolism.

My Eastern interpretation of *Vampyr* will show Dreyer creating his own archetype—in fact, a Daoist archetype, as I will show—right out of his collective unconsciousness. This archetype moves between the yin and the yang in his search of inner processes. In his wanderings, he demonstrates the will of the unconscious corresponding with the Eastern knowledge of the supernatural that had influenced Jung into developing his theories. A text one should mention here is *The Secret of the Golden Flower*, a translation by the German sinologist Richard Wilhelm of the Daoist classic *Taiyi jinhua zongzhi*, purportedly authored by the ninth-century Tang Dynasty Daoist immortal Lü Dongbin (the contents transmitted orally until it came into print in the later part of the seventeenth century). The translation, along with a commentary by Jung, was published in 1929. An English translation followed in 1931. Dreyer's production of *Vampyr* occurred around the time of the publications of the translations of *The Secret of the Golden Flower*, which conceivably may have exerted some influence on Dreyer's singular conception and conceptualization of the film.

The book contains the esoteric secrets of *neidan* (the inner elixir) developed by Master Lü Dongbin toward achieving Daoist immortality. In the section "Text and Explanation," Wilhelm explains the origins of the book. He remarked that the practice of these "secret traditions" was to achieve a state of "soul lifting [one] above all the misery of life," and the methods used were "magical writing, prayer, sacrifice, etc., and, in addition to these, widely prevalent mediumistic *séances*, by means of which direct connection with the gods and the dead is sought."[20] The book teaches that "by the union of the spiritual principle in men to the correlated psychogenetic forces one can prepare for the possibility of life after death, not only as a shadow-being doomed to decay, but as a conscious spirit."[21] "The spiritual principle, now fitted for an independent continuation of life in the spirit-body, created out of its own forces, deserts the earthly body, which remains behind as a drying shell like that abandoned by a cicada."[22] Harold Coward informs us that Jung "strongly nourished" his "sense of the existence of psychic parallelism or correlations between inner and outer events" from reading *The Secret of the Golden Flower* (and other translations of Chinese classics by Wilhelm, including the *Yijing*, and the Buddhist-Daoist manual of inner alchemy, *Huimingjing*).[23] For his psychiatric practice, Jung coined the term "synchronicity" to refer to the parallelism and correlations of the inner and the outer, and particularly, "in the shifting of the center of gravity of the personality from the ego to the Self."[24] The self is the "virtual point between the conscious and the unconscious."[25] If we follow this principle, the hero of *Vampyr* is doing nothing more than synchronizing the inner and the outer, to shift his center of gravity from his ego to the self. The hero's experience is a direct experience of this interrelationship. The film is transcendental, then, in the East-West sense. It transcends the Western ego to reach into the Eastern self.

The wanderer Gray

We may take transcendence simply to mean transcending one's identity and consciousness, transcending all borders to reach the world beyond. From our perspective, this is the transcendence of the Dao conjoining East and West in a field of existence and, equally, nonexistence. We can begin with the hero, Allan Gray (the name given in the German version released under the Criterion Collection published in 2008 that is the basis for this study of the film). He is ostensibly a Western gentleman who wanders into a genial French countryside carrying fishing equipment, looking like "a dapper young man on holiday," as Anna Powell describes him.[26] Powell writes further that "we discover nothing else about him," that he is "a stranger forced to investigate and experience the mystery of the place," and that he is "our perpetually aghast surrogate rather than a character in his own right."[27] On closer inspection, following Powell's extended descriptions of the protagonist ("fixed facial intensity," "sleek-backed hair," "liquid protuberant eyes"[28]), we can recognize Gray as a gaunt, dark-complexioned Eastern-looking gentleman rather than a typical Westerner.

The fact that he is a traveler and "a stranger" carrying fishing equipment marks him out as a carefree Daoist wanderer. He could well have come out of the first chapter in the *Zhuang Zi*, entitled "Carefree Wandering" ("Xiaoyao you"). Wandering is a central concept in Daoist thought, which holds that one wanders infinitely in limitlessness beyond limitlessness itself (*wuji zhi wai fu wuji*). The fishing equipment reminds one of the chapter's allusion to fish (as well as to birds, about which more later) and to the master Zhuang Zi's fondness for fish and fishing. The fish imagery in Daoism is associated with "the unrestrained human spirit"; the "jovial movement of fish in the water" inspiring early Daoists "to project an ideal of spiritual freedom" in such imagery.[29] Although we do not see any fish, the fishing net and the rods carried by Gray easily convey an impression of fish and of Gray as an angler-wanderer. (Only cynics or detractors would think that the net is for catching vampires.)

In addition, Gray is seen "coming up from the river bank," the angle of the camera suggesting "that he is virtually arising from the water,"[30] which boosts the substance of Daoist imagery in the opening scene based on the symbolism of fishing in Daoist mythology.

From all these signs, we can discern a Daoist and an Eastern identity in Gray and that he has wandered into the West. The Western location also radiates another dimension of Daoist and Eastern thought, which is that the West connotes death. Among Chinese, going to the West means that someone has passed on. In the film's opening scenes, we can clearly deduce that Gray has wandered into the West that is the realm of the dead. This is immediately signified by the man with the scythe, described as "the reaper" in the original script.[31] The reaper makes his presence felt throughout the opening scenes as he goes to the river to call for the ferryman, an allusion to Charon, the ferryman at the River Styx—these traditional symbolisms in European mythology doubly underline the West as the realm of the dead (or, to take a more local perspective, it is Hades, "the Greek realm of the undead," to quote Nash[32]). The Eastern viewpoint of the West as the realm of the dead/undead is a stunning transposal of the Western perception of the East as the source of immortality, or "demi-immortality," as J. Jeffery Franklin has characterized it, a state of existence exemplified by characters in nineteenth-century fiction who have acquired immortality "through a combination of occult spirituality and alchemy."[33] Perhaps the most iconic figure of this type is Dracula. In Bram Stoker's novel, Jonathan Harker describes his journey into Dracula's domain as being like "entering the East."[34] Of even greater interest, from our Eastern perspective, is that these Oriental "demi-immortals" tend to live in the West. This could well be the motivation for Allan Gray's wandering to the West (Figure 6.1).

The concept of the West as the nether region sets the stage for our "passive acceptance" of the supernatural, as Carroll says, "no matter how incredible or unintelligible the story as a whole appears."[35] In this region, the state of consciousness no longer pertains. The film exerts an immersive, penetrative quality from its very first image and sequence. This immersion makes us completely synchronous with being in the land of the dead where death is the generalized state and life is localized, the living being that of the living dead or of a dream in which one sees one's own corpse carried out for burial. The West, then, as the nether region is effectively the primary reason why the

Figure 6.1 Gray, the fisherman and vampire hunter.
Vampyr, Producer: Carl Dreyer.

film is as it is, vague and indeterminate, perpetually enveloped in a grey haze that dissolves any distinction of day and night.[36] S. S. Prawer calls *Vampyr* a "grey-and-white film."[37] Grey is the leitmotiv—and literally, the light motif—of the film, symbolizing the theme of vagueness ("blackness suggesting whiteness," as Prawer puts it[38]). White, on the other hand, represents death. (White, traditionally, is the color of death in the Chinese mind.) Gray's name is a "'speaking' name," as Prawer lets on.[39] His name reflects not just the lighting motif of the film but also his own state of existence. What is Gray doing in this realm of the dead? The answer, logically, is that he himself is dead but his name denotes that he may not be dead. Rather, he is in the grey area between the living and the dead.

The introductory intertitle before the fade-in tells us that Gray had "immersed himself in the study of devil worship and vampires" and, "preoccupied with superstitions of centuries past, he became a dreamer for whom the line between the real and the supernatural became blurred." His "aimless wanderings" had led him to a secluded inn in the village of Courtempierre. That the village has a name suggests that Gray is anchored in a real-world setting where people are alive, not a metaphorical world of the dead. The intriguing issue of Dreyer's West is that we are not just in the realm of the dead but also of the living. This may well be the main cultural differentiation in the interpretation of the West from Dreyer's own Western viewpoint. The Eastern viewpoint is of the West as the resting place of the dead. If we merge Dreyer's viewpoint with the Eastern viewpoint, we may come to a certain interchange and crossing where things are not what they are. We can see the film as a cross-cultural East-West film in the metaphysical geographical sense of the term, making use of Eastern motifs hardly analyzed in the literature but necessitating, in any case, a cultural interpretation. Some accounts of the film refer to certain intersections reached by the filmmaker and his protagonist. David Bordwell, for instance, refers to "overriding differences of inner and outer, subject and object,"[40] resulting in Gray ultimately possessing "the mystery of death."[41] Jonathan Rosenbaum speaks of Dreyer applying a paradigm to the film of "a 'closed' world of fate and an 'open' world of freedom perpetually counterposed, each unmasking the other to create an exalted realm where the natural and the supernatural, the physical and metaphysical can breathe the same enlightened air."[42] These words by Rosenbaum and Bordwell summing up the abstractions of Dreyer's vision in *Vampyr* point to some kind of transcendental tradition that would seem to lie outside of Western liberal progressivism or even the Christian church. The abstractions suggest possibilities for other readings of Dreyer's world, and it is our contention that Dreyer evokes Daoist concepts and motifs to underline his themes of life and death. The individual's intercessions with the mysteries of life and death are an experience into the metaphysical realm of the Dao. These Eastern underpinnings of the tale seem more apparent because of the film's vague structuring of Christian symbolism as a rather inept response toward vampirism, as I will shortly explain. Instead, we see conspicuous elements and currents of Eastern concepts rising out of the Western framework of the vampire tale.

To boost our claim that the film denotes Eastern dogmas, it is necessary to briefly address the issue of Christian religiosity in *Vampyr* that seems to derive from the general opinion of Dreyer as a religious director. Since Dreyer's last film before *Vampyr* was the intensely religious *The Passion of Joan of Arc*, there may be a tendency to see *Vampyr* as a kind of companion piece to *Passion* for its apparent religiosity inherent in the subject matter. According to Mark Nash, Dreyer's films carry on a religious discourse. The films rehearse "the playing out of politico-religious doctrinal struggles within the context of a patriarchal order marked by Judaeo-Christian monotheism"—and Nash cites "witchcraft" as the problem addressed in *Vampyr*, along with films like *Day of Wrath*, *The Passion of Joan of Arc*, and *The Parson's Widow*.[43] Clearly, in this company, *Vampyr* is the weakest as a Christian reaction against witchcraft. Dreyer's vampire tale is mostly just "transcendental" in a highly abstract way, and perhaps, Dreyer may have in mind some kind of Christian transcendence for his characters. There is really no Christian doctrinal "struggle" to speak of in the film. It is not particularly strong as a Christian testament against vampirism (conversely, the film may be seen as a crisis of Christian faith due to the onset of the nihilism of death). Rather, it seems primarily obsessed with the occult. Dreyer shows shadows of crucifixes and other ornaments as the symbols of Christian faith which seem hardly effective against the vampires; contrast this with the film *Dracula* (1931) where Dracula is immediately repulsed by Christian symbols.[44] Part of the reason for this is that *Vampyr* "is very much a transitional film," as Nash points out, being one of the first horror films of its type at the dawn of the sound era: its transitional character "is marked in the fantastic text as incoherent, uncertain."[45]

The incoherence and uncertainty may be interpreted as Dreyer's noncommitment to a Christian reaction to the fantastic (as if such a reaction were expected of Dreyer). This rhymes with Schrader's view of Dreyer as a noncommitted transcendental filmmaker—and "Dreyer's lack of commitment begets a similar lack of commitment in the spectator."[46] However, our Eastern analysis challenges this notion. Dreyer is a transcendental filmmaker for his commitment to other forms of spirituality and psychology, and the spectator is immersed in this transcendence, fascinated, as Dreyer is, with the vampires who represent an alternative kind of religion. At the same time, Dreyer is much captivated by the occult since he shows equally the shadows of ghosts and other symbols of the supernatural arts. All this fascination is filtered through Allan Gray, not just Dreyer's alter ego but also the viewer's. Gray shows mainly curiosity rather than repulsion toward what he sees. Gray is almost a secular hero or else he is like an academic whose research interest is vampires. He enters their milieu as though he was doing fieldwork on this species, using himself to experiment with their world of death and other goings-on. Gray might also be doing some kind of spiritual exercise in contemplating death so that he can meet it without fear, which is what Daoism proposes. Gray obviously belongs to an Eastern faith, and it does not seem very important to denote what faith it is. Rather, what is important is his faith in the supernatural. Gray, then, manifests the Eastern wisdom implicit in the text and the story of *Vampyr*. He is the Eastern specter of Dreyer, or Dreyer's Eastern Other, and his knowledge and wisdom is the outgrowth of Dreyer's understanding of the basic theme of the metaphysical crossing between the external world and the inner spirit.

The tale of the vampire is essentially a pretext for a contemplation about mysticism and death, and it is through an Eastern interpretation that we may better grasp the inner matter at hand. The film then offers an inner experience of the Way, or the Dao, through its hero's dealings with mystical forces and his wanderings in the realm of the dead. We might say that Gray's quest is to achieve the immortality of being a Daoist transcendent (*shenxian*) in which state one acquires "the power to reinvent one's own physical, spiritual, and social self."[47] The vampire has, after all, achieved such a state, even if it is only one of "demi-immortality," which I would interpret as a more perverted kind of immortality, and this is the risk that Gray takes in his quest. The hero's wandering into the Western sphere of the dead and the supernatural is thus to search for the transcendence of true immortality. The wandering is of a free will; we might even say that Gray is not consciously aware of the wandering. Described as "aimless" in the words of the intertitle, this kind of wandering already suggests a kind of transcendence—the transcendence of consciousness in psychological terms but in Eastern terms a transcendence of reality and the transposition of the mind into the unknown of the Dao. Gray is in a state of wandering in the realm between his consciousness and the unconscious which we may call the Dao manifested in the film as "a world in which nothing, or everything is real," as Tom Milne describes the world of *Vampyr*.[48]

The state of wandering locates the opening scenes into an Eastern aesthetic perspective, since it is these scenes that convey the first sense of disorientation in the viewer, the starting point of the vagueness of the film. Gray is a wanderer but he is not as conscious that he has wandered into the region of the dead or that he himself may be dead, which is why the film inserts "portents of death," as Bordwell puts it, into his arrival at the inn.[49] We see shots of the reaper, unmatched with the shots of Gray wandering into the inn. There is no continuity in space between them as Dreyer crosscuts between the two figures although Gray, at one point, looks out of the window from his room apparently to check if what he is seeing is the reaper. Gray needs some time to orient himself into this Western region, and the word "orient" is suggestive here since Gray, finding himself in the West, experiences a veritable feeling of *dépaysement* in settings which seem entirely real, as Philippe Parrain tells us (the contrary effect of real settings adding to the disorientation).[50] He has literally to find the sun for direction (he does, for example, at the end of the film). He finds the sun after undergoing his adventures and, crucially, his experience with death. In his death experience, his body detaches from his self. He sees his own corpse lying in a coffin, and the vampire and her entourage seemingly paying their last respects over his corpse. They carry the coffin away for burial.

Gray's wandering being a total immersion into the vampire's domain compels a certain attitude of the hero's passive acceptance of all that he sees and experiences. He shows a sense not so much of fear, although this is palpable, but of wonder. We can intuit these two emotions as a disconnect between East and West—fear as a Western reaction and wonder as an Eastern one—only for Dreyer to emphasize more on the Eastern sensibility of wonder. Gray is motivated to wander by the very fear that he feels. Fear is engendered through his meeting of the man with the disfigured face inside the inn, and the old man who enters his room as he sleeps to leave behind a book that must be opened in case of his death. The old man later turns out to be the father of the two girls, Leone and Gisele, victims of the vampire. He is indeed shot to death. The fear that Gray intuitively feels may be a standard Western reaction to unusual phenomena. Dreyer certainly accounts for this fear by cutting to scenes of Gray's reactions. For example, he quickly walks away from the disfigured man and goes into his room, shuts the door, and disappears off screen but returns immediately to the frame to turn the key, locking the door. (The camera's track to the keyhole capturing Gray's hand in close-up reemphasizes the fear.) These scenes and those which take place soon after, of the father entering Gray's room and Gray reacting in fear, are never matched in the same space. They are "discrete entities," as Bordwell says, "different action strands" which are crosscut by Dreyer, therefore avoiding "the smooth sequentiality of traditional scenic construction, creating time gaps during which the absent cause can operate."[51]

Bordwell maintains there is an absence of cause in the events that we see. There appears to be no causal relationship between scenes. Based on this principle, the fear that is palpable in Gray does not seem related to what he sees. Is Gray really afraid? Subsequent shots show Gray moving on doggedly to discover more of the same phenomena that he encounters inside the inn. He is nothing if not persistent. Fear, obviously, does not deter him. Fear seems to have no purpose other than being a generic factor in horror movies that Dreyer evokes in an obligatory and perfunctory manner (this is rather similar to Dreyer's use of Christian symbols, which are more like clichés that he dispatches with cursorily). In *Vampyr*, it seems to drive Gray toward more wandering, and Gray shows that he is an intrepid wanderer. In this sense, there is a continuity in the mise-en-scène, a continuity provided by Gray's incessant movements between "discrete entities" and "time gaps" that are spatial and temporal boundaries which Gray seeks to exceed. This is a function of his wanderings. The wandering motif therefore determines the lack of continuity or the absence of cause that we perceive. The wandering itself is of course not the kind of wandering that we take for granted. It is a wandering compelled by one's unconsciousness, a matter of pure chance.

There is a Daoist conviction behind Gray's wanderings that he will come across death, the portents of which are prominent in the opening scenes. Death is one of the themes in the *Zhuang Zi* and many of its stories teach us not to fear death, since we naturally fear it. One should welcome death as the path to the world beyond, and it may even be something to be experienced, just as we see Gray experiencing it, as if it was a trial run for the real thing. Gray is certainly mindful of the sage's instruction of attaining transcendence: "Slough off your bodily form, dim your intelligence, forget all relationships and things, join in the great commonality of boundlessness."[52] There is reason to think that Gray has attained the status of an adept—if nothing else, he is a superior wanderer—since he has now unrestricted "access to the supernatural," in Noël Carroll's words.[53] Gray has wandered beyond the bounds of humanity, where the distinction between life and death has broken down.

Eastern symbolisms

Gray's wandering inspires wonder, something signified by his protuberant eyes, which perhaps also display fear at the same time. This is, basically, the mood or temperament, if not the theme, of the first third of the film, covering the sequences of Gray's arrival at the inn, the events inside the inn, and Gray's trek to the dilapidated lair of the vampire, lured by shadows. The sense of wonder cancels out the fear. Fear is then the transitory state to a greater sentiment, and I invoke Indian rasa theory to refer to the sentiment of *adbhuta* (wonder or awe), which I feel captures the prevailing mood of the sequence in the dilapidated building housing the vampire's lair. In the *Natyasastra*, the ancient Indian manual of dramaturgy, it is stated that the *adbhuta* sentiment (translated as the marvelous sentiment) arises out of the heroic sentiment (*vira*),[54] and this is how we can see the *adbhuta* expressed in the sequence. It follows from the heroic wandering of Allan Gray. The heroic sentiment is characterized by "energy, perseverance, optimism, absence of surprise, and presence of mind" among "[such other] special conditions [of the spirit],"[55] an apt description of Gray's character. The *adbhuta* sentiment is achieved through determining factors such as "sight of heavenly beings or events" and "entrance into a superior mansion, temple, audience hall (*sabha*)," among other determinants, and is represented by "wide opening of eyes, looking with fixed gaze, horripilation."[56] Such descriptions apply roughly to the sequence in spirit, not in letter.

Drawn by shadows, Gray wanders into the lair where he sees more shadows, first, inside the house, the shadow of a one-legged soldier who climbs up a ladder. Gray is then led upstairs, and on his way, he sees the vampire, an old woman, whom he instinctively avoids (the vampire is introduced by the shadow of an overhanging bat). Upstairs, he sees the soldier seated on a bench and his shadow joins him, appearing in the same pose as if unified with its body. All this inspires an initial sense of wonder rather than fear, and the wonder deepens when more shadows appear, putting on an exuberant shadow dance. This part of the sequence is truly awe-inspiring, marvelous in the fantastic sense as well as in the cinematic sense. The shadow dance reminds one of Indonesian *wayang kulit* and Chinese *piying*. The Malay-speaking community throughout Southeast Asia has adopted the word *wayang* to mean cinema. The Chinese word for cinema, *dianying*, meaning literally "electric shadows," is adopted from the *piying* (shadow puppetry). Shadows are thus culturally resonant in Eastern Asian communities as pre-cinematic cultural forms that have "cinematic qualities."[57]

Apart from this cinematic impression, the shadows express the theme of the detachment of consciousness from one's body, this very theme constituting perhaps the key to the appeal of *The Secret of the Golden Flower*. Thus, the shadows relay an Eastern sense of *hun* (spirit-soul, or the animus) in the depictions of the shadow dance (the shadows are the spirits of dead criminals who have joined the vampire in her lair) and of the soldier's shadow acting as if separated from the body, eventually to rejoin it. The *hun* then rejoins the *po* (the anima or the body-soul). All these are concepts from Daoism glimpsed in *The Secret of the Golden Flower*. In Daoism, the *hun* is a higher element than the *po*. It soars upon death while the *po*, linked to the body, sinks to the earth and decays.[58] This is borne out in the case of the soldier: we see his *hun* mounting a ladder, and at the end of the film, he falls down the staircase to death. We see the same principle of *hun-po* later applied to the remarkable sequence of Gray's vision of his own corpse.

The sequence of Gray's wandering in the vampire's lair is also notable for showing other Daoist motifs or symbols. As Gray wanders through the building, he sees, and we observe among various artifacts and objects, skeletons and skulls, wheels, an open casket with clippings of paper strewn all over, and a parrot in a cage. The skeletons and skulls may be generic horror symbols, but they take on an Eastern inflection when we consider the Daoist context of Gray's wandering. They recall the episode in the *Zhuang Zi* where the master encounters a talking skull in a dream (he had seen the skull during his travels, taken it back with him to use as a cushion to sleep on). Clearly, they presage a later scene in the chateau where Gray has a dream of a skull, and its skeletal hand reaching out with a bottle of poison. In a previous scene, Gray had given his blood to Leone and weakened by the transfusion falls into sleep and dreams that his blood has spoken to him. Later, he encounters the skull and they have a "communication." We can see this as a variation of the Zhuang Zi dream. Zhuang Zi tells the skull that he can arrange for it to be human again, with bones, flesh, tendons, and skin. The skull refuses the offer, and the moral of the dream is that human existence is not all that it is cut out to be. In Allan Gray's dream, the voice, which could also be the voice of the skull, tells him to follow it, "We shall become one soul, one blood," "death is waiting." Gray is awakened by the manservant at this point to save Leone's life as she is about to take the poison, but Gray does not absolutely refuse the skull for he does follow it, the suggestion already planted in the dream, to the point where he has his death experience, in the sequence where he sees his own corpse.

The skull was associated with the vampire in the sequence at her lair and it is therefore all too clear whose identity the skull represents when it appears to Gray. If the vampire is death itself, the skull may suffice as an objectification of her spirit-soul (*hun*), but other objects, with Daoist signatures, augment her personality and her aura of death. Perhaps the most intriguing is the wheel. As the shadows dance, the camera tracks laterally across the wall and comes to the threshold of a huge barn-like hall where the vampire appears, in long shot, by the entrance and orders "Silence!" The scene is marked with wheels, two giant ones by the entrance, one on each side of the vampire, and several suspended above, with one whirling around and another swinging slightly left and right, like a pendulum. The wheel will later (Figure 6.2) feature as a symbol at the end of the film, where it spells death for the doctor, but as the vampire already signifies death, the wheel represents a more ambiguous symbol in relation to her. Daoism speaks of a celestial potter's wheel, which signifies the cycle of life and death. Jung refers to the mandala symbolism as a magical wheel, which works "an effect" (of an "enclosing circle" or a "charmed circle") on a target (as well as on oneself).[59] The wheel, then, suggests the vampire's power to deliver the same cycle. Given that the vampire is the embodiment of evil, the destruction of this power is necessary. However, Gray appears to submit to this

Figure 6.2 Symbols associated with the vampire.
Vampyr, Producer: Carl Dreyer.

power, perhaps understanding that the wheel symbolizes the encirclement of both good and evil, and that one's fate should decide where one falls. He goes through a controlled experiment, as it were, to experience death, overseen by the vampire. He experiences death as a dream during which he sees the vampire and her associates looking down on his corpse. Taken away for burial, he wakes up just in time to help the manservant in opening the vampire's tomb and destroy her.

The wheel is a prefiguration as well as a representation of Gray's experience of life and death resulting from his contact with the vampire. The movements of the wheel also characterize Gray's movements. During the sequence inside the lair as he wanders through it, he comes up through a trapdoor, with the camera moving contrariwise from him past an open coffin, and we see paper clippings strewn all over it. The clippings look like Daoist *lingfu*, spiritual or magic figurines and talismans usually hung up over coffins to prepare the dead for its journey into the West. The camera rests for a second on a shingle with the words "Docteur du Médicin" lying on the floor beside the casket, before it swivels back to Gray who is seen continuing into the corridor, as if trying to evade the implications of what he sees. The shingle, obviously, is a reference to the vampire's chief acolyte, the doctor, who clearly practices the black magic of death. I should note here that Gray's countermovements from scenes of "death portents" (to use Bordwell's words) constitute a motif in this first third of the film. Gray instinctively moves away from the disfigured man at the inn, from the vampire at her lair and from the coffin with the paper clippings. Then, like a pendulum, he swings back toward more death portents during his adventures at the chateau, and, finally, his own death experience.

In his further wanderings, Gray passes through a room which looks like a laboratory where the doctor performs his alchemy (the skulls and skeletons are seen here: the skull, a symbol of science in the Spanish Inquisition segment of Dreyer's 1921 historical epic *Leaves from Satan's Book* now the very symbol of black magic). He then meets the doctor and after a short dialogue, during which the doctor denies there are children or dogs in the house (the voices of which Gray claims to hear), he ushers Gray out of the house. After Gray leaves, the doctor obsequiously welcomes the vampire into his office (her presence indicated by a door that opens by itself, but she appears from another room). As the vampire walks up the corridor, Dreyer crosscuts with images of skulls.

The association between the vampire and the skull images would then make it obvious as to who appears to Gray in his dream at the chateau (a skeletal hand offering him poison). In the office, the vampire passes a bottle of poison to the doctor. A parrot in the cage squawks and the doctor walks past it to deposit the bottle on a mantle.

The parrot is a reference to the fish-bird imagery in Daoism representing the spiritual freedom and Daoist ideals and mode of life expressed in the first chapter of the *Zhuang Zi*, "Carefree Wandering." There, a giant fish transforms into a giant bird, emphasizing "the metaphor of flight, or traveling beyond the limitations."[60] Caged, the parrot is obviously not free and unable to travel beyond the limitations. The caged parrot may also indicate the doctor himself who is not free because he is under the evil influence of the vampire and that he has lost his original nature and needs to regain it. Indeed, the consequence is that he regains it through death, with the help of the parrot, which at the end appears as a shadow, associated with the ghost of the chatelain. The ghost haunts the doctor and the one-legged soldier, bringing about their deaths (the soldier falls down the stairwell, while the doctor suffocates to death by flour grind by the great wheel of the mill).

Death and the wheel

Gray's progression from the vampire's lair to the chateau appears to slow down the momentum of his wandering. Once inside the chateau, the events take a turn to the more conventional horror traits of the vampire tale. They make up the middle third of the film. Leone has been bitten by the vampire and comes under her spell; the chatelain is killed, shot by the one-legged soldier; Gray plays the hero who saves Leone (who wanders out again into the woods and is again bitten by the vampire); Leone becomes more vamp-like, gazing seductively at her sister Gisele; the doctor enters and tries to give her poison, making it so that she takes it herself; Gray gives blood and has his dream where the skull appears; he is awakened by the manservant so that he can prevent Leone from taking the poison. In this segment, the book given to Gray by the chatelain takes over as a determining factor of the narrative. It makes the narrative more static in this middle section of the film, and much less interesting. Gray is compelled to read the book rather than to wander. The scenes of the pages of the book are far less wondrous than what one sees in the scenes of Gray's wandering in the previous sequence set in the vampire's lair.

The book, entitled *The Strange History of Vampires* by one Paul Bonnat, deals with the kind of clichés that now form part of the cinematic lore of vampires. It plays a counterproductive role in the narrative in as much as it provides a moral, Christian, context to the events in Courtempierre. Thus, vampires are evil and their destruction to be expected. Allan Gray, however, entertains another notion of vampires, which is to see them as a way of getting even deeper into the recesses of the supernatural or the numen. The world of nature around him in Courtempierre appears to be the Dao-site of this numen. Allan Gray may come across as an archetype of a modern Western man in search of "*knowledge* instead of *faith*, which is the essence of the Western forms of religion," to quote Jung.[61] "Modern man abhors faith and the religions based upon it. He holds them valid only so far as their knowledge-content seems to accord with his own experience of the psychic background. He wants to know—to experience for himself."[62] Gray, thus, wants to experience for himself just what the world of the vampires entails for his soul, or his spirituality. In our Eastern interpretation, he is a Daoist wanderer who has wandered into Courtempierre and partakes of its mystery, replete with its dangers, immersing himself deep inside this field of "synchronistic" phenomena.

We may observe that the book renders Gray as an inactive hero, as if making him pause to consider the moral questions of his quest for gnosis. This becomes a problem for the film because reading is stasis and Gray is a wanderer who also needs to play the role of a hero saving the lives of Leone and Gisele. Dreyer overcomes this problem by transferring the reading to the manservant, a secondary character. This makes it possible for Gray to resume his role as the hero and savior. Gray gives blood to Leone, which weakens him, and he therefore cannot read (instead he has the dream of the skull); he becomes a wanderer again in the last third of the film, where he has his dream experience of death. Bordwell considers the book to be a symbol of intelligibility, "the means of mastering the absent cause."[63] I would rather see it as a structural device that gives more weight to Gray's passivity as he engages with the chatelain's family and entourage. The book's function is to postmark the nonaction of Gray, the scenes of the book gesticulating the hero's passivity. That Gray is a passive hero is not a mere perception. It is an ideal type conforming to the Daoist concept of passive nonaction (*wuwei*). This concept characterizes Gray's entire presence in the film. Although Gray is driven along by events into actual participation which tries to turn events around (e.g., his giving blood to Leone, his stopping of Leone in the nick of time from taking the poison, and his presence at the destruction of the vampire), it is not he who drives the stake into the vampire but the manservant.

The ideal of *wuwei*, nonaction, must be cultivated among Daoists to reach a stage of spirituality. Commentators have spoken of it as a skill, in fact, "a form of action," that is distinguished by "fine-tuned responsiveness," "non-deliberative spontaneity," "effortlessness," and "enjoyment."[64] Also connected with the concept is a theme of flow. One flows along spontaneously with events and harmonizes with constant changes and tumult. Mostly, Gray leaves things to work out for themselves. He does not take the initiative to be heroic, as, for example, destroying the vampire. His participation in the narrative is more like a spontaneous flow into the events. Thus, he flows into the famous sequence of his death experience. His animus (*hun*) detaches from his anima (*po*); he lies in the coffin as a corpse as if in a sacrifice-experiment presided over by the vampire and her associates. Taken out for burial with his eyes wide-open, he sees the world outside through a glass frame, very aware (and one might say he is "enjoying" the experience), and the whole sequence thus demonstrates a remarkable confluence of subjectivity and objectivity. This is the acme of flow experience, and it allows Gray to reach the endpoint of his wandering.

Gray's "death" completes the wheel, so to speak, of his wandering and his contact with the vampire and the chatelain's family. The wheel of Gray's experience denotes his cycle of life and death and his detachment of animus and anima as a positive engagement with his unconscious. *The Secret of the Golden Flower* states that the animus loves life and the anima seeks death.

> All sensuous pleasures and impulses to anger are effects of the *anima*; it is the conscious spirit which after death is nourished on blood, but which, during life, is in direst need. Darkness returns to darkness and like things attract each other. But the pupil understands how to distil the dark *anima* so that it transforms itself into Light (*yang*).[65]

Ever the pupil, Allan Gray learns to distil the dark anima and transform itself into Light in his flow into unconscious and out of it. Gray is the Western cinema's wanderer par excellence with *wuwei* (nonaction) as his modus operandi. He flows with nature, the unconscious Dao, letting it determine the outcome of events. In his death dream, he sees Gisele imprisoned in the lair and when he comes out of the dream, rescues her. He does not even need to destroy the doctor and the one-legged soldier. The forces of the supernatural destroy them. Gray and Gisele walk in the forest to the light of day (see Figure 6.3).

The wheel at the mill grinding the flour, which suffocates the doctor, comes to a stop, and thus we reach the central discrepancy with the Daoist cycle of life and death. The wheel stops because the doctor is not an immortal since he perverts the notion of immortality by dabbling in the black art. We might see this stopping as an aesthetic decision by Dreyer to mark the ending of the film—and would it not constitute the stasis which, as Schrader tells us, is the "final test of transcendental art"?[66] However, Schrader may be right to say that there is no stasis in Dreyer, and in *Vampyr*, this is due to the motif of wandering which seems endless for the protagonist Allan Gray. Gray achieves no stasis because he is no longer in the West (i.e., the land of the dead, the

Figure 6.3 Gray and Gisele walk toward the light and out of the West.
Vampyr, Producer: Carl Dreyer.

realm of his unconscious) but in the land of the living. His destiny is to wander still into another cycle.

Notes

1. Boerge Trolle, "The World of Carl Dreyer," *Sight and Sound*, 25 (3), 1955, p. 125.
2. Schrader, *Transcendental Style in Film*, p. 118.
3. Kirk Bond, "The World of Carl Dreyer," *Film Quarterly*, 19 (1), 1965, pp. 34–35.
4. Robin Wood, "Carl Dreyer," *Film Comment*, 10 (2), 1974, p. 13.
5. David Bordwell, *The Films of Carl-Theodor Dreyer* (Berkeley and Los Angeles: University of California Press, 1981), p. 93.
6. Alison Peirse, "The Impossibility of Vision: Vampirism, Formlessness and Horror in *Vampyr*," *Studies in European Cinema*, 5 (3), 2008, p. 163.
7. See S. S. Prawer's discussion of such influences in the chapter on Dreyer's film in *Caligari's Children* (Oxford: Oxford University Press, 1980), pp. 138–63.
8. Schrader, *Transcendental Style in Film*, p. 112.
9. Carl Dreyer, "Thoughts on My Craft," *Sight and Sound*, 25 (3), 1955, pp. 128–29.
10. Schrader, *Transcendental Style in Film*, p. 120.
11. See Mark Nash, "*Vampyr* and the Fantastic," *Screen*, 17 (3), 1976, p. 38.
12. Ibid., see p. 35, 40, and 43.
13. Tzevetan Todorov, *The Fantastic: A Structural Approach to a Literary Genre*, trans. Richard Howard (New York: Cornell University, 1975), p. 24.
14. Carroll, "Notes on Dreyer's *Vampyr*," p. 109.
15. Ibid., p. 106.
16. Ibid., p. 111.
17. See Richard Wilhelm, *The Secret of the Golden Flower: A Chinese Book of Life*, trans. Cary F. Baynes (London: Kegan Paul, Trench, Trubner and Co. Ltd., 1947). Jung's words were uttered in a memorial speech dedicated to Richard Wilhelm included as an appendix in the book; see pp. 147–48.
18. Wood, "Carl Dreyer," p. 14.
19. Ibid.
20. Richard Wilhelm, "Origin and Contents of the T'ai I Chin Hua Tsung Chih," *The Secret of the Golden Flower* (London: Kegan Paul, Trench, Trubner and Co. Ltd., 1947), p. 3.
21. Ibid., p. 4.
22. Ibid.

23 Harold Coward, "Taoism and Jung: Synchronicity and the Self," *Philosophy East and West*, 46 (4), 1996, p. 480.
24 Ibid., p. 481.
25 Carl Jung, "The Detachment of the Consciousness from the Object," Commentary by C. G. Jung, in Richard Wilhelm, *The Secret of the Golden Flower: A Chinese Book of Life*, trans. Cary F. Baynes (London: Kegan Paul, Trench, Trubner and Co. Ltd., 1947), p. 123.
26 Anna Powell, *Deleuze and Horror Film* (Edinburgh: Edinburgh University Press, 2005), p. 132.
27 Ibid.
28 Ibid.
29 Zuyan Zhou, *Daoist Philosophy and Literati Writings in Late Imperial China: A Case Study of* The Story of the Stone (Hong Kong: Chinese University Press, 2013), p. 176.
30 Johannes Weber, "'Doctor! I'm Losing Blood!' 'Nonsense! Your Blood is Right Here': The Vampirism of Carl Theodor Dreyer's Film *Vampyr*," in D. Fischer-Hornung and M. Mueller (eds.), *Vampires and Zombies: Transcultural Migrations and Transnational Interpretations* (Jackson: University Press of Mississippi, 2016), p. 193.
31 See the screenplay included in the booklet *Writing Vampyr*, published by the Criterion Collection, New York, 2008. The English translation of the screenplay (by Dreyer and Christen Jul) is by Oliver Stallybrass.
32 Nash, "*Vampyr* and the Fantastic," p. 31.
33 Franklin, *Spirit Matters*, p. 165.
34 Bram Stoker, *Dracula* (Oxford and New York: Oxford University Press, 1983), p. 1.
35 Carroll, "Notes on Dreyer's *Vampyr*," p. 112.
36 David Rudkin sees this as one of the technical defects of the film. "Little trouble seems to be taken to distinguish night from day: were there budgetary or schedule constraints?" he asks. See Rudkin, *Vampyr* (London: British Film Institute, 2005), p. 26. By Dreyer's own account, he had wanted to use grey as the style throughout the film after discovering an accidental lighting effect at the start of shooting. See Prawer, *Caligari's Children*, pp. 146–47.
37 Prawer, *Caligari's Children*, p. 153.
38 Ibid., p. 145.
39 Ibid., p. 147.
40 Bordwell, *The Films of Carl-Theodor Dreyer*, p. 114.
41 Ibid., p. 115.
42 Jonathan Rosenbaum, "Vampyr: Der Traum des Allan Gray [Vampyr: The Strange Adventure of David Gray]," *Monthly Film Bulletin*, January 1976, p. 180.

43 Mark Nash, *Dreyer* (London: British Film Institute, 1977), p. 19.
44 J. Jeffery Franklin makes the claim that Dracula is "tied to the history of Christian symbology—crucifixes, the Host, holy water, sanctified ground," and consequently is "the most deeply religious figure in the novel." See Franklin, *Spirit Matters*, p. 172.
45 Nash, "*Vampyr* and the Fantastic," p. 43.
46 Schrader, *Transcendental Style in Film*, p. 125.
47 Sing-chen Lydia Chiang, "Daoist Transcendence and Tang Literati Identities in *Records of Mysterious Anomalies* by Niu Sengru (780–848)," *Chinese Literature: Essays, Articles, Reviews*, 29, 2007, p. 2.
48 Tom Milne, *The Cinema of Carl Dreyer* (New York: A. S. Barnes and Co., 1971), p. 119.
49 Bordwell, *The Films of Carl-Theodor Dreyer*, p. 97.
50 See Philippe Parrain, *Dreyer, cadres et mouvements* (Paris: Lettres Modernes, 1967), p. 13.
51 Bordwell, *The Films of Carl-Theodor Dreyer*, p. 96.
52 See Mair, *Wandering on the Way*, p. 99.
53 Carroll, "Notes on Dreyer's *Vampyr*," p. 108.
54 Bharata-Muni, *The Natyasastra*, Vol. 1, trans. Manomohan Ghosh (Calcutta: Asiatic Society of Bengal, 1951), p. 107.
55 Ibid., p. 114.
56 Ibid., p. 116.
57 See Anne Ciecko, "Theorizing Asian Cinema(s)," in Ciecko (ed.), *Contemporary Asian Cinema* (Oxford and New York: Berg, 2006), p. 13.
58 See Wilhelm, *The Secret of the Golden Flower*, pp. 14–15.
59 See Jung's "Commentary," in Wilhelm, *The Secret of the Golden Flower*, p. 100.
60 Steve Coutinho, *Zhuangzi and Early Chinese Philosophy: Vagueness, Transformation and Paradox* (Aldershot, Hampshire: Ashgate, 2004), p. 72.
61 See Carl G. Jung, *Collected Works*, Vol. 10 (Princeton, NJ: Princeton University Press, 1970), p. 84.
62 Ibid.
63 Bordwell, *The Films of Carl-Theodor Dreyer*, p. 112.
64 Nathaniel F. Barrett, "*Wuwei* and Flow: Comparative Reflections on Spirituality, Transcendence, and Skill in the *Zhuangzi*," *Philosophy East and West*, 61 (4), 2011, p. 682.
65 Wilhelm, *The Secret of the Golden Flower*, p. 81.
66 Schrader, *Transcendental Style in Film*, p. 120.

7

Eastern Principles in Sam Peckinpah's Westerns

Peckinpah and the East

This chapter focuses on the Westerns of Sam Peckinpah to examine how they have absorbed Eastern philosophical principles. The director made his mark in the genre with his second feature film, *Ride the High Country*, released in 1962, but it was not until *The Wild Bunch* (1969) that he exerted his greatest impact on the genre. There have been mutual interactions and influences between the Western and the Eastern genre that is felt to be the most compatible to the Western, namely the jidaigeki (literally, period drama) in the Japanese cinema. The most notable example of this interaction has been the various remakes of Kurosawa's *Seven Samurai* (1954) as Westerns. The first remake was *The Magnificent Seven*, directed by John Sturges, and this was itself remade in 2016 by Antoine Fuqua. *The Wild Bunch* can also be seen as an unofficial remake of Kurosawa's film.[1] I will discuss the Eastern influence of *The Wild Bunch* and Peckinpah's other Westerns in more detail below, but first, it is incumbent to note that Peckinpah displays more generic Eastern influences in a latter film in his career, namely *The Killer Elite* (1975), a non-Western. Here, the Eastern influence is far more apparent through plot elements, action styles featuring sword fighting and other martial arts, and the use of East Asian actors. The film contains a climactic action scene employing the kind of swordplay seen in Japanese *chanbara* and *yakuza* movies or in Hong Kong martial arts movies. The plot deals with a conspiracy to kill an Asian political leader under the protection of Mike Locken, a hired private agent from a quasi-secret agency, played by James Caan. This character, crippled in the leg and in the arm early in the film by his partner who has betrayed him, goes on to master Asian martial arts during the process of his recovery. Indeed, it is his mastery of

Eastern martial arts that facilitates his recovery, restoring him back to health and into the regular business of his type of employment. Such a theme recalls the 1967 Hong Kong swordplay classic *The One-Armed Swordsman*. The film seems so immersed in this whole tradition that *The Killer Elite* is probably the one most obvious example of Peckinpah's "Eastern" manner. However, there are less than obvious examples in his Westerns, and I argue that it is in the Western genre that Peckinpah shows a far deeper engagement with Eastern philosophy.

Most commentaries on Peckinpah, written by European and American critics, do not address the Eastern character of his work nor acknowledge that there is anything Eastern about it, unless it is something obvious in a work like *The Killer Elite*. The closest they would do so is to acknowledge Peckinpah's debt to Kurosawa. His Westerns would seem completely inimical to any Eastern reading, but I will try to show below that it is in the Westerns more so than in something like *The Killer Elite*, one of his lesser works, that we can best appreciate the Eastern nature of Peckinpah. Peckinpah's own personal affinity for the East may well have been a crucial factor in the creative ways he has absorbed Eastern concepts into his Westerns, although this aspect of his creative life has not been well documented nor brought to light by writers. Peckinpah had a connection with the East early in his life. He had been to China as a marine from 1945 to 1946. David Weddle claims in his biography of the director that Peckinpah "had begun to dabble in Zen and had taken up with a Chinese girl from a good family" toward the end of his service in China.[2] According to Weddle, the girl was a young communist but did not convert Peckinpah to her Marxist views, he being "too deeply inculcated by the rugged individualist creed of the American West."[3] Nevertheless, we can assume that the relationship was a formative one for Peckinpah and that this affair as well as his whole experience in China instilled other Eastern beliefs and ideas in him.

Straw dogs

From his experience in China, Peckinpah very likely maintained a lifelong interest in Eastern philosophy. The title of *Straw Dogs*, possibly his most controversial film, released in 1972, is stark evidence of this interest. It comes from the *Daodejing*, chapter 5:

> Heaven and Earth are not benevolent
> All things are like straw dogs
> The sage is not benevolent
> All humans are like straw dogs
>
> (My translation)

The concept of "straw dogs" (*chugou*) is probably difficult to comprehend for most people and has become quite controversial for its implications which are interpreted as being immoral, amoral, and antihuman.[4] The controversy really has to do with the Daoist interpretation of *ren*, a Confucian principle that is usually translated as benevolence but can also mean humanism, rather than with the conception of the straw dogs. The Daoists assert a non-anthropocentric understanding of *ren*, relating it to their idea of nature. In the *Zhuang Zi*, it is stated that "humaneness and righteousness are not attributes of humanity."[5] Therefore, the sage is not benevolent if we think of this as disavowing an anthropomorphic view of the natural and physical world. The straw dogs, as described in the *Zhuang Zi*, are sacrificial offerings

> packed in bamboo containers wrapped with patterned embroideries. The impersonator of the dead fasts before taking them out. After they have been displayed, passers-by trample their heads and spines, grasscutters gather them for lighting cooking fires. That's all they are good for.[6]

Hans-Georg Moeller considers the straw dogs to be Daoism's anti-humanist reaction against Confucian rituals, particularly its "emotional obsession with death":

> Like heaven and earth, the Daoist sage is not especially "humane" and not particularly concerned with human beings. For the Daoist sage, human beings are not essentially different from dogs—not even from *straw dogs*! Human beings vanish from life just as straw dogs from a ritual performance. Just as straw dogs turn into fuel for the fireplace, human beings will not turn into heavenly ancestors but, rather (for instance), something as nonhuman as the wood for a crossbow.

Moeller goes on to say that all this does not mean that the sages "dislike or even despise humankind; they are simply not more or less attached to this species than to any other."[7] The British philosopher John Gray invokes the straw dogs as the title of his book calling for a Daoist non-anthropocentric approach to the world.[8] In underlying the concept, Gray declares that "humans can never be other than straw dogs": "If humans disturb the balance of the Earth they will be trampled on and tossed aside."[9] All humans are an inherent part of natural phenomena just like "straw" and "dogs" (not the sacrificial objects offered to Heaven and Earth). "In this manner, the statement becomes a metaphor for the self-regulatory order of nature, which provides for all without Heaven and Earth doing anyone favors," as Rudolf Wagner tells us.[10]

Peckinpah has prominently evoked the straw dogs concept in his film *Straw Dogs*, which is not a Western but is "the most 'Western' of all of Peckinpah's films not set in the Old West in that it features a violent, Western-style 'shoot-out' at the end," as Michael Bliss has put it.[11] I will not discuss it here at length as a Western, but of all of Peckinpah's films, it enjoys pride of place in this chapter for its obvious reference to Eastern philosophy via the quote of the Daoist text. What is the significance of the quote in the context of the film and of Peckinpah's Westerns? The film *Straw Dogs* is set in contemporary England in a rural village where an American mathematician David Sumner (played by Dustin Hoffman) lives with his young English wife Amy (Susan George). Peckinpah builds up an incremental sense of negativity and antagonism between all the characters, not least between David and Amy. In the bloody climax, David defends his home against a group of rowdy and venal male inhabitants in the village who had earlier raped his wife, unknown to him. These characters are emblematic of a community stuck in "a pre-Oedipal stage" of development "characterized by unrestrained phallic power and by aggressive behavior, which is not repressed and internalized but directed outward to the world," as Rory Palmieri describes it.[12] That Peckinpah specifically invokes the straw dogs principle is seemingly a rationalization of the film's primitive violence that is highly graphic and shocking. Because of Peckinpah's tendency of showing such violence, the principle illustrates the generic violence of Peckinpah's films taken altogether, attesting to "the extreme savagery of the world and its characters" which then compel the "primacy of passion over reason," in the words of Jim Kitses.[13] However, it would be wrong to assume that the concept of the straw dogs is fully explicable as a trope for human violence in a savage world and therefore a rationalization of violence.

In his analysis of the film, Michael Bliss zooms in on David as the sly, catalytical force of savagery. David is an intellectual and academic who might readily remind one of the "sage" of the original Daoist text cited. Bliss links the text to the psychology of David, who becomes a rather reprehensible figure in Bliss's eyes, acting in a self-serving way by confronting the rowdies "in a ritual offered toward a presumably violent god who must somehow be placated."[14] Bliss's unsympathetic reading of David confers on him the perversion of the sage (often misread as inhumane) who "engineers the attack on the farm so that he might dispassionately sacrifice the gang in order to shore up his insecure masculinity."[15] In fact, we might see David as himself a part of the action driven by some inevitable force of animal reaction in which humans are sacrificial victims. David's reaction implicates him in a chain of violence which has nothing to do with the non-benevolence of the sage. In fact, human affairs function to distort the idea of non-benevolence. The whole straw dogs principle is therefore used ironically by Peckinpah who shows us "a supposedly cultured man acting on the level of an animal" and therein gives us "a chilling view of human nature."[16] While this view is more pertinent to the film *Straw Dogs*, Peckinpah has used this Daoist principle in other films, primarily in the Western *Ballad of Cable Hogue* (1970), which was the film he made before *Straw Dogs*, and in *The Wild Bunch*, the film made before *Ballad*. He would also use it as a leitmotif in later films, as I will demonstrate. Thus, it is one of the key Eastern ideas determining the "Eastern" in Peckinpah. How it relates to Peckinpah's films may constitute another whole chapter in itself, but I can only address its rudimentary aspects here.

Because of Peckinpah's penchant for screen violence, one may (mis)understand it as a commentary on the human propensity for savagery and violence in the world of Peckinpah's cinema. *Straw Dogs* features violence more primeval and virulent than anything Peckinpah had done up to that point in his career or would do thereafter.[17] However, Peckinpah's films are not solely about violence but they raise other concerns of human affairs. The straw dogs principle itself implies a certain cosmology of the Dao, if we return to its original quotation from Lao Zi's *Daodejing*, which would be more to the point of Peckinpah's Eastern temperament. The concept applies to *Ballad of Cable Hogue*, which is one of the gentlest of Peckinpah's films, in fact, a comic Western with song interludes, containing very little violence. The film serves as a broader frame to understand Peckinpah's worldview of the West—and the principle fits squarely into this personal worldview. One could call the film a very Daoist Western which deals with nature and the human response to its environment. As such, the concept of "straw dogs" applies more to the immutability of nature and nature's detachment toward all things. Nature is a non-anthropomorphic entity, and the sage is like nature, an impartial and objective entity that cannot treat human beings subjectively with human feelings. Accordingly, the humans in Peckinpah's films are entities that must find their way in the harsh natural environment of the world, not separate, privileged entities but part of the geophysical environment. "Species cannot control their fates. Species do not exist."[18] If only we can communicate and empathize with nature and be as one with it, we might be sage-like.

The theme of *Ballad of Cable Hogue* is precisely Cable Hogue's communication and commiseration with nature, with the desert and the animals, established right in the opening scene in which Hogue walks right up to a lizard and they mutually hiss at each other. "Sorry, old timer, but you're only part poison, and I'm hungry for meat," says Cable to the lizard (see Figure 7.1). Hogue is a straw dog who fits into the void of nature and becomes a part of it, submitting to its wholeness which thus determines his fate. On the other hand, we can also say that he is a straw dog in the sacrificial sense because he has human feelings whose socio-secular concerns (with finding gold and then finding water) make

Figure 7.1 Cable Hogue and the lizard.
The Ballad of Cable Hogue, Producer: Sam Peckinpah.

him vulnerable or all too "human." He also seeks revenge on his partners who betrayed him. The film shows Cable Hogue (played by Jason Robards) able to survive in the wilderness almost out of a divine courtesy from God, and the film has been interpreted in a Christian sense by some writers, based on the fact that Peckinpah had a "biblical upbringing" and that he was prone to cite from the Bible in his films.[19] However, part of the comic mood of the film is that Peckinpah injects a strong dose of irony right at the core of his apparently Christian moral. This is the purpose for the existence of the character of the Reverend Joshua Duncan Sloane (played by the British actor David Warner). The final sermon preached over Cable Hogue's grave by the Reverend Joshua describes Hogue's affinity for and his communion with nature. It is a fine expression of Daoist philosophy.

> When Cable Hogue died, there wasn't an animal in the desert he didn't know. There wasn't a star in the firmament he hadn't named, there wasn't a man he was afraid of. Now the sand he fought and loved has covered him at last. Now he has gone into the whole torrent of the years, of the souls that pass and never stop.
> Hogue lived and died here in the desert, and I am sure Hell will never be too hot for him. He never went to church. He didn't need to. The whole desert was his cathedral. Hogue loved the desert, loved it deeper than he could ever say. He built his empire but was man enough to give it up for love, when the time came.

The sermon paints a portrait of Cable Hogue as the very representation of an iconoclastic, independent Daoist spirit. However, while it is notable as a eulogy of Cable Hogue, it is also an ironic testament of Christian faith since it comes out of the mouth of the supposedly Christian pastor, portrayed in the film as a very flawed and hypocritical Christian. The sermon, of course, underlines the irony of Peckinpah's vision of nature and man's relationship with it, not so much with God. The character of the dubious reverend embodies the irony. One might say that he is just the right man to deliver such a sermon. We can see then that the Eastern meaning of Peckinpah is subsumed under a layer of Western, Christian, veneer, and that a Daoist affirmation of nature and one's communion with it must be dressed up in Christian clothing. The performance of David Warner's Joshua Duncan Sloane portrays this "dressing up" in Christian garb very aptly, and his character (possibly Peckinpah's most endearing) is a symbol that stands for looking at something beyond the obvious. Most would see him as a fake preacher but to my mind, he is a freethinking subversive straying from the path of Christianity.[20] He could even be a sage in the Daoist sense, one who observes the workings and manners of "straw dogs" in the Western setting. He is himself a straw dog in his own human weaknesses and natural tendency toward hypocrisy. In this way, however, he is self-reflexive, his hypocrisy being essentially a self-conscious mannerism, which is why the character is so engaging. We could well say that Joshua Duncan Sloane is Peckinpah himself, but critics generally do not seem to acknowledge this gentle and ironic side of his personality. Rather, they see in him the "savage" persona that seems to define his films (e.g., Kitses and Stephen Prince have both utilized this very word in titling their respective discourses on Peckinpah: "Sam Peckinpah: The Savage Eye," in Kitses's book *Horizons West*, and Prince's book is called *Savage Cinema*).

In Peckinpah's more violent Westerns, his characters fit into the natural world as they are infantile and violent. It is a theme in *The Wild Bunch*, stated in the opening scene where the children torture scorpions with ants. This motif of children torturing animals is repeated in *Straw Dogs*, where children oppress a dog in the cemetery, somewhat rubbing in the allusion to the straw dogs principle (which, then, unfortunately, allows for misinterpretations of the principle as a justification of violence). If we follow the standpoint of the principle in the Daoist context, there is no moral rectitude in Peckinpah's characters. They may achieve some kind of nobility in their violence, a theme best exemplified by the sacrifices of the Bunch in the last bloody climax of *The Wild Bunch*. The theme also applies to the hero of the post-Western *Bring Me the Head of Alfredo Garcia* (1975), about which more below. The concept of "straw dogs" postulates that human violence is an objective factor in nature because there is no benevolent force to determine otherwise. *The Wild Bunch* illustrates this point in the scene of the children and the ants and scorpions in the credit titles sequence. Though the children may look innocent and beatific, they do not represent a benevolent force.[21] Only certain codes devised by human beings can control the urges of violence. However, human codes of behavior may not be enough. In Daoist thought, the Dao (the Way) that is constructed is not true and all within it is therefore untrue. A communion and flow with nature is the way forward. Thence, Peckinpah poses a dilemma of human behavior. How do we become true to our nature? It is of course no accident that his characters, who are not intellectuals or scholars, are primal forces of nature but yet seek some form of transcendence. Nature is thus that entity postulated by the concept of the straw dogs—the nature of Heaven and Earth that treats all things like straw dogs.

Peckinpah's Westerns almost without exception pose the question of how we become true to our nature, a Daoist premise with which Peckinpah explores character and violence. All of them deal with incalculable violence and the lack of harmony between peoples. His characters demonstrate the Daoist idea that people delight in following difficult paths and stray from the main road (the Way). They do not cultivate harmony in themselves and therefore cannot find harmony in the world. The brave and the bold will perish, for they tempt fate, and fate conquers all things. Peckinpah's Westerns show his characters tempting fate, and they achieve a certain kind of epiphany through violence. How does one transcend violence given that the Daoist philosophy emphasizes oneness and harmony with nature? Peckinpah does not give any ready answers and his violence in the Western form is perhaps too dependent on the American context—on its national framework of history, myth, and convention—to be really understood in a general sense. Robert Warshow famously stated that the chief appeal of the Western was that it "offers a serious orientation to the problem of violence such as can be found almost nowhere else in our culture."[22] The "Western" nature of Peckinpah portrays, and some might say even celebrates, violence as if in substantiation of Warshow's words and his Westerns remain even today exemplary of this maxim. In *Ballad of Cable Hogue*, the hero has certainly done his share of violence, but as noted, the film is actually one of Peckinpah's least violent. To this extent we might say that it is the one film in Peckinpah's oeuvre in which he earnestly attempts to answer the question of how to transcend violence. It is a contemplation of violence and nature as well as of one's relation to the land. The hero is not entirely free of secular, or even, political concerns, to be sure—and there is a political layer to the film, a show of patriotism, that seems to suggest the necessity for some kingly authority, a rule of law and order, as a counterweight against violence. This is like a cliché of the genre, which seems surprising in a Peckinpah film. I am referring to the scene of Cable raising the American flag over

Cable Springs. In this instance, it seems that apart from a Daoist vision of a natural affinity with the land, there is in essence what we might call a rustic Confucianist sense of order, a thirst for stability, and love of country that rises above Cable's animal spirits, as it were. Thus, Peckinpah's resort to a rare expression in his cinema of overt patriotism marries his Daoist vision with his concerns for society and the state, as if to say that it is the state that can solve violence.

The sociopolitical meaning of the flag-raising scene is rather allegorical, as John M. Gourlie elucidates:

> To feel how remarkable the scene is, we must remember that its innocent and reverent patriotism was filmed in 1970 when the Vietnam War raged on, and the flag was often the symbolic brunt of the war protestors' anger and frustration. The film offers a moment of pure peace and simple love of country, utterly unattainable in 1970, and redemptive at any time, putting us back in touch with a fundamental value as it does.[23]

Peckinpah, of course, cannot be detached from his American context. Stephen Prince tells us that Peckinpah "was an engaged observer and commentator on the dynamic and memorable history of the period through which he lived and during which he directed his best films."[24] His films undoubtedly gain in measure when we see them as chapters of American history and allegories of contemporary politics, but this is somewhat beyond the scope of this chapter.

Having come this far in assessing Peckinpah's Eastern quality, we should now ask the following question: Is there a contradiction between the Western side of Peckinpah and his Eastern side? In our methodology of explaining the Eastern side of Peckinpah, we do not compare differences of national or cultural formations. Rather, we think of the genericity that links the Eastern and the Western. In doing so, we may see how the Eastern Peckinpah is a natural outgrowth of the Western Peckinpah, particularly in considering action principles of bravery, loyalty, giving and keeping one's word, and the conflict between individualism and the social. These Western values (i.e., values of the genre if not of the whole Western society) are also values and preoccupations of Confucian societies. From the Eastern perspective, the Western's preoccupations mirror Eastern-Confucian values. These values may be naturalized into the Western context such that they are unrecognizable in

Eastern form, and thus, in this way, East and West are illusions in the ultimate reality that is the Dao.

Word and action

In this section, we will discuss another dimension of the Eastern side of Peckinpah, where he shows greater affinity for Confucian principles as opposed to Daoist ones, although there is a great deal of overlapping between the two philosophies as Peckinpah has evoked them. While Peckinpah has undoubtedly taken an integrative, eclectic approach in his Eastern influences, it basically reflects the same state of eclecticism in Chinese culture itself. A film like *The Wild Bunch* shows this eclecticism at its most interesting insofar as a Confucianist code of ethics drives its main theme. At the same time, the general sense of the film seems enmeshed in an amoral, antihuman environment of the Daoist straw dogs principle. The film poses a stark complementarity between these two schools of thought, each accounting for some aspects of the Bunch's behavior and actions. The contradictions that arise are natural to the sense of eclecticism in which Peckinpah meshes the philosophical contrarieties together into his volatile and often unpredictable Western setting.

The characters of *The Wild Bunch* are outlaws and bandits, classic bad men rather than honorable or respectable men of the West. However, the members of the Bunch act by a code to stick to each other and, more importantly, to act by one's word (Pike Bishop makes passionate speeches about these two concepts), and most importantly, to die for it. This is rather like the Confucian credo of the chivalrous *xia* warriors of Chinese historiography in which one's word is one's bond, action must follow one's word, and one is not afraid of death in carrying out the word.[25] This action code operates in Eastern epics that are equivalent of the Western, such as Kurosawa's *Seven Samurai*, of which *The Wild Bunch* is a reworking.[26] In Kurosawa's film, there is something Zen-like about his samurai heroes that signify the subliminal deep-rootedness of the code. The Zen-concentration of the samurai is to seek a realization of their code in the form of expressive and physical action, thus to "achieve unity of knowledge and action and realize the effect of practice and vision advancing together simultaneously."²⁷ Peckinpah ingests this action code and its Zen principle, making it a prominent theme in *The Wild Bunch*, although it was also a theme in his earlier Westerns *Ride the High Country* and *Major Dundee* (1965).

A classic expression of this code is the scene where the Bunch finally decide to confront Mapache (Emilio Fernández) in a last attempt to rescue their Mexican partner Angel (Jaime Sanchez). Pike Bishop, the leader of the Bunch (William Holden), says, "Let's go!" and Lyle Gorch (Warren Oates) rejoins, "Why not!" The communication is straightforward and tacit at the same time, conveying a Zen-like meeting of minds among warriors who then spring into action spontaneously without too much soul searching. Peckinpah gives further play of the signification of this "action" by showing the Bunch walking deliberately into Mapache's lair, knowing that they might not come out alive. This extraordinary sequence manifests the action principle of the old Chinese proverb *ming zhi shan you hu, pian xiang hushan xing* ("knowing full well that the tiger is in the mountain, we walk straight into it"), which is well known to any Chinese schoolboy and is quoted in the classic action-adventure novel *The Water Margin*. The scene is also a memorable illustration of the Confucian precept of *yan bi xin, xing bi guo*—to stand by one's word and to realize an outcome with action. This Confucian principle (from *Analects*, 13:20) effectively powers the whole narrative of *The Wild Bunch*. Pike Bishop's command "Let's go!" tersely demonstrates the notion of the word (*yan*). Lyle Gorch's response "Why not!" demonstrates that the word *must* inspire trust (*bi xin*). The subsequent walk of the Bunch is a literal demonstration of *xing bi guo*: the word *xing*, meaning action, can also mean walk, and thus the walk scene conveys literally a walking toward action, illustrating the Bunch's resoluteness to achieve an outcome (Figure 7.2).

Peckinpah had inaugurated this *xing bi guo* principle in *Ride the High Country*. The climactic scene showing the two aging gunfighters Gil Westrum (Randolph Scott) and Steve Judd (Joel McCrea) walking to meet the Hammonds in a frontal shoot-off expresses the same kind of action code that motivates the Wild Bunch into their iconic walk. There is no need for soul searching; it is practically a gratuitous act, with little or no forethought over the matter: "Partner, what do you think?" "Let's meet them head-on, half-way, just like always." "My sentiments exactly." The walk transforms Gil Westrum and Steve Judd into typical *ronin* or

Figure 7.2 The Bunch walking into the tiger's lair.
The Wild Bunch, Producer: Phil Feldman.

a *youxia* (wandering *xia*) who act by their own code of action with no fear of death. The walk is a transparent manifestation of the code. For Westrum, this final act redeems his character for he had earlier deceived Judd who had then cast him out as friend and partner. By joining Judd in this final walk, he reverts back into his noble and selfless nature. Action forms character or it reaffirms it, and loss of life is a part of such action, a true test of one's character.

In *The Wild Bunch*, the word "word" is evoked in several scenes, but most dramatically during a heated exchange between Pike Bishop and Dutch Engstrom (Ernest Borgnine) regarding Deke Thornton's "word" given to the railroad. "It's his word!" says Bishop. "That ain't what counts! It's who you give it to!" Engstrom remonstrates. Peckinpah renders the concept of word (*yan*) in a poignant and complex fashion. It is a motif of the relationship between Pike Bishop and Deke Thornton (Robert Ryan) and it appears to guide the way in which both men interact across the space that divides them (Pike among the Bunch and Thornton among the bounty hunters who are hunting the Bunch to kill them). Those scenes where they chance to eye each other at crucial moments of violence denote this (Thornton taking aim at Bishop with his rifle but hesitating to shoot in the opening massacre scene, and later in the train robbery scene where Thornton is on the bridge where he stops briefly during the chase to take aim at Bishop). Clearly, there is an abstract exchange of what passed between the two men in these scenes. It is an abstract treatment of *yan bi xin* (that one should stand by one's word). What is striking is that Peckinpah manages to convey both the conceptual resonance of *yan bi xin* (what passes between Bishop and Thornton) and the concrete action of *xing bi guo* (the Bunch's walk to the final shootout with Mapache's army).

On another level, *The Wild Bunch* works as a counterweight against Confucianist concerns of word and action in its depictions of the Bunch as an amoral group making deals with whoever can ensure their survival and quench their thirst for gold. Thus, they make an alliance with Mapache, a bloodthirsty general who has his own notions of honor or even "morality." (Mapache is not without virtues of courage and loyalty.) Mapache represents in his own way the Daoist vision of an amoral center in the universe with which humans engage, often at their peril. In the American Western context, he represents a reaction against the liberal-humanistic expressions of the Bunch. Dutch Engstrom is the representative of this "liberal" strand of thought. "We don't hang nobody," he says, drawing a line between the Bunch and Mapache. However, the Bunch is a mass of contradictions. From our Eastern perspective, I would see the contradictions as amounting to a conflict between their Confucianist predilections and the Daoist pull of amorality. Confucian morality needs a consensus of pure will from the Bunch. Daoist amorality saps at this will since human instincts of selfishness and self-preservation take over. Michael Bliss has pinpointed the contradictions of the Bunch and their adherence to "sticking together." "Despite being outlaws who believe that they live by a code, the Bunch continually subvert it," Bliss writes, pointing out that "Pike's code of 'stick[ing] together' is compromised by the Bunch's avarice, self-interest, and (on the part of the Gorches) racism."[28] Bliss analyzes these contradictions within the context of American capitalism and its social order. The violence of the Bunch is seen as "a dramatization of the history of the United States itself, whose past and present are riddled with treaties ignored, promises broken, agreements unmet."[29] To Bliss, *The Wild Bunch* "never resolves the issue of human beings' fundamental nature" but the film nevertheless

> functions as a critique of the society that made the Bunch what they are: a group of men unable to penetrate their socialized responses to the ultimate truth—that they are tragically representative of the predominantly anomic society in which they live.[30]

Bliss overstates his case somewhat. As a film, *The Wild Bunch* can only be true to its portrayal of the Bunch. It examines the Bunch's contradictions and their ultimate will to act. We might say that the Bunch resolves their fundamental nature by their deaths through acting (*xing bi guo*: the word *guo* indicates a result, a resolution). However, this is not to say they have resolved the contradictions of their world, or the contradictions of their nature, in accordance with the straw dogs principle. From a philosophical point of view, it is impossible that the Bunch would remain consistent in their attitudes. Humans "have a gift for self-deception, and thrive in ignorance of their natures," as John Gray tells us.[31] "Arising from our animal natures, ethics needs no ground; but it runs aground in the conflicts of our needs."[32] Accordingly, the Bunch cannot resolve the contradictions of their nature, if we see such contradictions in terms of the conflict between Daoist anarcho-amoralism and Confucian principles, though by their resolute action at the climax, they appear to have thrown their weight to Confucianist principles.[33] In effect, the Bunch embodies the film's contradictions which stem from the impulses within the set of Eastern philosophies it invokes (Confucianism and Daoism). As an American artist, Peckinpah naturally offers his own responses and retorts to the Confucianist inklings in the action codes inevitably transforming them into American codes embedded in an American context. For me, this is ultimately the fascination of a film like *The Wild Bunch*.

Peckinpah's Chan poetic cases

By the time Peckinpah came to make *Pat Garrett and Billy the Kid* (1973), his incorporation of Eastern philosophy into his Westerns had become even more abstract, and in this section, I will discuss two representative examples of such abstraction, a scene from *Pat Garrett and Billy the Kid* and another from *Bring Me the Head of Alfredo Garcia*. Both examples testify to Peckinpah's Eastern content through moments of illumination that are akin to Zen poetry. Since I will be referring more to Chinese Zen poetry, I will use the Chinese word for Zen, which is Chan, in order to distinguish Peckinpah's affinity for Chinese philosophical principles as opposed to his Japanese influence that stems directly from Kurosawa's samurai films. Chan is another dimension of the Eastern principles that can be discerned in Peckinpah's cinema and what may be peculiar about this particular component is that he has applied it more along the style of a mannerism, or an idiosyncrasy. Earlier, I demonstrated Peckinpah's incorporation of the straw dogs principle which functions more or less universally in his films. Now, with the examples that I am referring to, we come to the stage of Peckinpah's Eastern "manner" in which he develops cinematic examples of Chan poetics. We will begin with *Pat Garrett*, where the cinematic Chan touches are sublime, whereas in *Alfredo Garcia*, the moment is more traumatic. Both are, in any case, moral. Although *Pat Garrett* functions as a continuation of *The Wild Bunch*'s preoccupation with both sticking to Confucianist principles and surrendering to Daoist impulses, the film is much too fragmentary or episodic to be analyzed as a systematic and comprehensive working out of this particular thesis. However, the film resonates more with the Daoist straw dogs principle. Both the eponymous characters are typical straw dog archetypes in Peckinpah's cinema. This central relationship unfolds on the dynamics of the sage's injunction of non-benevolence, and the Daoist aspect of the film is therefore more prominent. The episodic quality of the narrative is more in the nature of a Daoist tract made up of parables and moral tales, many of which can be freely interpreted through the vantage of Chan poems, such as the poignant episodes of Billy's shootout with Alamosa Bill, and Garrett's enlistment of Sheriff Baker to help capture Black Harris. For lack of space here, I will focus on another episode that I consider exceptional, being a far more abstract instance of Chan affect.

My case study is the scene of Pat Garrett (James Coburn) resting by the river, taking time off from his long and arduous mission of tracking down Billy the Kid and to kill him. As he rests, he hears shots fired and so alerted, he sees an old man on a raft shooting at a bottle thrown into the water by a child. Garrett, in response, draws his pistol to fire at the same bottle, just short of hitting it. Now, the old man fires at Garrett, just close enough to force him to stand up, get his rifle, and aim it at the old man as he leans on a tree. They point their rifles at each other. The children on the raft take cover. Garrett and the old man eye each other but the raft drifts out of range, and Garrett finally holds his rifle aloft, signaling the end of the "challenge" between the two men. There is indeed that sense of a challenge, as between two knights who meet each other by coincidence and must fight it out as an impulse of their nature. A seemingly playful manner is implicit but there is more than a hint of tragic circumstances. Though a short scene, it reaches near-metaphysical proportions such that even a figurative meaning is elusive if one were to search for it. The best way to see it is as a cinematic equivalent of a *gong'an* (*koan* in Japanese) which means "public case." These are stories or sayings of past masters that function as pedagogic materials for studying and mastering the principles of Chan Buddhism. In the examples of Peckinpah's sequences (in *Pat Garrett* and *Alfredo Garcia*, which I will come to shortly), Peckinpah was effectively creating "public cases" that are inserted into his filmic narratives as moral incidents, allowing for some commentary on the characters and their moral stature. These incidents serve as moral guidance for the viewer to understand the nature of the characters and their circumstances. In referring to Peckinpah's examples, I am not arguing that Peckinpah had a religious purpose nor am I suggesting that he was a Buddhist, although the definition of a Chan poem is that it is a type of sermon or preaching that casts some Buddhist reflection or illumination onto the reader. Rather, I am holding them up as cinematic "public cases" in which Peckinpah infuses Eastern content through the utilization of Chan poetry.

There is a long tradition of Chan poetry in both China and Japan, and I will attempt to put Peckinpah's cinematic Chan imagery within this tradition. I will also try to define the imagery by matching them with quotes from Chan poems. The central images from the scene quoted above from *Pat Garrett and Billy the Kid* are the drifting raft and the faux shootout between Garrett and the old man. An almost religious sense of epiphany is felt in this short segment, which, after all, is the effect of a Chan poem (or Peckinpah's Chan-like poetic imagery). In that sudden awakening, Garrett reflects on his inner struggle and moral quandary that has resulted from his betrayal of Billy the Kid. His faux shootout with the old man seems like a mutual conversation, but for Garrett, it is a deep reflection on his self, recalling the Chan poetry of Shi De, a Tang Dynasty monk:

> I laugh at myself, old man, with no strength left
> inclined to piney peaks, in love with lonely paths
> oh well, I've wandered down the years to now
> free in the flow; and floated home the same
> > a drifting boat[34]

The scene occurs in a seemingly empty space of the narrative, with no real connection to the rest of the film, but, in fact, it can be connected to a previous scene in which the motif of drifting down a river in a boat is stated. Garrett has called on his friend Sheriff Baker (Slim Pickens) to help him arrest Black Harris (L. Q. Jones). At first, Baker is reluctant to help. He is more interested in building a boat, which, when finished, he is going to use "to drift down this damn territory." As Paul Seydor has written, the boat evokes "an almost childishly pathetic dream of flight and escape that will soon be dashed when Baker is shot and staggers off and sits beside the river, dying as his wife looks on, helpless and weeping."[35] Seydor points out that the boat anticipates the raft episode, but he does not really explain the associations between the two scenes. The associations can only be made clear if we see the river scene as a Chan *gong'an*, with supernatural inklings of death and destiny. Garrett is haunted by the expectation of death as a final deliverance of justice on those who betray others and sell out their souls. Such an interpretation is probably only possible if we acknowledge that there is a spiritual dimension to the scene in the religious style of Chan poetry. Otherwise, one appreciates it for its realistic manifestation of the Western lifestyle: "The raft and the family it carries suggesting something of the oppressive squalor that was much of frontier life."[36]

Since the film, in its special restored version (available on DVD), is framed as a flashback narrative in between Garrett's own death, the whole film is practically a dirge on Garrett's life. The narrative looks back on his relationship with Billy the Kid, his relentless pursuit of Billy, and finally his shooting of Billy. All the supporting characters appear as a chorus commenting on Garrett's life as he carries out his mission to kill Billy. (Peckinpah himself appears in a brief scene at the end telling Garrett to "get it over with.") The raft episode assumes an emblematic significance reminding the viewer of Garrett's gamble with death and his date with destiny. Garrett has a presentiment of his own death. Earlier, he had looked on at Sheriff Baker as he lies by the river dying. Now Baker returns, as it were, drifting down the river. The old man on the raft is also the personification of Yama, the King of Hell and the God of Death in Eastern lore, coming to get Pat Garrett.

Peckinpah's obsession with death and character is reprised in his next film, the contemporary Mexican Western *Bring Me the Head of Alfredo*

Garcia (1974). The film is a variation of Kurosawa's *Yojimbo* with its cynical character, Bennie (Warren Oates), at odds with all sides, trying to achieve a catharsis "that sets the corrupting influence of lucre against the purifications of ritual violence," to quote Stephen Prince.[37] The film is also a variation of *Pat Garrett and Billy the Kid* with Bennie in the Pat Garrett role, hunting for the head of Alfredo Garcia and bringing it to the business interests who have initiated the hunt. The catalytic point of the film is when Bennie has located Alfredo's grave and has opened the coffin to cut off the head. Just as he is about to do so, two Mexican hit men who have been following Bennie knock him out cold. As he regains consciousness, Bennie finds himself buried in the grave and discovers that his girlfriend Elita (Isela Vega) is dead, interred alongside him. Following this traumatic discovery, Bennie encounters three members of Alfredo's family. They tell him that the two strangers have stolen Garcia's head. Bennie shouts at them to get out of his sight, but one of them looks at him intently. "Damn your eyes!" he curses the man. Like Pat Garrett, Bennie is a haunted figure. His bargain with the business interests for a small fortune in exchange for the head of Alfredo Garcia causes a trail of death, including the death of the woman he loves. Bennie "rises from the grave to wreak vengeance on the businessmen who hired him."[38] This leads Bennie into the most harrowing portion of his journey where he goes through "the purifications of ritual violence" in a vengeance quest, but as Peckinpah has envisaged it, it is really a quest for self-redemption. In Peckinpah's treatment, Bennie becomes psychopathological and neurotic as he keeps talking to the head of Alfredo Garcia placed in a bag on the passenger seat of his car. The viewer can only conclude from this behavior that his character can be saved through his own death. The money no longer matters. Bennie decides ultimately to find El Jefe, the man who commissioned the hunt for Alfredo Garcia's head. Thus, he goes straight into the tiger's lair, following the example of the Bunch in *The Wild Bunch*, and kills El Jefe (Emilio Fernández, the same actor who played Mapache).

The whole Gothic episode of Bennie's rising from the grave, the discovery of his girlfriend's corpse, his encounters with the men at the graveyard, and his monologue inside the car can be interpreted as another Chan *gong'an* in Peckinpah's Eastern Westerns. As Bennie engages in his monologue inside the car, he swears again at the man who had looked at him, thus showing

Figure 7.3 Bennie rising from the grave.
Bring Me the Head of Alfredo Garcia, Producer: Martin Baum.

that Bennie is clearly seized by a moral conscience and overwhelmed by a sense of guilt. He is aware of the aphorism that when a person looks at you, he can see right into your heart (*xin*, a word that is coextensive with mind). The look is a mirror of the mind, and the idea that Bennie's mind is soiled, quite literally, from being buried, is an illustration of the famous Chan poem (by the patriarch Shen Xiu) (Figure 7.3):

> One's body is like the Bodhi tree
> The mind is like a clear mirror
> Be sure to polish it at all times
> Do not let the dust taint it.
>
> (My translation)

Bennie's body, which has just come out of the ground, is like an uprooted Bodhi tree, and his mind is the mirror tainted with dust. The experience is traumatic, made worse by the discovery of the dead Elita buried beside him. His sense of guilt at Elita's death sparks a process of self-questioning and an awareness of his flawed character. The episode therefore represents the turning point in Bennie's life where he seeks to clear his mind (and heart) of the dust, which explains his sensitivity to being looked at. The eyes function like the refracted mirror into his mind. When we look into it, we see clearly that his mind/heart is soiled and corrupted. Bennie's whole experience constitutes a Chan experience that involves words, eyes, and Chan itself.

words
an enchanted film across the eyes
ch'an
floating dust on the mind
yet all ins and outs become one
with one twirl of the lotus
and the chilocosm whole in my body[39]

The experience, then, constitutes a reset of Bennie's mind: Chan "is the floating dust on the mind" that drives Bennie toward redemption, while his words (his conversations with the head) are "an enchanted film across the eyes." Though it is Chan that resets his mind, Bennie is a classical "straw dog" (Chan, of course, is not without Daoist connotations since historically, Daoist principles were absorbed by Buddhism) who contains all the contradictions of his existence: the chilocosm whole in his body. The Chan experience concentrates his consciousness of self and his contradictions, driving him toward the violent action of the finale and his redemption.

Like Kurosawa's hero in *Yojimbo*, Peckinpah's hero transforms violence into a ritual of "purification." Peckinpah's violence has a much bleaker consequence for his hero, though in death, Bennie becomes noble. As a straw dog, Bennie is a sacrificial object who reacts against the forces of authority in his own heroic way. At the same time, Bennie is a child of nature, and the motif of the children seen in Peckinpah's other films therefore recurs in a disturbing fashion. His talking to the head is Peckinpah's Gothic modulation of the straw dogs principle of communicating and commiserating with nature (compare Cable Hogue in the desert talking to the lizard and to God in *Ballad of Cable Hogue*).

I said that Bennie is ennobled through his final act of violence. Essentially, *Alfredo Garcia* ends on an Eastern-inspired moment of action in which Bennie resembles the historical Chinese assassin Jing Ke, who attempted to kill the Emperor Qin. Jing Ke penetrates the palace of the Emperor by masquerading as a diplomat. He unfolds a map and draws out a dagger hidden at the end of the scroll to carry out his assassination of the Emperor. (This was the basis of Chen Kaige's *The Emperor and the Assassin* [1998].) Peckinpah does a variant of this by showing Bennie taking out blocks of ice inside the basket that holds the head of Alfredo Garcia. He then draws out a gun to shoot El Jefe. As he makes his escape, Bennie is shot by El Jefe's minions, but he has already achieved his aim while the original Jing Ke could not kill the Emperor. Bennie thus becomes a chivalrous hero in the tradition of the Chinese *xia*-assassins, and we can only record this achievement in cinematic history if we adopt an Eastern outlook on the film and its hero. The film works as a meditation on his flawed nature through the Chan-Gothic moments which ultimately lead him toward his final redemption, achieved through his act of violence and his own death.

The borrowings from Chinese conventions show that Peckinpah's action concepts are generically Eastern as Peckinpah evolves from his Westerns to the contemporary action thriller *The Killer Elite* (1975), his next film after *Alfredo Garcia*. As noted before, the action in *The Killer Elite* is derivative of martial arts movies from the cinemas of the East. The action firmly suggests a mainstream Asian Cinema style embodied in the popular Hong Kong and Japanese action formulas of martial arts combat. Alas, despite some interesting aspects, its achievement is not on a par with Peckinpah's best Westerns and its Easternness comes across as somewhat hollow. This chapter's analysis of Peckinpah's Westerns suggests that the director captured Easternness through direct evocations of action principles and a poetic mode, integrating them into the settings of his Westerns. It is ultimately to the Westerns that we have to turn in order to judge what is Eastern about Peckinpah.

Conclusion

While Peckinpah's Westerns are more consistently Eastern in essence, some are probably more Eastern than others. Limited space precludes a comprehensive analysis of this topic in this chapter. In addition, it may be argued that *Ballad of Cable Hogue* is more Daoist and *The Wild Bunch* is more Confucianist, with a Daoist counter-thesis, while other films show only fragmentary qualities of Eastern aesthetics and philosophy. Peckinpah's eclecticism ensures that all his films share overlapping Eastern concepts and conceits. The straw dogs principle runs through all of them as a strong motif of philosophical commentary, including those that I have not had the space here to discuss in any depth, such as *Major Dundee*, *Junior Bonner* (1972), *The Getaway* (1972),

Cross of Iron (1977). There is the theme of the struggle over Confucian values of loyalty and word, social commitment and individualism. The films, therefore, share commonalities of Eastern action codes integrated into the Western genre mode. (*Cross of Iron* is a war movie but can work as a Western; *Junior Bonner* and *The Getaway* are more like contemporary Westerns: *Junior Bonner* is also about family, another "Eastern" value that makes it more distinctive than most Peckinpah films, and it too is a gentle, moderate work with next to no violence.) The Eastern character of Peckinpah is very much an unexplored subject and there is a great deal about his work to warrant further research. A comparative analysis of Daoism and Confucianism in Peckinpah's cinema is one such area. The straw dogs principle alone can probably justify multiple chapters in a volume on Peckinpah's Eastern nature. Indeed, Peckinpah's work can fall into separate categories of Daoist, Confucianist, and even Buddhist concerns. Only when Peckinpah's Eastern side is recognized and studied in all its aspects can we fully comprehend the director and his obsessions.

Notes

1. On the many remakes of *Seven Samurai*, see David Desser, "Remaking *Seven Samurai* in World Cinema," in L. Hunt and W.-F. Leung (eds.), *East Asian Cinemas: Exploring Transnational Connections on Film* (London and New York: I. B. Tauris, 2008); and D. P. Martinez, *Remaking Kurosawa: Translations and Permutations in Global Cinema* (New York: Palgrave Macmillan, 2002). Desser discusses the connections between *The Wild Bunch* and *Seven Samurai* in *The Samurai Films of Akira Kurosawa* (Ann Arbor: UMI Research Press, 1982), pp. 142–44.
2. David Weddle, *Sam Peckinpah "If They Move . . . Kill 'Em"* (New York: Faber and Faber, 1994), p. 58.
3. Ibid., p. 59.
4. See Robert E. Allinson, "Moral Values and the Daoist Sage in the *Dao De Jing*," in B. Carr (ed.), *Morals and Society in Asian Philosophy* (Richmond, Surrey: Curzon Press, 1996), pp. 162–65.
5. See Mair, *Wandering on the Way*, p. 76.
6. Ibid., p. 136.
7. See Hans-Georg Moeller, *The Philosophy of the Daodejing* (New York: Columbia University Press, 2006), pp. 136–37.

8 Gray, *Straw Dogs*.
9 Ibid., p. 34.
10 Rudolf G. Wagner, *The Craft of a Chinese Commentator: Wang Bi on the Laozi* (Albany: State University of New York Press, 2000), p. 266.
11 Michael Bliss, *Justified Lives: Morality and Narrative in the Films of Sam Peckinpah* (Carbondale and Edwardsville: Southern Illinois University, 1993), p. 11.
12 Rory Palmieri, "*Straw Dogs*: Sam Peckinpah and the Classical Western Narrative," *Studies in the Literary Imagination*, 16 (1), 1983, p. 33.
13 Jim Kitses, *Horizons West: Directing the Western from John Ford to Clint Eastwood* (London: British Film Institute, 2004), p. 202.
14 Bliss, *Justified Lives*, p. 160.
15 Ibid.
16 Ibid., p. 163.
17 Western critics have generally shied away from analyzing the straw dogs concept as it relates to the movie's violence. Instead, to explain the violence, most critics bring up allusions to Robert Ardrey's books, in particular *The Territorial Imperative* and *African Genesis* as key influences on Peckinpah.
18 Gray, *Straw Dogs*, p. 3.
19 Steven Lloyd, "The Ballad of Divine Retribution," in M. Bliss (ed.), *Peckinpah Today: New Essays on the Films of Sam Peckinpah* (Carbondale and Edwardsville: Southern Illinois University Press, 2012), p. 50. Michael Bliss has also noted the Christian references in *Ballad*: see the chapter "This Cactus Eden" in *Justified Lives*, pp. 127–41.
20 Richard Jameson calls the character a "proto-hippie" and notes that it was Peckinpah's "gesture of demystification" to have him appear on a motorcycle (recalling the bike riders of *Easy Rider*) in the film's climax. See Jameson, "The Ballad of Cable Hogue," *Film Comment*, 17 (1), 1981, p. 40.
21 The children motif in Peckinpah's films evokes the Daoist vision of the child possessing inherent goodness. The child is not aware of its own goodness. There are several references to the child in the *Daodejing* likening harmony and goodness to a newborn babe. Peckinpah's references to the child appear to evoke this Daoist notion, as, for example, in *The Wild Bunch*: "We all wish to be a child again, even the worst of us, maybe the worst most of all" (spoken by the old man in the Mexican village).
22 Robert Warshow, "Movie Chronicle: The Westerner," *Partisan Review*, 21 (2), 1954, p. 201.
23 John M. Gourlie, "Peckinpah's Song of Songs: *The Ballad of Cable Hogue* (1970)," *Journal of American Culture*, 14 (2), 1991, p. 97.

24 Stephen Prince, *Savage Cinema: Sam Peckinpah and the Rise of Ultraviolent Movies* (Austin: University of Texas Press, 1998), p. xviii.
25 The *xia* code of action is recorded in Sima Qian's *Shi Ji* (*Records of the Grand Historian*) in the chapter "Youxia liezhuan" ("Biographies of Wandering *xia*").
26 See Desser, *The Samurai Films of Akira Kurosawa*, p. 140.
27 Nan Huai-Chin, *The Story of Chinese Zen*, trans. Thomas Cleary (Boston, MA, Rutland, VT, and Tokyo: Charles E. Tuttle Co., 1995), p. 76.
28 Michael Bliss, "'Back Off to What?' Enclosure, Violence, and Capitalism in Sam Peckinpah's *The Wild Bunch*," in S. Prince (ed.), *Sam Peckinpah's* The Wild Bunch (Cambridge: Cambridge University Press, 1999), p. 115.
29 Ibid., p. 125.
30 Ibid., p. 126.
31 Gray, *Straw Dogs*, p. 116.
32 Ibid.
33 One could say that the Bunch encompasses a synthesis of Daoism and Confucianism. That the two schools form "a mutually complementary and harmonious whole" is a common view among Chinese scholars. See Li Zehou, *The Chinese Aesthetic Tradition*, trans. Maija Bel Samei (Honolulu: University of Hawai'i Press, 2010), p. 77.
34 See Jerome P. Seaton and Dennis Maloney (eds.), *A Drifting Boat: An Anthology of Chinese Zen Poetry* (Fredonia, NY: White Pine Press, 1994), p. 37.
35 Paul Seydor, *Peckinpah The Western Films: A Reconsideration* (Urbana and Chicago, IL: University of Illinois Press, 1997), p. 284.
36 Ibid., p. 287.
37 Prince, *The Warrior's Camera*, p. 233.
38 Ibid.
39 From the twelfth poem of the "Mountain Poetry: Twenty Poems" by the Ming Dynasty Chan monk Hanshan Deqing. See Seaton and Maloney (eds.), *A Drifting Boat*, p. 159.

8

Make Way for Tomorrow, America's Confucian Classic

Filial Piety as American doctrine

Leo McCarey's *Make Way for Tomorrow* (1937) is a most uncommon American film classic from the Golden Era of Hollywood cinema. It is likely the one Hollywood classic that Asians would feel instantly at home with, since it deals with family values, not least of which is filial piety (*xiao*, in Chinese). This refers to the debt that children naturally owe to their parents and their obligation to look after them in old age. (I will hereafter refer to "filial piety," "filial care," "filial devotion," and "filial duty" as interchangeable expressions of *xiao*.) It would be no exaggeration to say that Asians can identify with the film as if it were dealing with their own lives. The film could really be about Asian characters, and the fact that it deals with Americans seems purely an accident. Its story, reminiscent of Ozu's 1953 classic *Tokyo Story* (McCarey's film is said to have inspired Ozu's[1]), is about two aging parents forced to live with their children after losing their home. The mother lives with the eldest son, George, while the father lives with the daughter, Cora, and they are, thus, separated. Tensions mount within both families as the parents cope with living in cramped quarters, and their presences are intrusive. Finally, the mother goes to live in a nursing home and the father goes to California to spend his old age with another daughter. Before their departure, they use up the time to tour old haunts in New York, nostalgically retreading their younger lives and enjoying themselves for the last time.

Although there is no evidence to suggest that McCarey was influenced by Confucianism, a Confucian ethos nonetheless pervades the film. Contradictory as it may sound, *Make Way for Tomorrow* is probably the first true Confucian classic in the American cinema. McCarey, a conservative Catholic, begins his film with the Biblical injunction to "Honor Thy Father and Thy Mother," words that might function as a Confucian call for filial piety. These words reverberate with those written in *Mencius* 5A4: "In being a filial son, nothing is greater than honoring one's parents. In honoring one's parents, nothing is greater than caring for them with the world."[2] *Make Way for Tomorrow* is all about filial devotion to one's parents—in an American setting. The narrative shows the degree and depth in which the principle is put into practice, or not, in the American home. In the Confucian practice, filial duty includes reverence (*jing*), nourishing (*yang*), caring when ill (*bing*), mourning (*sang*), and sacrificing (*ji*).[3] Except for mourning and sacrificing, all the other essentials are depicted in the film, which works fundamentally as a critique on the practice of these duties. What makes the film an extraordinary Confucian work is its focus on reverence, implicit in the call to "Honor thy father and thy mother." Confucius counseled obedience of and reverence for one's parents as important outer forms to demonstrate filial devotion. The Master said, "Nowadays it's taken to mean just seeing that one's parents get enough to eat. But we do that much for dogs or horses as well. If there is no reverence, how is it any different?" (*Analects* 2.7).[4] Without reverence, there is nothing really to distinguish the worth of filial piety or to differentiate one form from another.

Robin Wood, the late champion of McCarey, has noted that from the moment of the "statement of intent" to "Honor thy father and thy mother," "the film that follows demonstrates definitively the impossibility of doing so, within the constraints of American middle-class existence."[5] The living conditions of the American family, as Wood tells us, "determined by the 'nuclear' model and the kinds of accommodation it requires, offer no space for an 'extended' family."[6] Wood might argue that the film is, in this way, very anti-Confucian. (Wood has actually stated that the whole movement of the film is "toward an affirmation of marriage and a denigration of the family,"[7] a contradiction in terms about which I will have more to say later.) To our way of thinking, the very American milieu of *Make Way for Tomorrow* and the emphasis on American middle-class conditions underlines the significance of the work as a Confucian classic, in a dialectical way. It works as an *American* interpretation of Confucian morality, something seldom seen on the American screen. It gives an American "face" to an age-old Confucian problem. When pressed further on filial piety, Confucius said, "The difficult part is the facial expression" (*Analects* 2.8).[8] McCarey depicts filial piety from an American perspective. We see the American faces in the parent-child relationship portrayed in the film, and we therefore see the universal problem of how to be filial. Asian audiences can find much in the film that mirrors their own condition. In a sense, it is irrelevant that the film is American, but yet, clearly, what makes it an outstanding work is that it is a very Confucianist work within the confines of American society.

Make Way for Tomorrow will then be analyzed as a Confucian film. All its elements fit the outlines of a Confucian work. The plot deals with an American family in which aging parents must rely on their children to house and look after them. While this suggests an empirical need at first, McCarey strives for a transcendental effect, which is very clear from his treatment of two perennial archetypes in melodrama, the old parents Barclay and Lucy Cooper (played by Victor Moore and Beulah Bondi, respectively). The basis of my Confucian interpretation then lies in McCarey's portrayal of this couple. McCarey shows the couple moving progressively toward a form of transcendentalism. It is classic melodrama, which can thus be defined as a tragedy striving for a transcendental form of emotional fulfillment. McCarey eschews sentimentality and achieves a near perfect expression of pathos in his two central characterizations. While McCarey was a devout Catholic, his work may be put within a broad tradition of American Transcendentalism, a movement inspired by Eastern religions, "especially Hinduism and Buddhism," as Arthur Versluis informs us.[9] Other writers have showed the affinities between Confucianism and Transcendentalist thinkers like Emerson and Thoreau as well as on later Pragmatist philosophers.[10] In the terms of the cinema, William Rothman has pointed out that Hollywood romantic comedies and melodramas "have 'Eastern' as well as 'Western' sources" due to the philosophical tradition of Transcendentalism in America, which "is a reflection of, and reflection on, the great impact of the introduction to the West of Asian religion, philosophy, and art."[11] *Make Way for Tomorrow* is an exemplary Hollywood melodrama representing a humane and benevolent contemplation of the family and old age, both major concerns in Confucian life philosophy. That it possesses Confucian sensibility should not be surprising at all in the light of Transcendentalism paving the way for Eastern philosophy to seep into American culture. In the Hollywood of the 1930s, Eastern themes and subjects were abundantly featured in films, from detective action thrillers of the Charlie Chan and Mr. Moto variety to China-set melodramas like *The Good Earth* (1937), Von Sternberg's *The Shanghai Express* (1932), and the "Eastern" films of Frank Capra, *The Bitter Tea of General Yen* (1933) and *Lost Horizon* (1937). Elizabeth Rawitsch's book *Frank Capra's Eastern Horizons* gives an astute examination of how Capra, typically seen as a nationalistic American director, was early "preoccupied with shifting representations of Eastern otherness."[12] This "Eastern" tendency in Hollywood is not limited to Orientalist films like those of Capra's. I contend that it can also apply to the normative American film, as I demonstrate through my analysis of McCarey's film in this chapter.[13] Hence, it is possible to view *Make Way for Tomorrow* as an Eastern film and McCarey as Hollywood's resident Confucianist at the time, particularly when it came to the business of making family-themed melodramas. *Make Way for Tomorrow* is just the very kind of melodrama that marks "American culture's ongoing conversation with itself, which is also a conversation with China (and with the rest of Asia as well)."[14]

Make Way for Tomorrow is a recently rediscovered work. Suppressed by its studio, it remained buried in the vault for a long time before being given its first home-video release in 2009, through the Criterion Collection. McCarey's film therefore has been given a new lease on life some seventy years after its release and that far from being outdated it carries its relevance even more solidly today, particularly in East Asian societies. Family remains largely an Eastern preoccupation and the resurgence of Eastern Asian societies through rapid economic development has refreshed and sustained the idea of Confucian values, perhaps ironically. In the United States, the family has been in decline over the years following the film's release, as a recent report by Haskins and Sawhill, published in the *Annals of the American Academy of Political and Social Science*, attests to.[15] Thus, McCarey's vision of family values and filial piety makes it a rare work in the West.

Make Way for Tomorrow is, in any case, a work of some perverseness. This is true in the sense of what Robin Wood calls McCarey's "irrepressible, instinctual anarchy," manifested more usually and normally in his early comedies (McCarey had worked with some of the great clowns of Hollywood, notably Laurel and Hardy and the Marx Brothers) but which is "ready to burst out anywhere."[16] A bit of that instinctual anarchy is evident in *Make Way for Tomorrow*.

It is a work of mighty contradictory impulses against Hollywood itself—against its creed of entertainment, rising above its genre, carrying a strong family message and a social critique about the plight of elderly parents. "The amazing thing is that it got made at all," writes Robin Wood, who also informs us that it "almost became a lost film."[17] McCarey's reputation as one of the more reactionary of conservative filmmakers during the notorious McCarthy witch hunt in American history probably casts a negative light on the film today (unjustly, of course). Yet, his anti-Communism might even make some sense on the film's Confucian theme. (McCarey's last film, *Satan Never Sleeps*, released in 1962, was a Cold War piece set in "Red China" about Catholic priests resisting the Communist presence in their mission.) McCarey's conservatism was no doubt an important factor in his conception of family values and the theme of filial duty and devotion toward one's parents.

Christopher Sharrett, in an analysis of *Make Way for Tomorrow*, has written that as "an intelligent conservative," McCarey "occasionally sees the flaws of the current society, but cannot posit anything but an affirmation of Catholicism."[18] Sharrett does not elaborate on how "an affirmation of Catholicism" could correct the flaws of society, but as far as the film describes the problems of a family, it would likely mean that McCarey believed in the Catholic doctrine of subsidiarity and that the ills of the society could be solved through its most immediate and smallest unit, the family. McCarey's depiction of the family was accompanied by a sense of social justice, a transparent theme which manifests as a critique on filial devotion, or the lack of it as a social trend in American society. McCarey may well be advocating a social community, with the family at the center, devoted to filial care and given the means of taking care of the old. This finds a parallel with the Confucian sense of justice on matters devoted to the family, and thus the Confucian stress on filial devotion as a solution to the social problem of taking care of one's aging parents. In a sense, the work's affirmation of Catholicism, as Sharrett asserts, shows its compatibility with Confucianism. That McCarey's film may be Catholic in spirit does not preclude its correspondence with Confucianism, of course, and my Confucian analysis of the film is undertaken on this understanding. There is actually a historical precedence in demonstrating the compatibility between Catholicism and Confucianism, through the work of the Jesuit missionary Matteo Ricci in the sixteenth century. (Ricci lived in China from 1582 to 1610 and was known by the Chinese name Li Madou.) His book, written in Chinese, *Tianzhu shiyi* (*The True Meaning of the Lord of Heaven*), published in 1603, marked a seminal attempt to marry Confucianist thought with Catholic doctrine. "Ricci was not only convinced that the Christian God was recognized by Original Confucianism, to the ancient Chinese sages he also ascribed ethical ideas compatible with Christianity," wrote John D. Young.[19]

Ricci, naturally, sought to stress what was more important to Christian doctrine. On the matter of filial piety, one of the major concerns in Confucianism, and of our present chapter, Ricci sidestepped this issue by seizing on the Confucian notion of *ren* (humanism, kindness, benevolence) to expound on "the two most important and significant aspects of Christianity— the love of God and humanity."

> Not only was Ricci's definition of love broader than Confucian *jen* [sic], but he also stressed that the love for God was more important than the love for any person, even one's parents: "Although one's parents are dearest to oneself, compared with God, they are only secondary." Ricci said that every person had three fathers, namely God, his monarch and his own father. God was the great lord and the great parent. One should, therefore, be most filial to him, the common father.[20]

Ricci thus described God as "the common father" (*gong fu*) to demonstrate the compatibility of the Confucian worldview with Catholicism. In other passages in the *Tianzhu shiyi*, he also referred to God as "the father for all purposes" (*wanling zhi fu*) and the "great father" (*da fu*). Clearly, Ricci did not disavow filial piety since one must be filial to all fathers in the Confucian value system but one's love of God "was more important than the love for any person, even one's parents."[21] This change of emphasis betrays Ricci's evangelizing efforts on behalf of his own faith but there was no doubt that through his comparative study of Confucianism in its ancient, more unattenuated form (not the neo-Confucianism of the society in which Ricci found himself), he discovered that it encompassed like-minded principles and ethics with Christianity.[22]

Given McCarey's conservatism, it may not be all that remarkable that *Make Way for Tomorrow* is more like an essentialist Confucianist work, but it is remarkable that it seems not to have anything much to do with Catholicism, in my view. Perhaps the corresponding match between Confucianism and Catholicism in the film is such that there is not much difference. The Confucianist ethos is directly signified by the moral injunction of "Honor Thy Father and Mother" at the beginning of the film. McCarey is effectively putting a strong Confucianist emphasis on filial piety as well as a Christian emphasis on taking care of the aged. It may be argued that his accent on the family makes him supposedly more Catholic but both Catholicism and Confucianism put the emphasis on the family and both are firmly rooted in classicism and ritual. However, the Confucianism in the film also stems from McCarey's social and political viewpoint toward the material. Clearly, McCarey sees the family as having social and political meaning, although he does not belabor the political by aligning it to any conservative cause, unlike in his later work *My Son John* (1952), which can also be analyzed as a Confucianist film, although I will defer it until another time. Here, the Confucianism of *Make Way for Tomorrow* lies in its inherently social and political implications which evolve from the material in an abstract fashion. I will show that the Confucian principles underlying the family rebound onto the wider political concept of the state.

The way of the family

Our interpretation of the film as a Confucian text rests on its theme of moral self-cultivation based on the parent-child relationship with which the film begins (see Figure 8.1). Our definition of family as depicted in the film is thus a social unit which is determined by the relationship between parents and their children, plus in-laws and grandchildren. All the members of the family share responsibility for meeting "the bodily, spiritual, and emotional needs of each other."[23] The path toward moral self-cultivation is through such a relationship and the fulfillment of responsibilities, in particular filial devotion and what the philosopher Jeffrey P. Bishop calls "family-oriented care."[24] The film explores this relationship internally, that is to say, within the inner circles of the family, but most interestingly, it also places the ethical relationship in various social contexts. The key scene of this contextual placement is the Bridge class scene in which Anita Cooper (Fay Bainter), George's wife, teaches a group of social climbers how to play Bridge, interrupted by the presence of Lucy. (I will return to this scene and thereafter refer to it simply as the "Bridge" scene.) The family must be in holistic association with society. This is the Confucian

Figure 8.1 The family at the beginning of *Make Way for Tomorrow*.
Make Way for Tomorrow, Producer: Leo McCarey.

understanding of the family. Because filial piety is the most prominent of the ethical obligations, society must consider its special role. This is ultimately the sociopolitical message of the film—or its political philosophy. I will hold that *Make Way for Tomorrow* is McCarey's model of inculcating family values and filial piety into American society. McCarey undoubtedly believes in these values sincerely and while his "anarchic" instincts appear to upset such values in the far from harmonious "family" scenes showing the old parents living in their children's homes, it would be far too negative to say that McCarey is anti-family. Even for a right-wing American anarchist, family values are the key to the stability and harmony of society, and "what is actually the norm in most families, even American families," as Jeffrey P. Bishop reminds us, "is a family of care—the family as the foundational context for living and even dying, despite the institutionalized structures and mythologies of American culture."[25] It is in this spirit of American family care that McCarey provides his critique of the family. His solution to the problem of care for one's aging parents is hardly a call to individual action of the solitary American kind but more a social awareness of ethical family values to be applied broadly. The film is a moral lesson, with McCarey functioning as a Confucian teacher showing the audience the Way—and it is very much a Way of the family as a collective unit.

The Way to individual self-cultivation lies within the family, where members are expected to nurture the right kinds of relationships with other family members, and particularly with one's parents. Here, then lies a special role for filial piety. McCarey is rather relentless in stressing this special role. The film begins with the scene of the children called together at the parents' home. They inform the children that they have lost the home. The children make temporary arrangements to house the parents. The film proceeds thereafter to show how the parents are coping individually with their children. The mother, Lucy, lives with eldest son George (Thomas Mitchell), but it is clear she makes for an intrusive presence in George's household from the point where we see her granddaughter Rhoda, with whom she shares a room, remove the portrait of her grandfather Barclay hanging on top of their beds and brings it out to the living room. George's wife, Anita, teaches Bridge lessons and they try to persuade Lucy to stay in her room during Bridge class night. (George tries to convince sister Nellie to take her for the night, but fails.) Lucy Cooper's relationship with her teenage granddaughter further exacerbates tensions with Anita. (She keeps a secret about Rhoda's relationship with an older man from Anita.)

Hints are dropped to move Lucy to the Idylwild Home for Aged Women. Meanwhile, Barclay Cooper, living with daughter Cora, falls ill. (A telling scene shows him sleeping on the couch in the living room and when the doctor calls, Cora quickly moves him into the bedroom.) The suggestion is made that he should live in the warmer climate of California with another daughter Addie (whom we never see in the film). Before Lucy goes to the nursing home, she spends a few hours in New York with Barclay, who will later take the train to California. The old couple deliberately misses the dinner reunion with their children to spend their last hours together at the Vogard Hotel, where they spent their honeymoon. In the scenes of the mother in George's apartment and of the father at Cora's house, McCarey shows the social tensions that exist in the parent-child relationship. Such tensions are only to be expected and are perhaps normal. Confucius suggests as much when he puts the onus on the young to show filial devotion to their parents.

Essentially, McCarey fields filial piety as a public good in American society. At the same time, he is aware of the limitations of filial piety in the modern

American family, and he is criticizing American society by showing how filial care is wanting or lacking a certain moral compulsion. McCarey is making a case for filial care, and he needs to be critical about the children, on whose shoulders they must carry the burden. The children go through the motions of taking care of their parents. This strikes at the heart of Confucius's injunction that while one can go through the motions of filial care, it is truly challenging to be filial. "Many people can go through the motions, but filial piety requires an individual to behave in such a way that a spirit of deep-seated respect or reverence for her parents and elders is a part of her demeanor," writes Erin Cline.[26] The concept of demeanor, or "facial expression" as Confucius has put it, underscores a major scene in *Make Way for Tomorrow* in which Lucy Cooper is placed in a situation where, first, shame, and then, reverence are equally brought into play. This is the Bridge scene where Lucy makes herself highly conspicuous by coming out to join Anita's Bridge class. As she gives her opening lecture, the maid brings out a rocking chair and places it right by the blackboard. Lucy comes out and sits on the chair. Her presence is so embarrassingly awkward that Anita must plead with her daughter to bring her out to the movies. Later, when she returns to the same room after coming home from the movies, she speaks on the phone to Barclay. She speaks so loudly that the Bridge players, social aspirants all, cannot help but listen in but, this time, they are visibly moved by their conversation and the pathos of their being kept apart ("We'll soon be together, for always"). The scene is extraordinary for its subtle social comedy and may in fact be a classic *echt*-McCarey moment that Wood defines as "moments of embarrassing intimacy" except that the intimacy here occurs on a broader social scale (it takes place in a room full of people), and hence, with a greater sense of embarrassment (see Figure 8.2).[27]

The Bridge scene occurs over two sections, both of which have to do with the idea of face. The first shows the presence of Lucy among the players as a kind of show of filial devotion but really emphasizing the embarrassment and shame of Anita and George, both conscious of class and status. The mother insists on showing herself rather than staying inside her room. Her action underlines the concept of filial devotion by hoping to show her son's pride in her. (Most Chinese in the audience will probably know this instinctively.) The second section shows Lucy's pathos, eliciting sympathy and reverence for

Figure 8.2 The public listens in on Lucy Cooper's phone conversation with Barclay. *Make Way for Tomorrow*, Producer: Leo McCarey.

her among the Bridge players despite their class-consciousness (they are all dressed in high-society fashion and occasionally show condescension to the old mother), and underlines the need for respect of the old. The Confucian theme of face comes across as a social comedy of manners, and through this comedy, it touchingly manifests, at the same time, the theme of respect and reverence for the old. The transition from comedy to pathos is perhaps typical of McCarey but the Confucian comedy of manners is a kind of bonus in the transition.

The Confucian emphasis on "facial expression" has to do with sincerity, or the difficulty in expressing sincerity. The concept of filial devotion is nothing if there is no sincerity, and it is precisely therefore one of the most difficult to realize in real life. (A person's real worth may lie in whether one is filial.) Here, in the Bridge scene, or its two sections, as I have compartmentalized them (the two sections being divided by the movie theater scene in between), McCarey puts the theme of filial devotion to the test of sincerity. It is the first such test in the film and it takes place in public (during the Bridge class). The scene becomes a McCareyan interpretation of the Confucian idea of sincerity, which is something to be contrasted with the Hollywood notion of sincerity. Robin Wood offers some McCareyan nuances of sincerity. According to

Wood, sincerity is a component in a pair of values that are "clearly central to McCarey's work" (spontaneity is the other value).[28] He writes,

> "Sincerity" is always a problematic concept: McCarey was doubtless, on a certain level, "sincere" when he aligned himself with the McCarthy witch-hunts. But a far deeper and very different sincerity animates, say, the last half hour of *Make Way for Tomorrow*, the Christmas play sequence of *The Bells of St. Mary's*, the Thanksgiving Day pageant of *Rally 'Round the Flag, Boys!* The former type offers the "sincerity" of a consciously held, "respectable" belief; the latter type the sincerity of spontaneous impulse. "Sincerity" becomes authentic only when it is fused with spontaneity.[29]

What is the kind of "sincerity" expressed in the Bridge scene, as I have analyzed it in terms of Confucian filial devotion? Is it a purely social kind of sincerity, which is that of a consciously held belief, a kind of sincerity often degraded by excessive sentimentalism and thus not be seen as "authentic"? McCarey does show his faith toward the family and his respect for the old, and he believes in their benefits for society. This is the Confucian sincerity of McCarey. Alternatively, we might ask, is it the kind of sincerity fused with "spontaneity" that Wood favors? Evidently, the Bridge scene contains elements of both sincerity and spontaneity, particularly when it comes to the scene of the phone conversation. It would be foolhardy to say that McCarey is not sincere in his belief of family and filial devotion. However, McCarey had wanted to demonstrate the difficulty of being sincere about filial devotion in modern America. Wood is cognizant of the impossibility of realizing filial piety in middle-class America, but does this mean that McCarey is therefore rejecting it and the family entirely? The answer is obvious. McCarey's sincerity has the effect of affirming family values and filial piety. Such values point the way to a good and harmonious society, and this makes *Make Way for Tomorrow* a political film. In Confucian society, there is "an explicit connection," as Erin Cline tells us, "between filial piety in the family and stability at the political level, suggesting filial piety constitutes the roots of political order."[30] Mencius evokes a common saying in Chinese society, *tianxia zhi ben zai guo, guo zhi ben zai jia* ("the root of all under heaven is the state, the root of the state is the family": *Mencius* 4A5).[31] Such sentiments would resonate with McCarey's conservatism and would be entirely compatible with his sense of values. The whole Bridge segment argues for a social agenda of family, filial devotion, and respect for the old. McCarey underlines its political sense not just by the content of the entire segment but also by staging it as a public scene, with Mother Cooper acting out a morality play about family to an audience. (The Bridge players gathered in George's apartment.) Due to this "public" nature, McCarey's sincerity is transparent, to be seen as a "'respectable' belief." He achieves the extraordinary effect of showing the private and intimate aspects of the family in an open public manner. This would be the height of sincerity.

That McCarey sincerely believes in the family is not in dispute, I think. However, Robin Wood has advanced the notion that McCarey disliked families "but loved couples."[32] Wood has argued this line insistently in his several writings on McCarey, basing his argument on the last sequence in the film where the old couple spend five hours together in New York. They meet in the park, walk on the sidewalk, and then go for a car ride where the driver, a car salesman, is trying to sell the car to the couple but gives them a free ride instead. He drops them off at the Vogard Hotel where they meet with friendly receptions from the hatcheck girl, the hotel manager, and finally, the bandleader, as they join a dance on the cabaret floor. The sequence ends with the departure of the father at the train station. This whole sequence functions like a movement that finishes in the "equalization" of the couple and rejects everything about the family, according to Wood. In the process of the couple's equalization, "presumptions of male privilege are invariably chastised," "gender differences are progressively minimized, the partners both modifying and enriching each other's attitudes and behavior patterns in a process of exchange and reciprocal learning."[33] "It is the traditional family, of course, that defines and reproduces the patriarchal gender roles and functions: its absence or negation is essential to the equalization of the couple."[34] In addition, the sequence closes with an "unmarrying motif" (the old man referring to his wife as "Miss Breckinridge") that finally announces "the systematic rejection of the family"[35] (Figure 8.3).

Wood's reading is fundamentally consistent with the perception of McCarey's creative anarchic instincts as a Hollywood craftsman of comedy and melodrama, compelling us to accept McCarey's complicity with the radical agenda of "equalization" of gender roles and the ultimate rejection of the family (this being the logical conclusion of the couple's equalization). The main point of contention, from our point of view, is the assertion of rejection.

Figure 8.3 A renewed courtship.
Make Way for Tomorrow, Producer: Leo McCarey.

Since Wood's reading rests on the foundation of the family, and our Confucian study of the film proceeds from this same foundation, there is a need to properly consider the ethical aftershocks of the rejection of the family. Confucian ethics demands filial devotion, which in turn influences the social order. *Analects* 1.2 states that a person "who is filial to his parents and respectful of his elder brother is rarely the kind of person who is inclined to go against his superiors and there has never been a case of one who is disinclined to go against his superiors stirring up rebellion."[36] The final sequence, though, appears to confirm the breakdown of filial devotion, and thus effectively, the breakdown of the family. In Confucian terms, this upends the whole sociopolitical order, but it is difficult to believe that this is McCarey's moral. Even if McCarey is criticizing the family, criticism does not imply negation of the family. There is a further issue of perspective that determines the critique. The sequence is told from the perspectives of the old parents, which makes it most unlikely that they would reject the family.

That the father and the mother would reject the family makes no sense, of course, from the Confucian point of view. If it was a rejection, it can only be thought of as a fantasy, functioning as a meta-critique of the family. The sequence plays out as another kind of fantasy—of the reversion to younger selves, and of renewed courtship through the "unmarrying" motif. This adds another dimension to the critical perspective. Wood's separation of the family and the "couple" is a reductive line of argument, but we may think of it as a constructive link into the Confucian perspective on family through an inverse correlation. Essentially, the "couple" becomes a son and daughter rather than a father and mother, two individuals on whom the notion of family would immediately implicate their lives instead of being freed from the family. However, the factor behind Wood's separation of the couple and the family is what I might call the Confucian conundrum. How does one subdue individual interests for family? McCarey's scope of the family may lie within the American context but its ethical frame of reference poses the same Confucian conundrum for the American individual as for his Chinese or East Asian counterpart. This conundrum is resolved, if we follow Wood's reading, by a rejection of the family. From the Confucian perspective, it is more likely to be resolved in favor of the family. A Confucian resolution would agree more with McCarey's conservative instincts, and the Confucian predilections of *Make Way for Tomorrow* make it arguably McCarey's most conservative film.

Wood's interpretation actually takes a more ambivalent view of McCarey, and this ambivalence is evident in the correlation between the couple and the family. For example, Wood makes much of the "unmarrying" motif, but it is very ambivalent because it can work in reverse. Wood has also written that the film constitutes a movement toward "an affirmation of marriage."[37] Barclay Cooper becomes a young man courting "Miss Breckinridge" and the courtship will of course end in marriage. Thus, the unmarrying motif is just as apt to function as a "marrying" motif.[38] Under the circumstances, the motif presents an interesting ethical idea along Confucian lines. Barclay effectively becomes a son and Lucy a daughter. They must marry each other according to the doctrine of filial piety. (It is their filial duty to marry, have children, and start a family.) The sequence then becomes a wish-fulfillment of filial piety from the perspectives of the old parents, a kind of starting over if it was ever possible to start all over again. The fantasy of courtship reverts naturally to the family as both an ethical concept and a kind of social necessity.

Because McCarey's theme and his entire narrative in *Make Way for Tomorrow* revolves around the family and the need of filial piety, there is no mistaking its compelling thrust nor the moral or didactic impulses. To imagine that McCarey would be totally against the family strains credibility. However, McCarey is delivering a critique of the family, a point that I have made several times above, and it is worth repeating here. It is permissible, under Confucianism, to criticize the family and to criticize one's parents. *Make Way for Tomorrow* is an American version of a Confucian critique in which McCarey presents a comprehensive valuation of the family from the perspectives of the old parents and that of their children. His attitude may be more critical toward the children but, as Robin Wood says, he is "too intelligent to sentimentalize the parents and put all the blame on the children."[39]

The last sequence of the parents spending five hours together contains some self-criticism. Both evoke their younger selves only to reflect critically on themselves. ("I was the town clown," says Barclay, and he acknowledges he is a failure, while Lucy says, "I think I slipped up someplace, though I tried always to be a good wife and mother.") Their failure, ultimately, is their uneasy relationships with their children, McCarey showing, most significantly, the tensions between Lucy and her daughter-in-law Anita. (They quarrel over Rhoda, Anita's teenage daughter who has confided her relationship with an older man to her grandmother.) Neither one of the old parents "is easy to live with," as Wood says,[40] and McCarey imparts the sense that he is also critical of the parents. This is done mainly through George, the eldest son, who is an interesting character functioning on both a subjective and objective level. Subjective because he himself has problems in looking after the parents, and objective because he understands them deeply and obviously has filial feelings toward them. His role seems to me to illustrate the Master's words in *Analects* 4.18: "In serving your father and mother, you may gently admonish them. But if you see they have no intention of listening to you, then be respectful as before and do not disobey them. You might feel distressed but should never feel resentful."[41]

On the whole, McCarey paints a fair and balanced portrait of the Cooper children as distressed but never resentful characters trying to cope with the problem of their aged parents. George is the only sympathetic character among the children, while the daughters are more mean-spirited: George, being the eldest son, is given the Confucian edge, or the benefit of the doubt, as it were. He has done his best, and functions as the conscience. At the end of the film, he reminds his siblings that they are "terrible." In Confucian terms, this self-criticism (or his expression of conscience) is a sign of filial piety. (George knows instinctively that his father would not be turning up for the reunion dinner with the children: "I kind of thought they'd like to be alone.") George is probably the most attentive to the idea of facial expression, striking the right face and showing the right attitude as a matter of propriety. In the *Book of Rites* (*Li ji*), it is written, "If a parent have a fault, the son should with bated breath and bland aspect, and gentle voice, admonish him. If the admonition do not take effect, he will be the more reverential and the more filial."[42] George's blandness and his timid character is the perfect complement to the concept of propriety in the parent-child relationship. This comes through vividly in the scene where it falls upon him to tell his mother she must move to the Idylwild home, only she anticipates this by telling him first. It is thus no accident that Lucy tells George that he was always her favorite child. George's sense of shame is palpable as he goes into his wife's room and says, "As the years go by you can always look back on this day and be mighty proud of me." It is important to recognize that his shame comes out of his filial piety, and that George has in fact conducted himself with the utmost propriety, showing reverence to his mother. (Thomas Mitchell's performance is therefore one of the most memorable in the film, alongside that of Beulah Bondi as the mother.)

Reverence of the old

The final sequence that Wood summarizes as a movement toward the rejection of the family can also be interpreted on another Confucian level, which is that of society's respect for the aged. This is perhaps a corollary theme arising out of the greater theme of the family and filial piety but McCarey turns it into a testament of his respect for old people rather than as a fondness for the couple. The whole sequence seems to be designed to demonstrate the well-known Chinese saying, from *Mencius* 1A7, *lao wu lao yi ji ren zhi lao* ("treat with reverence one's old and all other old people everywhere"[43]). Here, once again, we have McCarey's didactic strain of emitting an ethical message by making a public show of it. The sequence is a public vindication of the old couple since it shows Barclay and Lucy relating to strangers (the car salesman, the hatcheck girl, the hotel manager, and the bandleader) and these strangers showing kindness and respect to the Coopers in return. Effectively, they show kindness and respect because they are old. (The aged theme is emphasized in the dialogue and in the actions of the characters—as for example, the bandleader stopping the more modern music his band is playing and switching to a more old-fashioned tune to accommodate the old couple.)

The public emphasis of the sequence underwrites the Mencian theme of respect and reverence for the old as a sign of universal human goodness. "If everyone would treat their parents as parents and their elders as elders, the world would be at peace" (*Mencius* 4A11); "Treating one's parents as parents is benevolence. Respecting one's elders is righteousness. There is nothing else to do but extend these to the world" (*Mencius* 7A15).[44] Erin Cline tells us that according to Mencius, one's natural moral capacities lie in the heart-mind (*xin*), the function of which is to reflect: "When it reflects, it gets things right; if it does not reflect, it cannot get things right" (*Mencius* 6A15).[45] Thus, Cline writes that the heart-mind "contains cognitive and affective faculties," and she gives us certain inflections of the concept whereby Mencius refers to "our natural moral tendencies together as the 'child's heart-mind' (*chizi zhi xin*), the 'innate heart-mind' (*liangxin*), and the 'fundamental heart-mind' (*benxin*)."[46]

McCarey directs the sequence to express *xin* in all the episodes involving the car salesman, the hatcheck girl, the hotel manager, and the bandleader. According to Wood, the car salesman episode marks the point "where a very good film becomes a great one" and McCarey "takes complete possession of his material, making it essentially his own."[47] I believe that McCarey has taken complete possession of his material by grasping the moment to express the inflections of *xin*, childlike, innate, and fundamental, in the various episodes. (The episode with the car salesman possesses all these shades of *xin*.) Wood, of course, has analyzed these scenes as a deconstruction of the family. My interpretation rests on their reaffirmation of the family as the ultimate result of their various expressions of heart-mind. McCarey's use of the *xin* concept achieves both cognitive and affective results. The episodes could very well have turned into a succession of maudlin moments but McCarey pushes the envelope on *xin* counterpoising it with the family and the notion of filial devotion (Figure 8.4).

The kindness-of-strangers theme can be taken as offsetting and counterbalancing the apparent "unkindness" of the children toward the old

Figure 8.4 The Coopers with the car salesman.
Make Way for Tomorrow, Producer: Leo McCarey.

parents in the prior scenes. However, there is more to the sequence than just this simple counterbalancing effect. It is meant chiefly to convey the total affective impact of *xin* in all its modulations: the parents showing the child's heart-mind in their reversion to youthful wish-fulfillment, and the various strangers their innate and fundamental heart-minds. Even the children, at the end, show a fundamental conscience, which is their fundamental heart-mind (*benxin*, which is often translated into English as "one's conscience"). The sequence connects everyone through the heart-mind (*xin*), everyone combining into a universal family, reinforcing the Mencian theme of treating one's parents as parents, elders as elders. The social or the public connotation of the family and the theme of social respect for the aged is articulated for the last time, complete with the private and intimate affections of heart and mind.

Make Way for Tomorrow ends on the Mencian theme of universal reverence for the old. Its unwritten concluding exhortation is "If everyone would treat their parents as parents and their elders as elders, the world would be at peace," thus complementing the opening words "Honor thy father and thy mother." It is what we might call a socially righteous ending. Robin Wood offers some "happy" endings for the film, one of which McCarey could have used but did not. (The children dart out to the railway station and drag Barclay out of the train, reuniting him with Lucy, and then promise to look after them.) Wood writes, "The ending we have is clearly the right one, the perfect one, for the film McCarey made. That it provides no solution to the social problems it raises is beside the point; it speaks most eloquently for the necessity of seeking one."[48] Here, Wood's point about seeking solutions is rather ambiguous. He notes that the "artistic rightness" of the ending is finally underlined by a theme of "necessary self-delusion" that runs through McCarey's work "but is particularly pervasive and insistent here."[49] This is Lucy Cooper's self-delusion that the old man will find a job and support them. This "necessary self-delusion" can be read as both an endorsement "of the necessity to "pretend" and as a critique of it," according to Wood.[50]

Thus, Wood underlines the ambiguity of the ending as he sees it. However, his discussion touches on the economic premise of finding a job as the necessary solution to the problem of the aged. I would suppose that McCarey's solution would be the Catholic principle of subsidiarity, of relying on the family rather than on society as such. The "self-delusion" that Wood speaks of is the self-delusion of the economic solution in times of depression, imposed on the individual (the old man is expected to find a job), but I think McCarey is pointing to the family as universal solution, which is where McCarey's Catholicism converges with Confucianism. Thus, the Mencian theme of universal reverence for the old offers the solution of the family as being at the root of the problem. For Mencius, it is the responsibility of families to cultivate all the virtues of filial piety, fraternal respect, and the elderly being properly cared for. For Mencius, "political problems often originate when people do not understand and cultivate proper relationships within the family."[51] China's solution for its current aging problem seems still to reside in the family, the only viable solution for a country that, according to the estimates of many economists, is growing old before it becomes rich. Indeed, among Chinese communities throughout Asia even today, it is the family that is expected to take care of their old parents.

The ending of *Make Way for Tomorrow* invokes the family as solution. It is an Asian ending, perhaps, bearing in mind its thrust toward Confucian righteousness. In this way, it is not as ambiguous as Wood makes it out to be. However, there is probably a depressing quality to it all, which Wood refers to as an essential McCarey quandary: "Is life in our culture so inherently and irredeemably depressing that 'pretending' is the only way to make it endurable, or is the escape into 'pretending' precisely the obstacle to doing anything about it?" Even if one thinks that relying on the family as a solution is a depressing thought, McCarey sees no other way out. The ending may not be as pessimistic as it is felt to be. Through the expressive heart-mind in the last sequence, I think McCarey emits the feeling that the Cooper children will come around and be realistic and righteous enough to take care of their aged parents. At least, I think George will do the right thing, and he will see to it, as best he can, that all the other children will do their bit. George's prominent role in the film as the eldest male child is not without Confucian overtones, after all, and in him, ultimately, lies the Confucian idealism of the filial son.

Conclusion

I have offered an analysis of *Make Way for Tomorrow* as an unusual Confucian melodrama to come out of the classic Hollywood cinema. Its unusual nature is made all the more evident by McCarey's approach, which is sincere and somewhat subversive at the same time. The Confucian theme of the film is perhaps of subsidiary importance when seen from a Western perspective. Robin Wood's claim that McCarey was really against the family, his heart beating instead for the "couple," suggests that any Confucian dimension of family present in the film would hardly be persuasive. From our perspective, Wood's is a reductive reading of the family. It can be even more reductive if one isn't into couples all that much, and that is to reduce the couple down to a single individual. In fact, this is what happens for much of the film. Barclay and Lucy are reduced to being single individuals cared for separately by their children. It seems to me that what may be most non-Confucian about the film is McCarey's preference for one single individual, and this is the old mother, in my view. Her image ends the film. She is all alone, but indomitable in spirit. Throughout the film, her character gains the most traction, while the old father seems shunted aside. It is perhaps no accident that the old mother is much stronger in terms of her health and that the old father falls sick when under Cora's care. This conveys the strength of her character (therefore, she is the anchor of the film), and the marginalization of the father.

Therefore, rather than saying that McCarey loves couples, in *Make Way for Tomorrow*, he loves the individual even more. Arthur Nolletti Jr. makes much the same point about individualism, but with regard only to the father.[52] The old mother, however, is the real emotional and intellectual center of the film. She is the emotional locus of the Bridge scene and she provides the intellectual response to her husband's self-doubt ("You don't sow wheat and reap ashes, Pa"). Fittingly, as Wood has demonstrated, it is the old mother who makes the case for "pretending" that the old man can find a job ("when you're seventy ... about the only fun you have left is pretending that there ain't any facts to face"). Thus, she carries the weight of this self-delusion at the end of the film, just the sort of self-delusion that kindles the spirit of individualism. As a result, one may say that McCarey loves the individual even more than McCarey loves the couple and that the character of the old mother becomes the focus of the film as the single strongest individual. McCarey's feeling for the individual, and for the mother rather than the father, makes his film less Confucian and more American.

Yet, even from such a reductive reading, one can justifiably place the character within the Confucian schema of things. The mother is submissive as wife to husband should be in the Confucian rules of propriety. She is sensitive to the feelings of her children, but she also emphasizes their filial duty, such as making her presence felt in the Bridge scene and reminding her husband at the end to tell Ellie to take care of him. The mother also submits to George's wish for her to move to the nursing home. (Thus, she submits to the patriarchal line of the family.) It seems to me that the mother is the most realistic, or pragmatic, person in the film, and while she talks about pretending that there are no facts to face, it is only her way of facing up to facts. She shows womanly and maternal instincts that appear to emphasize her secondary role, and this comes through particularly in the final sequence where she engages her husband in the fantasy of renewed courtship. Therefore, her behavior is very Confucian, and it is perhaps McCarey's anarchic fancy to view her as an un-Confucian female individual in a Confucian drama about family, made in Hollywood—and I am not sure that McCarey had wanted to make any ideological point about individualism as an American solution to the problem of taking care of the old. Since the film is about a problem of great social dimensions, the solution rebounds back either to the family or to society as a whole. The individual, McCarey seems to imply, is helpless. However, the film achieves its transcendental end point through its focus on the individual figure of the mother.

In the final analysis, McCarey delivers a most untypical film for a Hollywood melodrama which easily discloses strains of Confucian values flowing out of its narrative about the family. As a Hollywood melodrama, it stokes some element of fantasy about the family, and thus it is only in this vein that we can accept Wood's line about the couple rejecting the family. Such a rejection is purely a fantasy in the minds of the aged parents and the circumstances of the children's predicament in taking care of them. McCarey broaches the fantasy of rejection as a meta-critique of the family, underscoring the problem of the aged and the necessity of filial duty. The family is the root of the problem and it is, surely, the solution to the problem but it is not an easy solution. McCarey does not pretend that it is easy for family members to look after their old. McCarey's vision and his wisdom is all the more striking for the director's Hollywood background seems entirely incompatible with Confucian themes—but McCarey's vision is not incompatible with the Eastern forethought into the issue. The Confucian values of the film—its call for filial devotion and reverence of the old—is no less McCarey's values.

Notes

1. I will not be doing any comparison between *Tokyo Story* and *Make Way for Tomorrow* as a method of teasing out the Eastern content and sensibilities of McCarey's film. My aim is to show *Make Way for Tomorrow* as an intrinsically Confucian film in its very American context and therefore in its own right. For a comparative study, see Arthur Nolletti, Jr., "Ozu's *Tokyo Story* and the 'Recasting' of McCarey's *Make Way for Tomorrow*," in D. Desser (ed.), *Ozu's* Tokyo Story (Cambridge: Cambridge University Press, 1997), pp. 25–52.
2. See Erin M. Cline, *Families of Virtue: Confucian and Western Views on Childhood Development* (New York: Columbia University Press, 2015), p. 22.
3. For a summary of these five duties, from the *Xiaojing* (*Book of Filial Piety*), see Ilhak Lee, "Filial Duty as the Moral Foundation of Caring for the Elderly: Its Possibility and Limitations," in R. Fan (ed.), *Family-Oriented Informed Consent: East Asian and American Perspectives* (Heidelberg, New York, Dordrecht, and London: Springer, 2015), p. 141.

4. From Burton Watson's translation, *The Analects of Confucius* (New York: Columbia University Press, 2007), p. 21.
5. Robin Wood, "From *Ruggles* to *Rally*; or, America, America! The Strange Career of Leo McCarey," *Film International*, 5 (27), 2007, p. 33.
6. Robin Wood, "Leo McCarey and 'Family Values,'" in R. Wood (ed.), *Sexual Politics and Narrative Film: Hollywood and Beyond* (New York: Columbia University Press, 1998), p. 153.
7. Robin Wood, "Democracy and Shpontanuity," *Film Comment*, January/February 1976, p. 15.
8. Watson, *Analects of Confucius*, p. 21.
9. See Arthur Versluis, *American Transcendentalism and Asian Religions* (New York and Oxford: Oxford University Press, 1993), p. 3.
10. See Matthew A. Foust, *Confucianism and American Philosophy* (Albany: State University of New York Press, 2017). Foust studies the influence of Confucianism on Emerson and Thoreau, and on the American Pragmatists Charles Peirce, William James, and Josiah Royce. He notes that the early Pragmatist, John Dewey, had lived in China from 1919 to 1921 and was so popular with the Chinese that they dubbed him "the Second Confucius" (p. 7).
11. William Rothman, "*The Goddess*: Reflections on Melodrama East and West," in W. Dissanayake (ed.), *Melodrama and Asian Cinema* (Cambridge: Cambridge University Press, 1993), p. 61.
12. Elizabeth Rawitsch, *Frank Capra's Eastern Horizons: American Identity and the Cinema of International Relations* (London and New York: I. B. Tauris, 2015), p. 8.
13. My analysis of McCarey's film radically departs from Rawitsch's analysis of Capra's films in her book. This is partly due to the films being so very different. I denote McCarey's film as an American film that is intrinsically Confucianist and therefore "Eastern," whereas Capra's films, such as *The Bitter Tea of General Yen* and *Lost Horizon*, are evidently Orientalist works. I am making no claims about *Make Way for Tomorrow* being Orientalist or that it deals with Eastern otherness and "shifting representations" (Rawitsch's catchphrase) simply because they do not apply at all.
14. Rothman, "*The Goddess*," p. 61.
15. See Ron Haskins and Isabel V. Sawhill, "The Decline of the American Family: Can Anything Be Done to Stop the Damage?," *American Academy of Political and Social Science*, 667, 2016, pp. 8–34. See also Mark J. Cherry, "Individually Directed Informed Consent and the Decline of the Family in the West," in R. Fan (ed.), *Family-Oriented Informed Consent: East Asian and American Perspectives* (Heidelberg, New York, Dordrecht, and London: Springer, 2015), pp. 43–62.

16 Wood, "From *Ruggles* to *Rally*," p. 33.
17 Wood, "Leo McCarey and 'Family Values,'" p. 151.
18 Christopher Sharrett, "Make Way for Tomorrow," *Cineaste*, Fall, 2010, p. 50.
19 John D. Young, *Confucianism and Christianity: The First Encounter* (Hong Kong: Hong Kong University Press, 1983), p. 35.
20 Ibid., p. 37. The principle of *ren* is, of course, not without relevance to filial piety since it is, in practice, oriented toward the family, as Rosemont and Ames point out. *Ren* "is not a principle or standard that has some existence beyond the day-to-day, family-grounded lives of the people who realize it in their relationships. *Ren* is fostered in the deepening of the relationships that emerge as one takes on the responsibility and obligations of family, and, by extension, of communal living, therein coming fully to life." See Henry Rosemont, Jr. and Roger T. Ames, *The Chinese Classic of Family Reverence: A Philosophical Translation of the Xiaojing* (Honolulu: University of Hawai'i Press, 2009), p. 23.
21 John D. Young points out that, being celibate, Ricci would not be partial to the injunction of filial piety since a requirement of being filial was to have children: see p. 36.
22 The effort to match Confucianism with Christianity is complemented later by efforts to match Confucianism with Democracy, as in the work of John Dewey. See David L. Hall and Roger T. Ames, *The Democracy of the Dead: Dewey, Confucius, and the Hope for Democracy in China* (Chicago, IL and Lasalle: Open Court, 1999), and Sor-hoon Tan, *Confucian Democracy: A Deweyan Reconstruction* (Albany: State University of New York Press, 2004). On a related idea, which is the equation of Confucianism with John Rawls's liberal theory of justice, see Erin M. Cline, *Confucius, Rawls, and the Sense of Justice* (New York: Fordham University Press, 2013).
23 See Jeffrey P. Bishop, "Dependency, Decisions, and a Family of Care," in R. Fan (ed.), *Family-Oriented Informed Consent: East Asian and American Perspectives* (Heidelberg, New York, Dordrecht, and London: Springer, 2015), p. 29.
24 Ibid., p. 28.
25 Ibid.
26 Cline, *Families of Virtue*, p. 14.
27 Wood, "Leo McCarey and 'Family Values,'" p. 161.
28 Ibid., p. 144.
29 Ibid., pp. 144–45.
30 Cline, *Families of Virtue*, p. 14.
31 My translation.
32 Wood, "Leo McCarey and 'Family Values,'" p. 145.

33 Ibid.
34 Ibid.
35 Ibid., p. 157.
36 Translation in Cline, *Families of Virtue*, p. 8.
37 Wood, "Democracy and Shpontanuity," p. 15.
38 I might add that the unmarrying motif is not all that obvious in the last sequence because the motif is fundamentally a comedic motif and the film is a tragedy. The motif works far better and clearly in McCarey's next film, *The Awful Truth*, a screwball comedy. It is a plot device driving the narrative, first through the divorce of the couple Jerry and Lucy Warriner (Cary Grant and Irene Dunne) and subsequently through each partner trying to prevent the other from marrying new partners. In the process, they go through a renewed courtship that can only end in their remarriage.
39 Wood, "Leo McCarey and 'Family Values,'" p. 153.
40 Ibid., p. 154.
41 Watson, *Analects of Confucius*, p. 34.
42 From James Legge's translation of *Li ji*. See *The Sacred Books of China: The Texts of Confucianism*, Part III, *The Li Ki* (Oxford: Clarendon Press, 1885), p. 456.
43 My translation.
44 Translations taken from Cline, *Families of Virtue*, p. 23.
45 Cline, *Families of Virtue*, p. 19.
46 Ibid.
47 Wood, "Leo McCarey and 'Family Values,'" p. 157.
48 Ibid., p. 163.
49 Ibid.
50 Ibid., p. 164.
51 Cline, *Families of Virtue*, p. 22.
52 See Nolletti, Jr., "Ozu's *Tokyo Story* and the 'Recasting' of McCarey's *Make Way for Tomorrow*," p. 45.

9

John Ford and Asian Family Values

The family in Ford

John Ford liked to say that he made Westerns, and these films reflect what critic Jim Kitses has called "the white point of view," or more explicitly, the perspectives of the Anglo/Irish/European migrants who settled the West.[1] As a result, most considerations of Ford are undertaken through this same point of view. That there are Eastern elements in Ford's films has not been seriously considered or discussed at all in the literature. I discussed Ford's Westerns in my previous book, *Eastern Westerns*, focusing on *The Searchers* (1956) as a wellspring of rasa sentiments and analyzing it from the mythical ur-perspective of the Indian classic *The Ramayana*.[2] Ford's American-ness easily hides whatever Eastern concepts and elements may be present in his films, and Ford himself does not appear to have any particular inclination toward Eastern thought or culture. However, his films are certainly susceptible to Eastern readings, as I have demonstrated in my previous book, and will demonstrate again below. In this last chapter, I continue my discussion on Ford on a broader and social level of Eastern themes, in particular Ford's susceptibility to Asian family values.

Ford's career shows great range and magnitude, spanning both the silent and sound periods and covering many genres. Since I have previously focused on the Westerns, the impression might be given that they are more conducive to an Eastern interpretation, but Ford did not just make Westerns and his vision is far more wide-ranging than a focus on a single genre might convey. His vision is also far more socially grounded in the universal structure of the family than might have been recognized. This cinematic social grounding on the family therefore entails a demand for a greater Eastern analysis of Ford's films for it is the family that still looms large over Eastern societies, and I would venture to say that Asian audiences are probably far more capable of appreciating Ford's films. Although the films may be perceived to be outdated by contemporary audiences and Ford's critical status largely forgotten or neglected, how his films would resonate even more today in the East is a testament of his depictions of familial relations emitting timeless emotions. Several of his non-Westerns are particularly instrumental for our purposes of engaging with Ford's films and the family as a motif. They are *The Grapes of Wrath* (1940), *How Green Was My Valley* (1941), and *The Quiet Man* (1951). All three films are among Ford's most honored works. He received the academy award for best directing for all of them, and *How Green Was My Valley* received the Best Picture of 1941. All are family-centric works and constitute a trilogy for the sake of analysis here.

The family is also at the center of his best known Westerns, including the so-called Cavalry Trilogy, *Fort Apache* (1947), *She Wore a Yellow Ribbon* (1949), *Rio Grande* (1950), and *The Searchers* as well as *The Man Who Shot Liberty Valance* (1962), these last two films among the most significant Westerns ever made. Most of Ford's films are essentially all about the family, even those that apparently deflect away from the family, such as *The Lost Patrol* (1934), about a company of men lost in a Middle-Eastern desert, and Ford's last film *7 Women* (1966), about a group of missionary women in China. These films are ultimately studies of familial-like units. Their lead characters make sacrifices to preserve a communitarian spirit, as if to uphold the dominion of the family.

A dominant subtheme in these family-centric films is the individual's role within the family unit, community, or group. This individual is basically male in Ford's world although in a film like *7 Women* it is female (although one could argue that this character, played by Anne Bancroft, is essentially acting like a male or like one of Ford's characteristic male heroes). This male individual, then, is often seen as a hard-headed type but with a soft core. In many Ford films, he is represented by John Wayne, but Henry Fonda, who also appeared in multiple Ford films, was probably a better archetype to convey the softness implicit in Ford's men. He breaks out of the family and embarks on a course of wandering to look for greener pastures on his own. This theme is evident in *The Grapes of Wrath*, *How Green Was My Valley* and *The Quiet Man*, which works as an unbroken trilogy in its portrayal of the family. All three films outline the theme of the individual whose role and status in the family is unstable. Economic conditions determine this instability in *The Grapes of Wrath* and *How Green Was My Valley*. The persona of the individual becomes even more unstable due to some emotional trauma even when he has achieved a measure of success on his own, as in *The Quiet Man*. The hero in *The Quiet Man* seeks personal and spiritual stability by reestablishing himself within the community and by marrying and setting up his own family, but not before settling disputes with his bride and *her* family.

The trilogy therefore supports a theme of how an individual is compelled to leave the family and to strike out on his own. Nevertheless, as he does so, he begins to yearn for the family and its sense of belonging. A counter-compulsion takes place within this individual that sees him return to the family. *The Grapes of Wrath* begins with the image of Tom Joad (played by Henry Fonda) who returns to his family after serving time in jail (Figure 9.1).

The rest of the film shows Tom unable to sustain his longing for home and settle down as a normal family man. In the end, he leaves again. The family itself is always on the move, the narrative detailing the migration of families from Oklahoma to California during the Great Depression. Thus, Tom Joad's

Figure 9.1 The return of Tom Joad.
The Grapes of Wrath, Producer: Darryl F. Zanuck.

departure does not seem as tragic as it would be in normal circumstances. At the end of the film, Ma Joad makes a valedictory speech which seems to regard the family more optimistically: "We're the people that live. They can't wipe us out. They can't lick us. And we'll go on forever . . . cause we're the people!" This speech, Vivian Sobchack tells us, is "less an assertion of social consciousness than of the indomitability of the family," and I would agree.[3] Sobchack's point was that Ford was less interested in the sociopolitical aspects of John Steinbeck's novel *The Grapes of Wrath* and that he was more family-oriented than socially committed. The novel was about proletarian class conflict in America of the Depression era, but Ford was more into crafting his own personal vision of the Joad family "as the basic unit of community" rather than, as Steinbeck has emphasized it, "a family of Man."[4] Ford's vision of the family was inevitably romanticized, lacking interest "in the specificity of history and politics and social problems."[5] However, in Ford's hands, the concept of the family exerts the sort of appeal that most Asians can easily empathize with—familial relationships, the attachments of sons and daughters to the parents, the family as a force and a unit that remains steadfast and permanent while members may come and go.

Where the family remains indomitable in Ford's vision, an individual who leaves, such as Tom Joad at the end of *The Grapes of Wrath*, is fundamentally committed to the family even though he acts on his compulsion to wander. It is probably significant that through most of the film, Tom attaches himself most to his mother. Tom's love for his mother attests to the Daoist feminine-cum-maternal principle contained in the *Daodejing*: "The origin of the world is its mother"; and this focus on the mother-son relationship in the film underlines its next principle "Understand the mother and you understand the child."[6] *The Grapes of Wrath* is one of Ford's family films that centers on the mother figure. Here she is practically the head of the family, the moral center, continuing a theme already established in Ford's previous films such as *Four Sons* (1928), and *Pilgrimage* (1933), illustrating Jim Kitses's comment that in Ford, "Men may act in history but it is through women and the family that they are connected to the human chain of life."[7] Thus, the family, through the figure of Ma Joad, remains constant and seemingly indestructible (Figure 9.2).

Ford's vision of the family is not a simplistic one. In Ford, the family can be as tragic as it is life sustaining. Ford, in fact, does not flinch from destroying

Figure 9.2 Tom Joad and his family.
The Grapes of Wrath, Producer: Darryl F. Zanuck.

his families. The sons wander away and the father dies, as in *How Green Was My Valley*. The return to the family does not mark a closure, as we see in *The Grapes of Wrath* and in *The Searchers*, both films beginning with a return to the family and ending with a departing, thus sharing a structural similarity. I mention *The Searchers* in order that we might see a difference in Ford's comprehensive vision of the family through his approaches to the Western genre and the non-Western. Though the family remains fundamental in the Westerns, it seems much more fragile as "the basic unit that sustained the individual."[8] The Westerns appear to take a more tragic view of the individual. *The Searchers* shows the individualistic hero's family destroyed. This tragedy of the individual in the Western may be attributed to the fact that Ford often portrays this type as one of the "men without women," a point made by Kitses and we should be reminded of his previous point that it is through women and the family that men are connected to "the human chain of life."[9] Thus, in *The Quiet Man*, a work that is as joyous as *The Searchers* is tragic, the individual male, Sean Thornton (played by John Wayne), finds happiness at last through his union with a woman Mary Kate Danaher (played by Maureen O'Hara) and his reversion to the family. Perhaps uncharacteristic for Ford, the individualistic hero of *The Quiet Man* does find closure in the family.

Ford rubs in the tragic theme of the Western man without a woman in *The Man Who Shot Liberty Valance* where Tom Doniphon (again played by John Wayne) goes to seed as the ultimate man without a woman, despite his best efforts to court and marry the woman he loves, Hallie (played by Vera Miles). He loses Hallie to Ransom Stoddard (played by James Stewart), the dude lawyer. Tom then retreats to a life of lonely decline after accepting that it is his destiny to help bring progress to the Wild West at the cost of sacrificing his love. This tragic dimension in Ford seems reserved for the Westerns or at least, the latter ones where Ford was effectively deconstructing the genre. However, he was trying to show how the family and society are inevitably connected, the family as the basic unit of society. Ford's Westerns reveal how a social unit must eventually evolve into a nation (the West becoming part of the United States as a modern nation state), and in this way, we might say that Ford was a historian of the family's evolution into the modern state. His films are political to the extent that they promote the family as American ideology. They are pertinent today in the context of a global Hollywood history influencing the social viewpoints of Asian societies—and they were pertinent back in the 1950s during the Cold War.

Ford's films, particularly his Westerns, have been located within the Cold War matrix of American foreign policy utilizing Hollywood films as instruments of soft power against communist influence from the late 1940s onward. Stanley Corkin and J. Hoberman have both written books to assess Ford's Westerns as Cold War vehicles emitting American values.[10] Generally, as Corkin states, Westerns "show the frontier as a place where the American ethos of the individual could be articulated and then recontained in a social structure that offered a moral order based on postwar U.S. assumptions regarding the nature of the world and the terms of Cold War international relations."[11] Ford's focus on the family is an important component of this Cold War effort. With a major part of the Cold War theater being in Asia, the family, occupying the center of Ford's films in both his Westerns and non-Westerns, serves as an important plank of the American foreign policy strategy. In this strategy, the family becomes an American "value" that could appeal to Asian audiences. This American value is framed more along the line of political conservatism, and it is no accident that conservative family values was the ideology behind the production company named Asia Pictures, established in Hong Kong in

1953, with CIA funding.¹² Asia Pictures functioned as a conservative bulwark against left wing and Communist ideology in Hong Kong and Southeast Asia.

Ford's family and Asian values

I have emphasized the family thus far because it is the one component of Ford's themes that can conspicuously and strongly link the director with Eastern values and sensibility. A conventional description of Asian culture is that life revolves around the family and that it functions as the microcosm of nations throughout Asia. The family is "a cornerstone of social order and an integral part of the centralised state system" in East Asian Confucian societies.¹³ Asian countries are highly family-centric despite the waves of industrialization and modernization. A dual track approach has developed in the modern transformation of the family. State power remains strong, but in the private sphere, "traditional norms and practices still define familial relations, and the family remains an active and effective regulator of the claims and expectations of its own members."¹⁴ This is not to say that the family unit is unaffected by modernity. What is more to the point is how it changes as underdeveloped nations react to the imperative of modernity and how that change casts an impact on nations that are developed.

Ford's family-centric films provide a mirror to Asian societies in cataloging some of this change. Even in America, "modernity threatens the personal quality of life and the closeness of familial relationships," and the family "has been under particularly intense pressure," according to Anne R. Pierce.¹⁵ Pierce's argument is that the family's development is obviously central to Ford. After all, his films show how the United States evolves from family unit to statehood, best demonstrated by *The Man Who Shot Liberty Valance* where the metaphor is that of an evolution from underdeveloped desert to developed garden. The film may actually work as a Confucian thesis of social order, where the character of Ransom Stoddard (James Stewart) takes on the guise of a Confucian scholar-cum-lawyer preaching the virtues of civilian law and order and participation in statehood in a primitive Western town. Its justification of family and the state (a very Confucian concept) is now impressed in the minds of viewers through the famous line "Print the legend."

Ford's Westerns detail the legendary aspects of the family's evolution into the modern state. There is a tendency in the majority, if not all, of these works from *Stagecoach* (1939) onward (*Stagecoach* being his first sound Western) to display a tragic outlook on the family's station out West, which somehow makes the concept of the family more solemn and noble. The family takes on a legendary aura as both institution and concept. *Fort Apache* seems exemplary in this regard, but one could also think of *The Searchers*. We may equate Ford's family out West with the Confucian family in the frontier kingdoms and all its preoccupations with social and state order while retaining its private nature of filial devotion between parents and children. Ford's Westerns may be seen as the most basic Confucian tracts of family and state in the American cinema, showing how the modern American state was fundamentally established from its Western development. (This is a basic theme of most Westerns.) Ford's family dramas in the Western genre are also the equivalents of the family dramas of the Japanese director Ozu Yasujiro, which emit a feeling of resignation and *mono no aware* (deep pathos and sad acceptance of things passing). *The Man Who Shot Liberty Valance* is, of all Ford's films, the one most suffused with *mono no aware*.

In the non-Western "family trilogy" that I have proposed above, the films function to denote how the family develops in the private sphere. Ford's families function in the same traditional ways as in Asian societies. *How Green Was My Valley* depicts how the patriarch exerts an active regulatory role over members of the family, which is very Asian. *How Green Was My Valley* is the most family-centric of the three films in its affirmation of traditional family values centered on the patriarch.[16] The individual does not stand out as in *The Grapes of Wrath* and *The Quiet Man*. However, the film depicts sons arguing with the father as a sign of incipient individualism. Tag Gallagher tells us that the movie is about "psychosis and the dialectics of individuality within family and social change."[17] The point about psychosis is exaggerated but the point about the dialectics of individuality is on the mark. The sons defy the father because of political division based on economic factors, and thus they go against the expectation of filial obeisance to the father.[18] Filial devotion remains nevertheless intrinsic in their behavior. The opposition to the father therefore works out as a dialectical engagement with the notion of filial duty.

Ford is unsparing in his vision of a family torn by division, and this is perhaps to his credit, but Ford does not deny the prominence of the family and its ethical significance. One could argue that Ford is romanticizing the family since his vision of the family is really limited to that of Huw Morgan as a child. To Tag Gallagher, "even Huw's family is a failure for it cannot tolerate discussion, and communication within it is severely circumscribed by patriarchal absolutism."[19] This is liberal reductionism. A closer viewing of the patriarch, as he is played by Donald Crisp, will reveal that he is not as absolutist as he seems and that the sons are rebellious not because of his perceived "absolutism." The father shows a measure of flexibility in interpreting his patriarchal authority, as when he calls his sons off the table for not showing good manners rather than for questioning his authority. Such flexibility of patriarchal authority is ethical in its own right, and it is a vanishing power. (Once the state and the law take over from patriarchal authority, such flexibility will no longer be operative;[20] Figure 9.3.)

The role of the individual within the family unit is probably a drama as much played out in Asian families as societies undergo modernization and industrialization. Change is of course implicit. Economic factors determine whether family members will remain or depart to find jobs elsewhere. This is

Figure 9.3 The patriarch and his family.
How Green Was My Valley, Producer: Darryl F. Zanuck.

evident in *How Green Was My Valley* where points in the narrative touch on sons leaving for America and elsewhere as economic migrants. (The film is set in a Welsh mining town.) This would strike chords in millions of Chinese families whose sons have migrated to the United States and elsewhere for economic reasons. The dispute between sons and father is a strand of the film's drama that is also very pertinent to modern Chinese families as an effect of how modernity and politics have an impact on traditional ways and the conservatism of the patriarch. Gallagher's point about the "dialectics of individuality" is as much an outcome that is pertinent to how the Chinese family has developed in more recent times as it is the result of the family in Wales. However, while there is change, the family itself has remained resilient and this is Ford's didactic message. Ford shows the traditional family changing as its members leave and the father dies. Ford catalogs this change while remaining nostalgic about the traditional form of the family. This nostalgia in itself is not without social and political significance.

The family as a sphere of nostalgia and yearning retains its imprint on the memories of individuals as development and modernization becomes overpowering forces compelling one to leave home and families to dissolve. *How Green Was My Valley* unfolds as a narrative told by the adult Huw Morgan who, as the film opens, is packing his belongings to leave the valley. The film constitutes the memory of Huw and, at times, it seems like a dream, particularly in the first section of the film showing the family united and working together harmoniously. "Who shall say what is real and what is not?" says Huw, immediately conveying an Eastern sense of life as an illusionary flow of sensations. Ford plays on this illusionary sense of the family by evoking the pathos and bathos of family life. Human feelings and emotions take precedence, conveying the ethical values of the family. Thus, the effect Ford achieves is an experience of family morality. It is the experience that counts. The portrait of the family is a positive collection of rituals, ceremony, and music, all of which Confucius would have certainly appreciated. The illusionary contingency of the family makes such a portrait even more valuable, as does its pastoral or country setting. *How Green Was My Valley* is relevant in Asian or Eastern contexts even as countries become more urbanized. Indeed, for some governments in Asia today, there is a stronger emphasis on family values as well as rural-village community values as modernization proceeds apace. The divide between urban and rural is a subtheme of modernization whereby rural values are valued over the urban. Increasingly, in Asia, "the idea of a countryside that acts as a repository of certain conservative cultural and moral values, in contradistinction to the chaotic liberal relativism of the city" is a refrain of the modern condition.[21] This theme is far from absent in the American cinema and the appeal of Ford's Westerns lies in the exposition of such a theme as history—a history shared between the West and the East in terms of modernization and rapid economic development. In Ford's Westerns, the Western hinterland is the historical repository of moral values, with the accent on the family and the community.

Ford's Irish other personality

Ford rearticulates the pastoral theme in *The Quiet Man*. The film is set in Ireland, Ford's ancestral home country but not the country of his birth. Though born in the United States, Ford took his Irish ancestry seriously and treated it in his films either as a prominent motif in a series of works, including his Westerns, or as a running motif throughout his oeuvre. This Irish identity in Ford is key to how we might identify Ford in Eastern terms. Jim Kitses has explained that Ford had grown up "with the sense of cultural dislocation many ethnicities experienced in a new polyglot nation."

> The Irish were frequently stereotyped as cartoon figures sustained by brawling and alcohol, an image that Ford himself, together with his characters, both variously reinforced and challenged. . . . Reflecting his own upbringing, the cornerstone of the world of the films was their powerful sense of family, the nourishing roots of the clan, the importance of home, the pain of exclusion.[22]

Kitses's words would more or less resonate with Asian immigrants. A Chinese immigrant, for example, would find the idea of family, the clan, the home most empathetic. I therefore see Ford's Irish identity as an indicator of his outsider mentality and cultural background corresponding with the Eastern Asian perspective with which we are trying to interpret Ford. Some critics hold Ford's portrayal of Irishness against him. For example, Jack Morgan rails against Victor McLaglen's portrayal of the Irish sergeant in the three Cavalry films, dismissing the character as a "crude ethnic caricature."[23] Morgan proclaims that Ford's films "evidence a kind of vestigial colonialist mindset, a trace of racial self-contempt going oddly hand in hand with a maudlin Irish boosterism."[24] *The Quiet Man* is probably Ford's most representative work in relation to his Irish background, and it too has been criticized as portraying stereotypes. From my Eastern viewpoint, I consider the film a major work of self-identification by an American director with an ancestral culture. It tells the story of Sean Thornton, an American citizen who returns to his land of birth to settle in his home village and marry a local Irish girl. Thornton has nostalgia for country and home. If we project Ford into his character, we sense this nostalgia even more profoundly. Unlike his character, Ford was born in America but, obviously, he retains psychic connections with Ireland. Ford has exploited his Irish identity to bolster his storytelling. Here, we trust both the artist and the tale. *The Quiet Man* is hardly ambivalent about the Irish identity in Ford, and I tend to see it as a rather radical turning point for Ford inasmuch as he appears to backtrack on his American identity by regressing to a cultural identity based on a country that was not his birthplace. At the same time, it also appears to negate modern values and looks back fondly to idyllic, even imaginary, values of an almost premodern society.

The Quiet Man is the kind of work that an ethnic Chinese director living in the United States or a diasporic Chinese community elsewhere (e.g., in a Southeast Asian country) could have made about China. The story of *The Quiet Man* is quite Eastern in its abstract romantic quality of clan roots, ancestral home, and family. Ford's Ireland is the very model of what diasporic Chinese would call "Tangshan" (the name usually given to China by older Chinese immigrants while younger migrants might call China by its proper name, Zhongguo). Sean Thornton also represents the Chinese immigrant who returns to his ancestral land and yearns for the sense of community and a common social identity. Thornton's anguish over his American identity, symbolized by his trauma over killing an opponent in a boxing match, may well be the kind of anguish suffered by Chinese immigrants, though obviously the causes of anguish may differ. Thornton seeks to assuage his trauma by reintegrating himself with a more natural world (his rustic family home), a thought that would occur to Chinese as a Daoist sense of naturalization.

That Thornton goes home to Ireland to marry a local village girl is something a Chinese immigrant might do on his return to his ancestral village—and it would be more pertinent for him to do so due to historic discriminatory legislation passed by Congress stopping Chinese women from migrating to America (the Page Act of 1875). Like Thornton, he would submit to the custom of matchmaking and then to conduct courtship under the watchful eyes of the marriage broker. He too may encounter initial reservations from the village inhabitants and problems with the girl's family over custom and rituals. He may be too liberal for his own good while the bride's family may want to stick to ceremony and custom. He might then confront the elder over the matter of a dowry after much to-and-fro concerning his willingness to fight and the growing feeling that he might be a coward. To prove himself, he eventually does fight (done in kung fu style), and finally, all would be resolved on the old proverb, "Only through fighting can two people truly know each other" (*buda bu xiangshi*). *The Quiet Man* could be rebranded Ford's Chinese immigrant experience. A Chinese viewer could see it as a narrative based on a common experience of family, home, and country.

In an essay entitled, "What *The Quiet Man* Said: Shifting Contexts and the Polysemy of the Text," Joseph Bierman writes, "Through shifts in the contexts that each viewer brings to the viewing experience, different meanings may be created from these common narrative events."[25] Bierman discusses *The Quiet Man* from the Irish perspective in an effort to reassess the film as a work that is not stereotypical and simplistically romantic. "*The Quiet Man*'s inclusion of Irish myths and stereotypes enables the director to question the dynamics by which they operate and the realities they purport to reflect."[26] I have tried to show that Ford's inclusion of Irish myths and stereotypes is really a method of universalizing a certain immigrant experience. Common grounds of family, home, and national or ethnic identity constitute the dynamics by which such myths and stereotypes operate. Ford's Irish identity is manifestly central to the dynamics. It is the one catalytic factor. Bierman denotes certain contexts in which Irish Americans could view the film much more meaningfully. For example, he mentions the economic migration to America brought on by the great famine from 1845 to 1852, and the political struggles in the Irish homeland. All these contexts provide the "nostalgic/romantic and political/economic meanings of the film."[27] Such contexts and conditions are probably generic to the immigrant narrative experienced by Chinese and other Asians who would probably respond to *The Quiet Man* in much the same way as an Irish-American viewer. A Chinese immigrant would surely feel the same nostalgia for home, his migration also brought about by economic realities, and most likely also compelled by political struggles back home (revolution against the Qing, rampant warlordism, and the civil war between the Nationalists and the Communists throughout the first half of the twentieth century).

Bierman asserts that although content and medium remain constant, "differing localized experiences and expectations of the medium may bring about shifts in the context portion of the mosaic."[28] He concludes that each viewer can construct his or her own context through "interaction with numerous diffuse texts" that are found in the film.[29] Following this assertion, Ford's film is open to interpretations. Bierman, however, does not expand on how the shifts of contexts might occur and from whose perspectives. His essay still places *The Quiet Man* firmly within the historical, social, and political contexts of Ireland, which is, of course, understandable. Presumably, Irish Americans and Irish people everywhere are the target audience of Ford's film. How other cultures interpret the film is something that has to be tested. If *The Quiet Man* is as polysemic as Bierman claims it is, it could probably withstand all kinds of cultural interpretation. What is interesting is that this potential multiculturalism predicates itself on the factor of Irish identity while Ford himself is American in nationality.

Knowing the self, knowing the other

Perhaps the most crucial aspect about Ford's Irish identity is that it represents a self-reflexive nature in Ford, the man and the artist. Furthermore, Ford employs this identity and ancestry to "read" other cultures and stories, projecting self into the Other. Ford used it to establish his working relationship with the Indians in his Westerns and the Indians made him a blood brother of various nations. He said the following:

> Perhaps it's my Irish atavism, my sense of reality, of the beauty of clans, in contrast to the modern world, the masses, the collective irresponsibility.

> Who better than an Irishman could understand the Indians, while still being stirred by the tales of the US Cavalry? We were on both sides of the epic.[30]

As best he could (which might not have been enough for some critics), Ford presented the Indian perspective in several Westerns, including *Fort Apache* and most of all *Cheyenne Autumn* (1964), his last Western and swansong to the genre. Even in *The Searchers*, the Indian Chief Scar (played by Henry Brandon) has a few scenes where he forcefully argues his side of things. *The Searchers*, in fact, has an interesting focus on the Indian that is definitely schizoid and paranoid, as manifested in the psychopathological character of John Wayne's Ethan Edwards. Ethan shows expertise in knowing the Indian (the Comanche subgroup Nawycha) and their custom and rituals while harboring a genocidal hatred toward them. The scene where he shoots out the eyes of a dead Comanche brave, "deriving a barbaric satisfaction in frustrating the Comanche belief in a passage to an afterlife," strikingly illustrates Ethan's behavior:

> For a man who continually interrupts sacred ceremonies among the settlers and treats religion with nothing but contempt, Ethan's conduct here seems strange, as if he actually believed in the religion of his enemies, rather than that of his family and the settler community. Of course, he does not, but his desire to avenge the forces inimical to society demands that he go so far as to understand Comanche beliefs and treat them more seriously than any of the other settlers do.[31]

The point to emphasize is that Ethan, while clearly quite deranged in his behavior, exhibits strategic knowledge of his enemy on the Chinese principle of "know thy self, know thy other" (*zhiji zhibi*), from Sun Zi's *The Art of War*. The film demonstrates Ford's knowledge of the Indian and his own internal self as represented by his character Ethan Edwards. Ford, however, portrays Ethan in a very complex fashion, and it may be said that Ethan is always on the verge of not knowing himself. Could we say the same of Ford? Perhaps. Yet it is noteworthy that he shows knowledge of the Other, even allowing for some measure of self-identification with the Other. Ford shows the Indians living "by principles that are certainly social, and many of their customs are noble," as J. David Alvis and John E. Alvis point out. "We observe sufficient indications of their distinctive practices to conclude that Ford credits the Indians with an integral way of life, which we today call a culture."[32] Ford used his Irish identity to reach out to an alien Other by identifying his own Irishness as itself an Other. This quality of projecting an Other is a remarkable factor in his work. In *The Searchers* it manifests as a paranoid and psychopathological attitude, whereas in other films he approaches a somewhat more objective and placid manner. (The two major works in this regard are *Sergeant Rutledge* [1960], about black cavalrymen, and *Cheyenne Autumn*.) This ability of Ford to project Otherness is unique among classical directors in the American cinema.

On *The Grapes of Wrath*, Ford had said that the story appealed to him because it reminded him of the Irish famine "when they threw the people off the land and left them wandering on the roads to starve." It was "part of my Irish tradition. . . . I liked the idea of this family going out and trying to find their way in the world."[33] *The Grapes of Wrath* was also a story of internal migration, about working migrants that is therefore a part of the immigrant experience. Again, a Chinese immigrant could certainly empathize with such an experience. Indeed, the story of *The Grapes of Wrath* could be a story of Chinese migrant workers themselves. In today's globalized world, the story could well be a story of any number of Asian migrant workers employed anywhere. In terms of character, Tom Joad would represent any one of the oppressed workers of the world. Ford probably identified with Tom Joad through his Irish identity, and this character would constitute the Other in his "Irish tradition." The identification of Ford with the Other projects onto a character who carries a certain sense of social concern. Tom Joad is a socializing animal rather than the rugged loner-individual. This is an Eastern trait that comes across from Ford's Other projection, making Tom Joad somewhat more special than Ford's other individualistic heroes. Though he leaves the family at the end, Tom gives a "socialistic" speech to justify his departure—his "I'll be everywhere" valediction. While prefaced by an ostensibly Christian undertone, the speech is quite Eastern in spirit (a sort of Daoist essentialism). Tom says he will become "the one big soul that belongs to everybody"; "I'll be all around in the dark; I'll be everywhere, wherever you can look":

> Wherever there's a fight so hungry people can eat, I'll be there. Wherever there's a cop beating up a guy, I'll be there. I'll be in the way guys yell when they are mad. I'll be in the way kids laugh when they're hungry and they

know supper's ready, and when the people are eatin' the stuff they raise and livin' in the houses they build, I'll be there too.[34]

The idea that Tom leaves at the end of *The Grapes of Wrath* as one of Ford's characteristic Western "individuals" is attributed by some critics to his insecurity, his psychopathology. Jim Sanderson advances the thesis that most of Ford's characters have "psychopathic traits" but that Ford builds on a literary tradition of American Romanticism that features such characters.[35] I noted before that there was a structural similarity between *The Grapes of Wrath* and *The Searchers*: the two lead characters return to the family and depart from the family and this indicates that both characters share the deep "psychopathic traits" of American tradition, as Sanderson has put forward. In this tradition,

> The psychopath has a chance to work "backward" through his psychological (and/or sexual) handicaps and thus cure himself and see a reality unobstructed by perceptions other than his own. He can grow and learn. If he lives, he can save himself and perhaps the world.

It would be significant, then, to note that Tom Joad and Ethan Edwards are native-born Americans and supposedly more prone to being "psychopathic." From an Eastern perspective, such individuals go through inner struggles about self and Other. In Daoist thought, this is a struggle for authentic being: "If there is no Other, there is no self" (*fei bi wu wo*), says Zhuang Zi.[36] Tom and Ethan also struggle to fit into society. *The Quiet Man* is interesting in that while its hero is a classic embodiment of both kinds of struggles, the film presents something of a break in that it has a happy resolution. Sean Thornton displays "psychopathic traits" as an American citizen. He is also Irish and returns to Ireland, apparently to get away from his "psychopathic" past. In Ireland, he finds a sense of community and establishes a family, although not before undergoing trials and tribulations. *The Quiet Man* emits an ideal and pacifying sense of identity, an Other-identification unproblematically manifested. In films like *The Grapes of Wrath* and *The Searchers* where there is a turning away from the home and the family at the end, Ford shows how his characters continue to search for an ideal identity and existence in life. This seems critical of the American identity, and by extension, the American polity, and it would be Ford's ultimate contradiction as an American artist. Kitses points out that Ford "was on both sides of the issue," trying to "serve the needs of the American imagination both in providing a bright romantic vision as well as to debunk it."[37]

Kitses avows that Ford showed an "allegiance to contradictory perspectives and dichotomous realities."[38] In Chinese philosophy, the yin and the yang principle approximates Ford's contradictory perspectives and dichotomous realities. In Chinese thought, the accent is on harmony, one side complementing the other in a union, rather than on contradiction or dichotomy. On the other hand, Ford, who was a military man, may well be applying Sun Zi's principle of *zhiji zhibi*, on his own work and life. There are inherent contradictions that arise. Thus, on the family, we see Ford covering contradictory angles from life affirming to life destroying. There are shifts from the self (*ji*) to the Other (*bi*). *The Searchers* is a tale about Ethan's family and about Chief Scar's family. The character of Debbie, Ethan's niece abducted by Scar, interconnects the families. (She has become his squaw.) The destruction of both her families is a mark of how the contradictions are unresolvable although Debbie alone survives. Ford shows the self (*ji*) in the form of Ethan Edwards turning away from the home at the end, probably in the realization that there is an unbearable agony in the knowledge of the self. Ethan is fated to wander in the hope of finding solace in the Way (*dao*). This is a tragedy in that so much violence was committed, and no one can hold Ethan accountable. However, *The Searchers* is a film that questions the individual self. From a Daoist perspective, the redemption of Ethan is possible if there is an acknowledgment of self as the pure self, one in tune with the *dao*. The wandering is the key, for in wandering, the individual experiences a freedom that brings him closer to nature and the "ceaseless self-emergence of life."[39]

Ford's contradictory perspectives often show up in his films as shifts of moods in the flow of life. *The Grapes of Wrath* is exemplary in this regard. As a family film, it carries all kinds of moods. One might call it a tragic film at heart or at its base, but Ford covers a range of moods, showing people close to their roots and close to the soil, as has seldom been seen in the American cinema.[40] Grandpa (played by Charley Grapewin) is essentially a comic figure who becomes tragi-comic as he dies. Al Joad (played by O. Z. Whitehead) has comic overtones as a character who then offers a contrast to Tom Joad, who has tragic overtones. Ma Joad (Jane Darwell) offers compassion, Pa Joad (Russell Simpson) a sense of frailty and weakness, the children innocence and perhaps indifference to suffering, Rosasharn a mixture of melancholy and desperate hope. While Tom Joad is the lead character, the family often subsumes him and therefore his tendency toward the tragic is never predominant.

Ford not only shows the family close to nature but also shows them responding to events and is essentially carried along by situations, a very Daoist sensibility. Ford is like a sage in his wisdom of understanding human nature in this way. In *The Grapes of Wrath*, he does achieve a harmony of sorts, the harmony of the yin and the yang in its illustrations of a variety of moods and situations. The Chinese saying *beihuan lihe* (joy and sorrow parting and meeting) applies to Ford in spades. A film like *The Grapes of Wrath* expresses *beihuan lihe* in rather controlled modulations. In a film like *The Searchers*, the shifts between joy and sorrow are quite drastically presented, sometimes separately, sometimes intermingling (an example might be those scenes involving Look, Martin's Indian squaw), and it becomes even cruder in later works like *Two Rode Together* (1961) and *Cheyenne Autumn* where we see comic interludes intruding into highly dramatic situations.[41] Yet, Ford understands that life is not just one or the other. There is a sense that Ford adjusts his sensibility to uncover the potential of human behavior in any situation. If a scene calls for tragedy, Ford trains his eye on the tragic, often to the poetic heights, and if there is comic potential, Ford mines it unashamedly.

Death and the family

Ford's tendency to show death further illustrates his sageness, and we might say this is his most Asian quality. Jim Kitses comments that *How Green Was My Valley* "describes the destruction of community and family, and culminates in the death of its patriarch. But in its closing moment, the film pirouettes to escape the bleakness—'Men like my father cannot die'—and returns to images of the Welsh mining village's bright past."[42] This is a somewhat hackneyed cinematic expression of the metaphysics of death but it is certainly in line with the idea of the family's sanctity and the worship of the patriarch. Indeed, the worship of one's dead parents in Chinese tradition is a custom very much indulged in by Ford in his cinema. *How Green Was My Valley* is very Chinese in this regard, since the whole film is Huw Morgan's remembrance of the dead. A darker aspect of death from Eastern myth seen in Ford concerns the depiction of the God of Death, Yama, seen in the form of Ethan Edwards in *The Searchers*. The representation of Ethan, in Western terms, is as an "epic figure," "the classic wandering hero," and "a mystery figure hovering over the community" (this is how Jim Kitses sees him).[43] However, in Eastern terms, Ethan is a metaphysical representation of death, presented clearly right at the opening. The film begins in darkness and the door opens showing Martha walking to the porch to look at a rider approaching the house. The rider, Ethan, represents death. He is riding forth to bring death and destruction to the family. Everyone in the house, with the exception of the little girl Debbie, will die, and, as the film progresses, Ethan searches for Debbie in order to kill her.

Ethan's countenance in this opening sequence already suggests that something is not quite right with the character. His look and his awkward gestures and movements imply that he is something of a ghost himself. Actually, he is Yama, the bringer of death. This metaphysical depiction of a death figure in the Western is not strange, of course. He actually takes a more or less benign form as the eponymous character of George Stevens's *Shane* (1953), for example (Yama can be both benign and malign), and in a much later work such as Sergio Leone's *Once Upon a Time in the West* (1969) where he manifests as the character of Harmonica (played by Charles Bronson). Ford portrays the Yama figure as a destroyer of the family and this is his most uncompromising expression of the inevitable in his cinema. Though Ethan finally does not kill Debbie, we still cannot escape the touch of the perverse in his exemption of death for Debbie. This may be a small mercy for Debbie for her life could be excruciating in a symbolic order where racism and prejudice still reign.

The Searchers is arguably Ford's darkest film about the family and one could ask why Ford perpetrated this unrelentingly bleak vision. An answer lies in Ford's self-reflexive nature and the depth he brings it to. The film's moral center shifts from the family to the individual. The story is about a wanderer who is unable to lose his self in nature, forever pulled back into the life of the social world—its politics, prejudices, and tragedies. Ford gives us a discourse on the individual's relationship with the family and the role the family plays in the dialectic between self and Other. *The Searchers* is a self-reflexive Western par excellence, allegorically rich yet also functioning as a metaphysical figure of thought in its totality. Ethan is both a metaphor of death and a human character caught in an inner struggle of knowing the self and knowing the Other. The struggle takes the form of an unending journey, and in one of his stops, Ethan implicates his own family. Death and the family are interconnected, and though it seems tragic, it also suggests a complementarity between nature and sociality. Ethan's wandering is to find his own nature, which appears not to fit into the sociality of the family, but Ford's dialectical vision also implies a complementarity between Ethan and the family. Aesthetically, Ford's sympathy lies with the family. The film begins in the enclosure of the home (which opens up to tragedy) and it ends with this same enclosure.

Like the Confucian obsession with death and the family, Ford's films deal with both in a commonplace manner. Ritual and communication interconnect death and the family. Ford's films are marked with rituals of death. Frequently seen in his films are funerals. His characters talk to the dead and worship them in their own way. Nathan Brittles in *She Wore a Yellow Ribbon* talks to his dead wife in the cemetery. *The Man Who Shot Liberty Valance* is, basically, a film about talking to the dead (Ransom Stoddard talking to the dead Tom Doniphon). In *The Last Hurrah* (1958), the hero, an Irish mayor in a New England town, played by Spencer Tracy, speaks to a portrait of his dead wife. The film is rather like a self-tribute, showing his last campaign for mayor, which he loses, and, at the end, he suffers a heart attack and dies. It becomes, finally, a paean to his own death. Death is everywhere treated in a ritualistic fashion. There is a scene showing the mayor visiting a wake of one of his dead constituents during the campaign, and he walks around the casket, his fingers knocking on the wood as if to wake up the dead man, or to recall him from his transference to the realm of the dead. This detail shows Ford in his element, comfortable with death, suggesting an Eastern sense that death is a transcendence of life and the transformation of things, and that taking care of the dead is a reflection of taking care of the living.

In conclusion, Ford's films about the family may today bring more attention to traditional values not least in Asia where the family is the pillar of societies in transformation. Economic and political reform and modernization of traditional societies entail a new set of values. They imply a criticism of traditional beliefs and morality, how they seem oppressive and out of tune with the modern world. Ford's films show both affirmation and implied criticism of family values, and, unlikely as it seems because Ford's films are so American, they are opportune to our present world as East and West become more interconnected. Perhaps the most Eastern quality about Ford is that his films are introspective and holistic in nature. His spare and simple style, his affinity with landscape and nature, is key to its Eastern quality. Finally, Ford's films portray aspects of the family which seem very Eastern in sensibility and moral values particularly in relation to Asian societies today. This free and natural congruence with the East makes Ford the original Eastern spirit man (*shen ren*) in the American cinema.

Notes

1 Kitses, *Horizons West*, p. 32.
2 See the last chapter in my book *Eastern Westerns, Film and Genre Inside and Outside of Hollywood* (London and New York: Routledge, 2017).
3 Vivian Sobchack, "*The Grapes of Wrath* (1940): Thematic Emphasis through Visual Style," *American Quarterly*, 31 (5), 1979, p. 615. The final scene was in fact not Ford's original ending (his preferred ending was the departure of Tom Joad). Darryl F. Zanuck added and shot the whole scene of Ma Joad's speech. See Joseph McBride, *Searching for John Ford* (New York: St. Martin's Griffin, 2003), p. 313.
4 Sobchack, "*The Grapes of Wrath*," p. 615.
5 Ibid.
6 From chapter 52 of the *Daodejing*. The English translation is from the online source http://gj.zdic.net/archive.php?aid=12881 (accessed February 3, 2017).
7 Kitses, *Horizons West*, p. 30.
8 Ibid.
9 Ibid.
10 Stanley Corkin, *Cowboys as Cold Warriors: The Western and U.S. History* (Philadelphia, PA: Temple University Press, 2004), and J. Hoberman, *An Army of Phantoms: American Movies and the Making of the Cold War* (New York and London: The New Press, 2011).
11 Corkin, *Cowboys as Cold Warriors*, p. 49.
12 For more on Asia Pictures, see Charles Leary, "The Most Careful Arrangements for a Careful Fiction: A Short History of Asia Pictures," *Inter-Asia Cultural Studies*, 13 (4), 2012, pp. 548–58. See also Sangjoon Lee, "Creating an Anti-Communist Motion Picture Producers Network in Asia: The Asia Foundation,

Asia Pictures, and the Korean Motion Picture Cultural Association," *Historical Journal of Film, Radio and Television*, March 2016 (online), pp. 1–22.

13 Xiaoming Huang, "Crafting the Modern State: Religion, Family and Military in Japan, China and Korea," in M. P. Amineh (ed.), *State, Society and International Relations in Asia* (Amsterdam: Amsterdam University Press, 2010), p. 39.

14 Ibid., p. 44.

15 Anne R. Pierce, "Modernity and the Destruction of Boundaries: John Ford's *The Grapes of Wrath*," in S. A. Pearson, Jr. (ed.), *Print the Legend: Politics, Culture, and Civic Virtue in the Films of John Ford* (Lanham, MD: Lexington Books, 2009), p. 60.

16 The emphasis on the family apparently came from the film's producer Darryl Zanuck who wanted to play down the more political aspects of labor strife in the story. Ford "fully embraced the plot of the family's dispersal and decline," according to Lea Jacobs. See Lea Jacobs, "Making John Ford's *How Green Was My Valley*," *Film History*, 28 (2), 2016, p. 58. Ford was not the original director of *How Green Was My Valley*. He replaced William Wyler, dismissed by Zanuck for long delays and much script revisions in the preproduction phase.

17 Tag Gallagher, *John Ford, The Man and His Films* (Berkeley: University of California Press, 1986), p. 199.

18 Filial devotion to the father is one of the five ethical relationships in Chinese society: the others are between sovereign and official, brothers, husband and wife, and friends.

19 Gallagher, *John Ford, The Man and His Films*, p. 188.

20 In present times, the decline of the family in the West has also meant the decline of the authority of the parents. Mark J. Cherry comments that "familial authority is routinely assumed to reach no further than that of trustee of the individual member's best interests and, moreover, as always properly subject to significant state oversight and governmental intervention. As a result, core family relationships are evermore undermined and subject to legal restrictions designed to deflate the significance of, as well as to marginalize the family." See Cherry, "Individually Directed Informed Consent and the Decline of the Family in the West," p. 55.

21 Alfian Bin Sa'at, "Hinterland, Heartland, Home: Affective Topography in Singapore Films," in T. Baumgärtel (ed.), *Southeast Asian Independent Cinema* (Hong Kong: Hong Kong University Press, 2012), p. 37.

22 Kitses, *Horizons West*, p. 32.

23 Jack Morgan, "The Irish in John Ford's Seventh Cavalry Trilogy—Victor McLaglen's Stooge-Irish Caricature," *Melus*, 22 (2), 1997, p. 35.

24 Ibid., p. 34.

25 Joseph Bierman, "What *The Quiet Man* Said: Shifting Contexts and the Polysemy of the Text," *Journal of Film and Video*, 63 (3), 2011, p. 32.
26 Ibid., p. 30.
27 Ibid., p. 33.
28 Ibid., p. 31.
29 Ibid., p. 43.
30 Quoted in McBride, *Searching for John Ford*, p. 291.
31 J. David Alvis and John E. Alvis, "Heroic Virtue and the Limits of Democracy in John Ford's *The Searchers*," *Perspectives on Political Science*, 38 (2), 2009, p. 74.
32 Ibid., p. 71.
33 Quoted in Sobchack, "*The Grapes of Wrath*," p. 615.
34 The film should rightfully have ended with Tom's valedictory speech. Instead, it now ends with a second valediction, namely Ma Joad's "We're the people" speech (Zanuck's added-on ending).
35 Jim Sanderson, "American Romanticism in John Ford's *The Grapes of Wrath*: Horizontalness, Darkness, Christ, and F.D.R.," *Literature Film Quarterly*, 17 (4), 1989, p. 231.
36 Authentic being "has no other, for it is totally Other—like a bell that only rings when it is struck, or a hollow tree that only sounds when the wind blows through it." See Møllgaard, *An Introduction to Daoist Thought*, p. 128.
37 Ibid., p. 41.
38 Ibid., p. 42.
39 Ibid., p. 124.
40 Early in the film, Ford presents a striking image of Muley (played by John Qualen), evicted from his land, squatting down and scooping up the soil with his hands. This image easily conjures up a comparative image of the Asian peasant, and more succinctly the notion of the "pribumi" or "bumiputera," which means "sons of the soil" (the former term is used more in Indonesia and the latter in Malaysia). Both are politically loaded terms used by the respective governments to justify preferential and affirmative action policies to win the support of their indigenous populations.
41 Readers are advised to read my chapter on *The Searchers* in my book *Eastern Westerns* where I deal with these shifts of mood and sentiments in more detail.
42 Kitses, *Horizons West*, pp. 40–41.
43 Ibid., p. 94.

Conclusion

The foregoing chapters, *quod erat demonstrandum*, constitute my case for adopting the Eastern approach. They have demonstrated a sustained application of the Eastern approach on films from the West and their directors. They have attempted to show how Eastern thought and principles have infused the spirit of Western films to attest to the oneness of the cinematic universe. The ultimate purpose of the Eastern approach is to merge the spirits of East and West in the interest of cross-cultural understanding if not transcendence. Whether this book has realized such a feat is up to the reader to decide, and some might argue that it smacks of a self-defeating kind of idealism (or romanticism, if one prefers). Western opinion remains all-powerful, and Eurocentrism is the rule rather than the exception in most academic and journalistic writing on film. For that reason, the project of this book may be regarded by some with bemusement as not merely idiosyncratic self-indulgence but an exercise in futility. It has nevertheless been carried through based on the need of working toward a balance of discourse, or, conversely, the need to redress the very imbalance that plagues the state of world affairs and the intellectual state of film studies—and I will have more to say on this question of balance below. It is obviously a point that presides over the proceedings of this book as the driving impulse for applying the Eastern approach. (In some ways, it may even cast a shadow over the whole book.) Very many film students, even those from Asia or the East, feel that they will never be able to understand film if they do not adopt the current practice and attitude of Western thinking on film. As demonstrated, this book has resolved to take the opposite view. Students will never be able to understand film if they do not adopt an Eastern outlook, an Eastern way of thinking, toward film. The Eastern approach encapsulates the idea and tactic of changing one's ways of observing and analyzing film through Eastern philosophy and concepts, to discern characteristics, motifs, and even cultural elements in films of the West. The book is entirely dedicated to the analysis of major classics of European and Hollywood cinemas. All these films have been observed and examined with my Eastern eyes and considered along Eastern philosophical lines of thought. They have been searched for inscriptions within their narratives that embed the conviction of Eastern ideas, hence allowing for the theoretical analysis and interpretations undertaken here. In broad Eastern terms, I have analyzed and brought out themes of philosophical and religious issues, interpersonal relationships, identity issues, matters of life and death or the cycle of birth and death, the nature of the world as object in opposition to the subjective self, the non-anthropocentric outlook, warrior values and action principles, family problems, filial piety, and social harmony. Thus, through the prism of an Eastern approach, I have sought to revalue and reify a corpus of Western films. I have striven to offer new critical perspectives on the canonical Western directors, who include Robert Bresson, Carl Dreyer, John Ford, Alfred Hitchcock, George Lucas, Leo McCarey, Jean-Pierre Melville, Sam Peckinpah, and Orson Welles, all of whom are considered auteurs of various degrees and all chosen for no particular reason except that their films show a propensity for Eastern content.

That I have focused on auteurs may be a misleading factor in this book, letting the reader to conclude that I have written another auteur study, and it is therefore incumbent upon me to set the record straight in this conclusion. In adopting an Eastern approach, I offer a very different conceptual view of these auteurs. My Eastern analysis is thus far from an exercise in classical auteur study. It is an exercise in deconstructing these respective directors' cultural contexts and their consonant social themes in the interest of cross-cultural interpretations. The films of these directors selected for analysis depend on their capability to evince Eastern content, as I have said earlier. Such content reflects the strength of innovation and the thirst for more philosophical substance in the respective works under study. My analysis can only be considered an auteurial study only because my focus on Eastern content brings out and confirms the status of the directors as auteurs and innovative thinkers. Otherwise, the analyses of their films selected here are based more on culturalist and philosophical ideas, given as cross-cultural platforms for greater interpretations and reevaluations, not specifically on the consistency of auteurist styles, motifs, or themes. In viewing these directors and their films through the Eastern approach, I hold them as models of the "Oriental West" (to use John Hobson's term), creative entities of received Eastern influences. My Eastern approach only brings out the Eastern content already inscribed or implied in the films but which were never made clear and analyzed by previous scholarship. The theoretical thrust of the book is not on the study of auteurs but on a corpus of content that is never brought to light.

Thus the book has given nine chapters to demonstrate the capacity of Western films to be analyzed and interpreted from the receptive point of view of an Eastern outlook on film. It is important to restate that the Eastern approach as it is used in this book gains its distinctive method from being applied to Western film and compared with Western ideas and theories. This is based on the Daoist principle of duality. In *The Book of Balance and Harmony* (*Zhonghe ji*), written by the thirteenth-century Daoist master Li Daochun, who preached the unification of Daoism, Confucianism, and Buddhism, it is stated, "With duality, there is sensing: with sensing, there is pairing of yin and yang in mutual interaction."[1] This approach, then, concerns itself with mutual interaction. To those who seek the redundancy of the approach, it may only be thought of as redundant if there was nothing to set off against it. Then, we might have attained a state of pure balance between East and West, or a state of complete negation of East and West, the concept of oneness that is, in Buddhist philosophy, a state of nonobjectivity. However, this is not the point of the book, for which the current task is a very preliminary exercise of comparing and interpreting. This writer has been drawn into the task on the principle of the Buddhist adage, "If I do not enter Hell, who will?" By and large, scholars in the West are not given to undertake any application of Eastern philosophy or concepts to films of the West, and, basically, they are not expected to. This therefore opens up some ground for scholars (and particularly Asian scholars) to analyze films from a non-West perspective. I have written this book in the hope of offering more pedagogical options for analyzing film. Many students in the West are learning Eastern languages and its cultures to engage the East, cognizant of its rise in present world affairs. Adopting an Eastern approach in analyzing Western films can be part of this learning process and facilitate more understanding of the East and its way of thinking. On the other end of the spectrum, students in the East routinely study Western theory barely recognizing Eastern contributions to the field. An Eastern approach to film studies can suggest how the East can complement the West and herewith I return to the question of balance. Rather than to suggest that the East and the West cannot meet, to use Kipling's saw, it is how the East and the West have met since past times and they have been in constant states of unbalance. The idea or need of balance is intrinsic in the reordering of international relations as multipolar occurrences of the future. The notion of balance, according to *The Book of Balance and Harmony*, is grounded in the center (*zhong*), in which the spirit (*shen*) resides and from where opportunities or potential (*ji*) emerge.[2] Working toward the goal of balance is therefore a compelling reason for writing this book because the world presently is unbalanced. This means that the spirit is nowhere in the center and potential is elusive. Though achieving balance is far from an easy task, our Eastern approach aims to turn and convince minds for such a balance. It does not aim to eradicate Western opinion, which is impossible. In fact, the idea of balance is to preserve Western ideas so that they can be counterpointed with Eastern concepts, motifs, and philosophy. East and West can complement each other, and they may achieve congruence in the form of a balance like the yin and the yang. In terms of film studies, the Eastern approach aims to instill a more comparative form of the study of films into the current stream of practice. A more balanced global outlook should in turn be reflected in film theory and film analysis, consistent with the rise of Asian countries onto the world stage. This demands a need in academic film studies everywhere for a deeper and comprehensive knowledge and understanding of Eastern or Asian cultural and philosophical perspectives. The shift to the East that international relations have experienced in recent times should be regarded as an opportunity to revamp film knowledge, and this can be achieved through applying a more objective and comparative discipline of East-West film studies or film analysis. The concept of an "Eastern approach" fits into this discipline. The East represents a change of outlook not only in the way that films from the East (or Asia) are studied but also on how we look at the films of the West. As such, while this book offers a certain resistance to Eurocentric theory, its purpose is primarily to add to existing knowledge through the evocation of Asian or Eastern theoretical or philosophical viewpoints which are then applied to the films of the West. Such application seeks to break the ground on which films are generally appreciated. The Eastern approach may otherwise be called Eastern theory, predicated on the principle that Western films are seen not just by audiences of the West but of the East, and the Eastern audience cannot be assumed to think in like manner with the Western audience. An Eastern viewer can resort to a rich tradition of Eastern philosophy and culture which can aid in the interpretation of Western films. Thenceforth, we come to the next important concept that flows out of the idea of balance. This is reciprocity. If there is balance between East and West, there is mutual reciprocity. Reciprocity is an important principle in Eastern learning. In the *Book of Rites* (*Li ji*), it is stated that what the rules of propriety value most is reciprocity. "If I give a gift and nothing comes in return, that is contrary to propriety. If the thing comes to me, and I give nothing in return, that also is contrary to propriety."[3] A balance of reciprocity leads to a golden mean of harmony and interdependence. However, since the question of balance is most unbalanced in the present day, reciprocity is not in balance. The West has been dominant for the last 200 years or so in world history, and the question of reciprocity is not such a matter of propriety for them as in the East. However, this does not mean that there is no need for it, only that Western hegemony has altered the necessity of such demand. East-West reciprocity has in fact been stuck in unbalance as long as the West has been in dominance but perhaps an opportunity for reciprocity has presented itself in our present times, and it may then go up another level of development.

I like to think that the Eastern approach by definition is inherently one of balance and harmony. This is hopefully demonstrated in the foregoing chapters. However, because the world is out of balance, it would be fair to say that the approach itself remains tentative and incomplete. What is the next stage of development for the Eastern approach? Is it applicable to all the films of the West? Is it compatible with the films of the global South? Are there films that are entirely resistant to such an approach? These questions may only find answers through more widespread application of the approach, but there will be many, no doubt, who will ask whether such an approach is absolutely necessary in film studies. While my own response to the question would be predictable, we may yet, above all, have to consider how the Eastern approach should ultimately function as its own self-negation where there is no longer any need for it. At that point, Eastern principles and philosophy are an absolutely integral part of any approach so that it is unnecessary to identify it. In the present state of unbalance, this thought is premature but even so, it sets up an abstraction of the future, from being to nonbeing, to follow Daoist thinking. If we have reached that stage we would have reached the pure state of oneness that is close to the Buddhist concept of emptiness (*sunyata*), "a field of infinite indeterminateness or inexhaustible possibility."[4] In order to reach there, we may be compelled to go deeper into the manifold levels of the Buddhist Hell and come out of it with a new consciousness of the self and the world. Christopher Nolan's *Inception* (2010) is a representation of this idea. Nolan takes us into the Mind-Hell, as it were, with levels of dream worlds posing as the layers of Hell. In the dream worlds time is stretched to a longer infinity than in our normal world. The characters are in the essence of time or inside time itself. In the phantasmal dream world, a longer span of time passes by in fleeting instances and in the end, we come back to our present reality, readjusting our new consciousness to our world of feeling and time. Nolan does not take us into the field of emptiness. Perhaps it is impossible to do so, but in unfolding the layers of the Mind-Hell, he suggests the possibilities. The characters experience the empty non-self (a negation of the self) while always mindful of the workings of the sentient world (the film cannot transcend its plot after all, which involves industrial espionage and infiltration through the invocations of dreams shared between the infiltrators and the victims). They experience the time of the non-self while at the same time remaining engaged with the time of one's cycle of birth and death.[5] They return to the world of suffering where the struggle continues to transcend the problems of perceiving and recognizing the world and its reality. Nolan's other films, such as *Memento* (2000) and *Interstellar* (2014), have also displayed the same capacity for showing the mind-suffering of the individual subject as a metaphor for one's immersion in the suffering of the sentient world and the potential that lies in journeying into the realm of emptiness—and they are certainly ripe for Eastern analysis. I bring up Nolan's work so as to convey the possibilities of the Eastern approach looking ahead. (A case could be made that he is the most "Eastern" of contemporary Western filmmakers.) However, the films are deadly complex such that the phraseology of "Mind-Hell" is appropriate to indicate the struggle of interpretation that lies implicitly in all the ways of the Eastern approach.

Finally, the struggle that this book represents is how to perceive and comprehend the films of the West from a non-West perspective. I could have taken the easier path by following the normal practice of analyzing these films and their makers from the standard "Western" perspective and the literature. In using an Eastern approach, I have followed my own direction to evolve a convergence in film analysis of Eastern and Western concepts, to explore how East and West are poised in tandem on a universal plane of interpretation and exploration of themes, both mundane and philosophical. I hope to show that such a book may yield productive and interesting results than merely following the established Western approach and resuscitating its conventional wisdom on these films. This may open up further vistas of analyzing films of both East and West in an ongoing process of "interpenetration" (*xiangru*) according to the Buddhist objective of "All are One and One is All."

Notes

1. Li Daochun, *The Book of Balance and Harmony*, trans. Thomas Cleary (New York: North Point Press, 1989), p. 7.
2. Ibid., p. 13.
3. From James Legge's translation of the *Li ji*. See *The Sacred Books of China: The Texts of Confucianism*, Part III, *The Li Ki* (Oxford: Clarendon Press, 1885), p. 65.
4. Nishitani, *Religion and Nothingness*, p. 267.
5. "We are born in time and we die in time," so Nishitani tells us. "'To be in time' means to be constantly within the cycle of birth-and-death." See Nishitani, *Religion and Nothingness*, p. 159.

Glossary

Ai ji sheng hen 愛極生恨
Beihuan lihe 悲歡離合
Benxin 本心
Buda bu xiangshi 不打不相識
Changqing 長青
Chizi zhi xin 赤子之心
Chuanqi 傳奇
Chugou 芻狗
Cike 刺客
Ci yijian shi, you wuqiong zhi qing, ci yijian hou, geng wu yu qing 此一見時，有無窮之情，此一見後，更無餘情
Dafu 大父
Dai lümao 戴綠帽
Dongfang 洞房
Fangfu ru du qirong zhi chuqian yue xiang 仿佛如賭其容之處前曰想
Fanying 反應
Fei bi wu wo 非彼無我
Fuyun youzi yi, luori gu renqing 浮雲游子意，落日故人情
Gongfu 公父
Gongan 公案
Huan you rensheng 幻由人生
Hunpo 魂魄
Jia zuo zhen shi, zhen yi jia, wu wei you chu, you huan wu 假作真時真亦假，無為有處有還無
Jianghu 江湖
Jiangshan yi gai, benxing nan yi 江山易改，本性難移
Kuhai wubian, huitou shi an 苦海無邊，回頭是岸
Lao wu lao yi ji ren zhi lao 老吾老以及人之老
Liangxin 良心
Lingfu 靈符
Miaoyong 妙用
Mingzhi shan you hu, pian xiang hu shan xing 明知山有虎，偏向虎山行
Neidan 內丹

Nüer shi shui zuo de gurou, nanren shi ni zuo de gurou 女兒是水做的骨肉，男人是泥做的骨肉

Nüxia 女俠

Ruoshui sanqian, zhi qu yipiao yin 弱水三千祇取一瓢飲

Ruxia 儒俠

Shenren 神人

Shenxian 神仙

Shuangxi linmen 雙喜臨門

Sida jie huanshe, xingqing bu xujia 四大皆幻設，性情不虛假

Sisheng you ming, fugui zai tian 死生有命，富貴在天

Tianxia zhi ben zai guo, guo zhi ben zai jia 天下之本在國，國之本在家

Tousheng guizi chang wei ren 偷生鬼子常畏人

Wanling zhi fu 萬靈之父

Wuji zhi wai fu wuji 無極之外復無極

Wuqiao be cheng shu 無巧不成書

Wuwei 無爲

Xiangbi 象比

Xiangru 相入

Xujing 虛靜

Yan bi xin, xing bi guo 言必信，行必果

Yi ganzi da fan yitiao chuan 一竿子打翻一條船

Yisheng wei sang, yisi wei fan 以生爲喪，以死爲反

Youyuan yu meinü 游園遇美女

Yuanfen 緣分

Zhiji zhibi 知己知彼

Bibliography

Alfian, Bin Sa'at, "Hinterland, Heartland, Home: Affective Topography in Singapore Films," in T. Baumgärtel (ed.), *Southeast Asian Independent Cinema* (Hong Kong: Hong Kong University Press, 2012), pp. 33–50.

Allen, Richard, *Hitchcock's Romantic Irony* (New York: Columbia University Press, 2007).

Allinson, Robert E., "Moral Values and the Daoist Sage in the Dao De Jing," in B. Carr (ed.), *Morals and Society in Asian Philosophy* (Richmond, Surrey: Curzon Press, 1996), pp. 156–68.

Alvis, J. David and John E. Alvis, "Heroic Virtue and the Limits of Democracy in John Ford's *The Searchers*," *Perspectives on Political Science*, 38 (2), 2009, pp. 69–78.

Ames, Roger T. and Takahiro Nakajima, *Zhuangzi and the Happy Fish* (Honolulu: University of Hawai'i Press, 2015).

Amineh, M. Parvizi (ed.), *State, Society and International Relations in Asia* (Amsterdam: Amsterdam University Press, 2010).

Anderson, Joseph, "When the Twain Meet: Hollywood's Remake of *Seven Samurai*," *Film Quarterly*, 15 (3), 1962, pp. 55–58.

Ansart, Olivier, "Embracing Death: Pure Will in *Hagakure*," *Early Modern Japan*, 18, 2010, pp. 57–75.

Auiler, Dan, *Vertigo, the Making of a Hitchcock Classic* (New York: St. Martin's Griffin, 2000).

Bandy, Mary Lea and Antonio Monda (eds.), *The Hidden God: Film and Faith* (New York: Museum of Modern Art, 2003).

Barr, Charles, "Au Hasard, Balthazar," in Ian Cameron (ed.), *The Films of Robert Bresson* (London: Studio Vista, 1969), pp. 106–14.

Barr, Charles, *Vertigo* (London: Palgrave Macmillan, 2012).

Barrett, Nathaniel F., "*Wuwei* and Flow: Comparative Reflections on Spirituality, Transcendence, and Skill in the *Zhuangzi*," *Philosophy East and West*, 61 (4), 2011, pp. 679–706.

Barthes, Roland, *Empire of Signs*, Trans. Richard Howard (New York: Hill and Wang, 1982).

Baumgärtel, Tilman (ed.), *Southeast Asian Independent Cinema* (Hong Kong: Hong Kong University Press, 2012).

Bazin, André, *Orson Welles: A Critical View* (Los Angeles, CA: Acrobat Books, 1991).

Benesch, Oleg, *Inventing the Way of the Samurai: Nationalism, Internationalism, and Bushido in Modern Japan* (Oxford: Oxford University Press, 2014).

Ben-gad, Shmuel, "To See the World Profoundly: The Films of Robert Bresson," *Cross-Currents*, 47 (2), 1997, pp. 230–35.

Bertolucci, Bernardo, "Untitled Tribute to Bresson," in J. P. Quandt (ed.), *Robert Bresson* (Toronto: Toronto International Film Festival Group, 1998). p. 529.

Beynon, David, "From Techno-cute to Superflat: Robots and Asian Architectural Features," *Mechademia*, 7, 2012, pp. 129–48.

Bhabha, Homi K., *The Location of Culture* (London and New York: Routledge, 2004).

Bharata-Muni, *The Natyasastra*, Vol. 1, Trans. Manomohan Ghosh (Calcutta: Asiatic Society of Bengal, 1951).

Bierman, Joseph, "What *The Quiet Man* Said: Shifting Contexts and the Polysemy of the Text," *Journal of Film and Video*, 63 (3), 2011, pp. 30–44.

Bishop, Jeffrey P., "Dependency, Decisions, and a Family of Care," in R. Fan (ed.), *Family-Oriented Informed Consent: East Asian and American Perspectives* (Heidelberg, New York, Dordrecht, and London: Springer, 2015), pp. 27–41.

Biskind, Peter (ed.), *My Lunches with Orson Welles* (New York: Metropolitan Books, 2013).

Bliss, Michael, *Justified Lives: Morality and Narrative in the Films of Sam Peckinpah* (Carbondale and Edwardsville: Southern Illinois University, 1993).

Bliss, Michael, "'Back Off to What?' Enclosure, Violence, and Capitalism in Sam Peckinpah's *The Wild Bunch*," in S. Prince (ed.), *Sam Peckinpah's* The Wild Bunch (Cambridge: Cambridge University Press, 1999), pp. 105–29.

Bliss, Michael (ed.), *Peckinpah Today: New Essays on the Films of Sam Peckinpah* (Carbondale and Edwardsville: Southern Illinois University Press, 2012).

Bond, Kirk, "The World of Carl Dreyer," *Film Quarterly*, 19 (1), 1965, pp. 26–38.

Bordwell, David, *The Films of Carl-Theodor Dreyer* (Berkeley and Los Angeles: University of California Press, 1981).

Bortolin, Matthew, *The Dharma of Star Wars* (Somerville, MA: Wisdom Publications, 2005).

Bowen, Jonathan L. and Rachel Wagner, "'Hokey Religions and Ancient Weapons': The Force of Spirituality," in M. W. Kapell and J. S. Lawrence (eds.), *Finding the Force of the Star Wars Franchise: Fans, Merchandise, & Critics* (New York: Peter Lang, 2006), pp. 75–93.

Brenez, Nicole, "The Secrets of Movement: The Influence of Hong Kong Action Cinema upon the Contemporary French Avant-garde," in M. Morris, S. L. Li, and S. Chan Ching-Kiu (eds.), *Hong Kong Connections: Transnational Imagination in Action Cinema* (Hong Kong: Hong Kong University Press, 2005), pp. 163–73.

Bresson, Robert, "Plongée dans le cinema," *Séquences*, January 16, 1959, pp. 23–26.

Bresson, Robert, *Notes on the Cinematographer*, Trans. Jonathan Griffin (Copenhagen: Green Integer, 1997).

Britton, Andrew, "Betrayed by Rita Hayworth: Misogyny in *The Lady from Shanghai*," in B. K. Grant and R. Wood (eds.), *Britton on Film: The Complete Film Criticism of Andrew Britton* (Detroit, MI: Wayne State University Press, 2008), pp. 232–42.

Browne, Nick, "Narrative Point of View: The Rhetoric of Au Hasard, Balthazar," *Film Quarterly*, 31 (1), 1977, pp. 19–31.

Burnett, Colin, *The Invention of Robert Bresson: The Auteur and His Market* (Bloomington and Indianapolis: Indiana University Press, 2017).

Butler, Judith, *Undoing Gender* (New York and London: Routledge, 2004).

Butler, Judith and Joan W. Scott (eds.), *Feminists Theorize the Political* (London and New York: Routledge, 1992).

Callow, Simon, *Orson Welles, Volume 2: Hello Americans* (New York: Vikinig 2006).

Cameron, Ian (ed.), *The Films of Robert Bresson* (London: Studio Vista, 1969).

Cameron, Sharon, "Animal Sentience: Robert Bresson's *Au hasard Balthazar*," *Representations*, 114 (1), 2011, pp. 1–35.

Caputo, John D., *On Religion* (London and New York: Routledge, 2001).

Carr, Brian (ed.), *Morals and Society in Asian Philosophy* (Richmond, Surrey: Curzon Press, 1996).

Carrée, Roland, "Il neige chez Melville," *Positif*, February 2011, pp. 72–74.

Carroll, Noël, *Interpreting the Moving Image* (Cambridge: Cambridge University Press, 1998).

Carroll, Noël, "*Vertigo*, the Impossible Love," in K. Makkai (ed.), *Vertigo* (London and New York: Routledge, 2013), pp. 71–88.

Castenada, Carlos, *Tales of Power* (New York: Washington Square Press, 1974).

Cavell, Stanley, *The World Viewed: Reflections on the Ontology of Film* (Cambridge, MA, and London: Harvard University Press, 1979).

Cavell, Stanley, "*North by Northwest*," in M. Deutelbaum and L. Poague (eds.), *A Hitchcock Reader* (Chichester, West Sussex: Wiley-Blackwell, 2009), pp. 250–63.

Chan, Wing-tsit, *The Way of Lao Tzu (Tao Te Ching)* (Upper Saddle River, NJ: Prentice Hall, 1963).

Chen, Jack W., "On Hearing the Donkey's Bray: Friendship, Ritual, and Social Convention in Medieval China," *Chinese Literature: Essays, Articles, Reviews*, 33, 2011, pp. 1–13.

Chen, Kuan-Hsing, *Asia as Method: Toward Deimperialization* (Durham, NC and London: Duke University Press, 2010).

Cherry, Mark J., "Individually Directed Informed Consent and the Decline of the Family in the West," in R. Fan (ed.), *Family-Oriented Informed Consent: East*

Asian and American Perspectives (Heidelberg, New York, Dordrecht, and London: Springer, 2015), pp. 43–62.

Chiang, Sing-chen Lydia, "Daoist Transcendence and Tang Literati Identities in *Records of Mysterious Anomalies* by Niu Sengru (780-848)," *Chinese Literature: Essays, Articles, Reviews*, 29, 2007, pp. 1–21.

Chow, Rey, "Postmodern Automatons," in J. Butler and J. W. Scott (eds.), *Feminists Theorize the Political* (London and New York: Routledge, 1992), pp. 101–17.

Ciecko, Anne (ed.), *Contemporary Asian Cinema* (London and Oxford: Berg, 2006).

Ciecko, Anne, "Theorizing Asian Cinema(s)," in A. Ciecko (ed.), *Contemporary Asian Cinema* (London and Oxford: Berg, 2006), pp. 13–31.

Cline, Erin M., *Confucius, Rawls, and the Sense of Justice* (New York: Fordham University Press, 2013).

Cline, Erin M., *Families of Virtue: Confucian and Western Views on Childhood Development* (New York: Columbia University Press, 2015).

Cohen, Paula Marantz, "Hitchcock's Revised American Vision, *The Wrong Man* and *Vertigo*," in J. Freedman and R. Millington (eds.), *Hitchcock's America* (New York and Oxford: Oxford University Press, 1999), pp. 155–72.

Cohen, Tom, *Hitchcock Cryptonymies, Volume 1: Secret Agents* (Minneapolis and London: University of Minnesota Press, 2005).

Coleman, Herbert, *The Man Who Knew Hitchcock: A Hollywood Memoir* (Lanham, MD, Toronto, and Plymouth: Scarecrow Press, 2007).

Collet, Jean, "Le drôle de chemin de Bresson à Balthazar," *Études*, July–August, 1966, pp. 80–91.

Conrad, Peter, *Orson Welles: The Stories of His Life* (New York: Faber and Faber, 2003).

Corkin, Stanley, *Cowboys as Cold Warriors: The Western and U.S. History* (Philadelphia, PA: Temple University Press, 2004).

Cornea, Christine, *Science Fiction Cinema, Between Fantasy and Reality* (Edinburgh: Edinburgh University Press, 2007).

Coutinho, Steve, *Zhuangzi and Early Chinese Philosophy: Vagueness, Transformation and Paradox* (Aldershot, Hampshire: Ashgate, 2004).

Coward, Harold, "Taoism and Jung: Synchronicity and the Self," *Philosophy East and West*, 46 (4), 1996, pp. 477–95.

Daidoji, Yuzan, *Code of the Samurai* (*Budo Shoshinshu*), Trans. Thomas Cleary (Boston, MA: Tuttle Publishing, 1999).

Davidsen, Markus Altena, "From *Star Wars* to Jediism: The Emergence of Fiction-based Religion," in E. V. D. Hemel and A. Szafraniec (eds.), *Religious Language Matters* (New York: Fordham University Press, 2016), pp. 376–89.

De Kosnik, Abigail, "The Mask of Fu Manchu, Son of Sinbad, and Star Wars IV: A New Hope: Techno-Orientalist Cinema as a Mnemotechnics of Twentieth-Century U.S.-

Asian Conflicts," in D. S. Roh, B. Huang, and G. A. Niu (eds.), *Techno-Orientalism* (New Brunswick, NJ, and London: Rutgers University Press, 2015), pp. 89–100.

Decker, Kevin S. and Jason T. Eberl (eds.), *Star Wars and Philosophy, More Powerful Than You Can Possibly Imagine* (Chicago and La Salle, IL: Open Court, 2005).

Deleuze, Gilles, *Cinema 2: The Time-Image*, Trans. Hugh Tomlinson and Robert Galeta (Minneapolis: University of Minnesota Press, 1989).

Desser, David, *The Samurai Films of Akira Kurosawa* (Ann Arbor, MI: UMI Research Press, 1982).

Desser, David (ed.), *Ozu's* Tokyo Story (Cambridge: Cambridge University Press, 1997).

Desser, David, "Remaking *Seven Samurai* in World Cinema," in L. Hunt and W.-F. Leung (eds.), *East Asian Cinemas: Exploring Transnational Connections on Film* (London and New York: I. B. Tauris, 2008), pp. 17–39.

Deutelbaum, Marshall and Leland Poague (eds.), *A Hitchcock Reader* (Chichester, West Sussex: Wiley-Blackwell, 2009).

Dirlik, Arif, "Chinese History and the Question of Orientalism," *History and Theory*, 35 (4), 1996, pp. 96–118.

Dissanayake, Wimal (ed.), *Melodrama and Asian Cinema* (Cambridge: Cambridge University Press, 1993).

Doty, Alexander, "Queer Hitchcock," in T. Leitch and L. Poague (eds.), *A Companion to Alfred Hitchcock* (Chichester, West Sussex: Wiley-Blackwell, 2011), pp. 473–89.

Douchet, Jean, "Hitch and His Public," Trans. Verena Andermatt Conley, in M. Deutelbaum and L. Poague (eds.), *A Hitchcock Reader* (Chichester, West Sussex: Wiley-Blackwell, 2009), pp. 17–24.

Dreyer, Carl, "Thoughts on My Craft," *Sight and Sound*, 25 (3), 1955, pp. 128–29.

Elliott, Paul, *Hitchcock and the Cinema of Sensations: Embodied Film Theory and Cinematic Reception* (London and New York: I. B. Tauris, 2011).

Estrin, Mark W. (ed.), *Orson Welles Interviews* (Jackson: University Press of Mississippi, 2002).

Fan, Ruiping (ed.), *Family-Oriented Informed Consent: East Asian and American Perspectives* (Heidelberg, New York, Dordrecht, and London: Springer, 2015).

Fan, Victor, *Cinema Approaching Reality: Locating Chinese Film Theory* (Minneapolis and London: University of Minnesota Press, 2015).

Feichtinger, Christian, "Space Buddhism: The Adoption of Buddhist Motifs in Star Wars," *Contemporary Buddhism*, 15 (1), 2014, pp. 28–43.

Fischer-Hornung, Dorothea and Monika Mueller (eds.), *Vampires and Zombies: Transcultural Migrations and Transnational Interpretations* (Jackson: University Press of Mississippi, 2016).

Foust, Matthew A., *Confucianism and American Philosophy* (Albany: State University of New York Press, 2017).

Franklin, J. Jeffery, *Spirit Matters: Occult Beliefs, Alternative Religions, and the Crisis of Faith in Victorian Britain* (Ithaca, NY and London: Cornell University Press, 2018).

Freedman, Jonathan, "From *Spellbound* to *Vertigo*, Alfred Hitchcock and Therapeutic Culture in America," in J. Freedman and R. Millington (eds.), *Hitchcock's America* (New York and Oxford: Oxford University Press, 1999), pp. 77–98.

Freedman, Jonathan and Richard Millington (eds.), *Hitchcock's America* (New York and Oxford: Oxford University Press, 1999).

Freedman, Jonathan (ed.), *The Cambridge Companion to Alfred Hitchcock* (Cambridge: Cambridge University Press, 2015).

Friedlander, Eli, "Being-in-(Techni)color," in K. Makkai (ed.), *Vertigo* (London and New York: Routledge, 2013), pp. 174–93.

Gallagher, Tag, *John Ford, the Man and His Films* (Berkeley: University of California Press, 1986).

Gourlie, John M., "Peckinpah's Song of Songs: *The Ballad of Cable Hogue* (1970)," *Journal of American Culture*, 14 (2), 1991, pp. 95–97.

Graham, Mark, "The Inaccessibility of 'The Lady from Shanghai,'" *Film Criticism*, 5 (3), 1981, pp. 21–37.

Grant, Barry Keith and Robin Wood (eds.), *Britton on Film: The Complete Film Criticism of Andrew Britton* (Detroit, MI: Wayne State University Press, 2008).

Gray, John, *Straw Dogs, Thoughts on Humans and Other Animals* (London: Granta Books, 2002).

Gunning, Tom, "In and Out of the Frame: Paintings in Hitchcock," in W. Schmenner and C. Granof (eds.), *Casting a Shadow: Creating the Alfred Hitchcock Film* (Evanston, IL: Northwestern University Press, 2007), pp. 29–47.

Hall, David L. and Roger T. Ames, *The Democracy of the Dead: Dewey, Confucius, and the hope for Democracy in China* (Chicago and Lasalle, IL: Open Court, 1999).

Harbemeier, Christoph, "Autochthonous Chinese Conceptual History in a Jocular Narrative Key: The Emotional Engagement *Qing*," in H. Joas and B. Klein (eds.), *The Benefit of Broad Horizons: Intellectual and Institutional Preconditions for a Global Social Science* (Leiden and Boston, MA: Brill, 2010), pp. 293–313.

Haskins, Ron and Isabel V. Sawhill, "The Decline of the American Family: Can Anything Be Done to Stop the Damage?," *American Academy of Political and Social Science*, 667, 2016, pp. 8–34.

Hayward, Susan, "French Noir 1947-79: From Grunge-Noir to Noir-hilism," in H. B. Pettey and R. B. Palmer (eds.), *International Noir* (Edinburgh: Edinburgh University Press, 2014), 36–60.

Hayward, Susan and Ginette Vincendeau (eds.), *French Film: Texts and Contexts* (London and New York: Routledge, 2000).

Heisig, James W. and John C. Maraldo (eds.), *Rude Awakenings: Zen, the Kyoto School, and the Question of Nationalism* (Honolulu: University of Hawai'i Press, 1994).

Hellmann, John, *American Myth and the Legacy of Vietnam* (New York: Columbia University Press, 1986).

Hemel, Ernst Van Den and Asja Szafraniec (eds.), *Religious Language Matters* (New York: Fordham University Press, 2016).

Hirata, Seiko, "Zen Buddhist Attitudes to War," in James W. Heisig and John C. Maraldo (eds.), *Rude Awakenings: Zen, the Kyoto School, and the Question of Nationalism* (Honolulu: University of Hawai'i Press, 1994), pp. 3–15.

Hobson, John M., *The Eastern Origins of Western Civilisation* (Cambridge: Cambridge University Press, 2004).

Hogue, Peter, "Melville: The Elective Affinities," *Film Comment*, November–December, 1996, pp. 16–22.

Holtzschue, Linda, *Understanding Color: An Introduction for Designers* (Hoboken, NJ: John Wiley and Sons, 2011).

Huang, Betsy, "Premodern Orientalist Science Fictions," *MELUS*, 33 (4), 2008, pp. 23–43.

Huang, Xiaoming, "Crafting the Modern State: Religion, Family and Military in Japan, China and Korea," in M. P. Amineh (ed.), *State, Society and International Relations in Asia* (Amsterdam: Amsterdam University Press, 2010), pp. 21–50.

Hunt, Leon and Leung Wing-Fai (eds.), *East Asian Cinemas: Exploring Transnational Connections on Film* (London and New York: I. B. Tauris, 2008).

Jacobs, Lea, "Making John Ford's *How Green Was My Valley*," *Film History*, 28 (2), 2016, pp. 32–80.

Jameson, Fredric, "Spatial Systems in *North by Northwest*," in S. Žižek (ed.), *Everything You Always Wanted to Know about Lacan . . . But Were Afraid to Ask Hitchcock* (London: Verso, 1992), pp. 47–72.

Jameson, Richard, "The Ballad of Cable Hogue," *Film Comment*, 17 (1), 1981, pp. 38–40.

Joas, Hans and Barbro Klein, *The Benefit of Broad Horizons: Intellectual and Institutional Preconditions for a Global Social Science* (Leiden and Boston, MA: Brill, 2010).

Johnson, William, "Balthazar," *Film Quarterly*, 20 (3), 1967, pp. 24–28.

Jones, Kent, *L'Argent* (London: British Film Institute, 1999).

Jung, Carl G., *Collected Works*, Vol. 10 (Princeton, NJ: Princeton University Press, 1970).

Kao, Karl S. Y. (ed.), *Classical Chinese Tales of the Supernatural and the Fantastic: Selections from the Third to the Tenth Century* (Bloomington: Indiana University Press, 1985).

Kapell, Matthew Wilhelm and John Shelton Lawrence (eds.), *Finding the Force of the Star Wars Franchise: Fans, Merchandise, & Critics* (New York: Peter Lang, 2006).

Kitses, Jim, *Horizons West: Directing the Western from John Ford to Clint Eastwood*, New Edition (London: British Film Institute, 2004).

Kline, Sally (ed.), *George Lucas Interviews* (Jackson: University Press of Mississippi, 1999).

Kolker, Robert, *Film, Form, & Culture*, Third Edition (New York: McGraw-Hill, 2006).

Lamb, Trevor and Janine Bourriau (eds.), *Colour: Art and Science* (Cambridge: Cambridge University Press, 1995).

Leaming, Barbara, *Orson Welles, A Biography* (New York: Limelight Editions, 1995).

Leary, Charles, "The Most Careful Arrangements for a Careful Fiction: A Short History of Asia Pictures," *Inter-Asia Cultural Studies*, 13 (4), 2012, pp. 548–58.

Lee, Ilhak, "Filial Duty as the Moral Foundation of Caring for the Elderly: Its Possibility and Limitations," in R. Fan (ed.), *Family-Oriented Informed Consent: East Asian and American Perspectives* (Heidelberg, New York, Dordrecht, and London: Springer, 2015), pp. 137–47.

Lee, Sangjoon, "Creating an Anti-Communist Motion Picture Producers' Network in Asia: The Asia Foundation, Asia Pictures, and the Korean Motion Picture Cultural Association," *Historical Journal of Film, Radio and Television*, March 2016 (online), pp. 1–22.

Legge, James, *The Sacred Books of China: The Texts of Confucianism*, Part III, *The Li Ki* (Oxford: Clarendon Press, 1885).

Leitch, Thomas and Leland Poague (eds.), *A Companion to Alfred Hitchcock* (Chichester, West Sussex: Wiley-Blackwell, 2011).

Li, Daochun, *Zhonghe ji (The Book of Balance and Harmony)*, Trans. Thomas Cleary (New York: North Point Press, 1989).

Li, Wai-yee, *Enchantment and Disenchantment: Love and Illusion in Chinese Literature* (Princeton, NJ: Princeton University Press, 1993).

Li, Zehou, *The Chinese Aesthetic Tradition*, Trans. Maija Bell Samei (Honolulu: University of Hawai'i Press, 2010).

Liu, Xiaogan (ed.), *Dao Companion to Daoist Philosophy* (Dordrecht: Springer, 2015).

Lloyd, Steven, "The Ballad of Divine Retribution," in M. Bliss (ed.), *Peckinpah Today: New Essays on the Films of Sam Peckinpah* (Carbondale and Edwardsville: Southern Illinois University Press, 2012), pp. 45–68.

Mair, Victor, *Wandering on the Way: Early Taoist Tales and Parables of Chuang Tzu* (Honolulu: University of Hawai'i Press, 1994).

Makkai, Katalin (ed.), *Vertigo* (London and New York: Routledge, 2013).

Martinez, D. P., *Remaking Kurosawa: Translations and Permutations in Global Cinema* (New York: Palgrave Macmillan, 2002).

McArthur, Colin, "*Mise-en-Scène* Degree Zero: Jean-Pierre Melville's *Le Samouraï*," in S. Hayward and G. Vincendeau (eds.), *French Film: Texts and Contexts* (London and New York: Routledge, 2000), pp. 189–201.

McBride, Joseph, *Searching for John Ford* (New York: St. Martin's Griffin, 2003).

McDonald, Matthew, "Death and the Donkey: Schubert at Random in *Au Hasard, Balthazar*," *The Musical Quarterly*, 90 (3/4), 2007, pp. 446–68.

McDowell, John C., *The Gospel According to Star Wars: Faith, Hope, and the Force* (Louisville, KY: Westminster John Knox Press, 2007).

McElhinney, Andrew Repasky, *Second Takes: Remaking Film, Remaking America* (Jefferson, NC, and London: McFarland and Company, 2013).

McGilligan, Patrick, *Young Orson: The Years of Luck and Genius on the Path to* Citizen Kane (New York: HarperCollins, 2015).

McVeigh, Stephen, "The Galatic Way of Warfare," in M. W. Kapell and J. S. Lawrence (eds.), *Finding the Force of the Star Wars Franchise: Fans, Merchandise, & Critics* (New York: Peter Lang, 2006), pp. 35–58.

Miller, D. A., *Hidden Hitchcock* (Chicago, IL and London: The University of Chicago Press, 2016).

Milne, Tom, *The Cinema of Carl Dreyer* (New York: A. S. Barnes and Co., 1971).

Misek, Richard, *Chromatic Cinema: A History of Screen Color* (Chichester, West Sussex: Wiley-Blackwell, 2010).

Miyamoto, Musashi, *Go Rin No Sho (The Book of Five Rings)*, Trans. Thomas Cleary (Boston, MA and London: Shambhala, 1993).

Modleski, Tania, *The Women Who Knew Too Much: Hitchcock and Feminist Theory* (London: Routledge, 2005).

Moeller, Hans-Georg, *The Philosophy of the Daodejing* (New York: Columbia University Press, 2006).

Mogg, Ken, "The Fragments of the Mirror: *Vertigo* and its Sources," (2016), *The Macguffin*, available at http://www.labyrinth.net.au/~muffin/vertigo_sources.html (accessed November 30, 2016).

Møllgaard, Eske, *An Introduction to Daoist Thought: Action, Language, and Ethics in Zhuangzi* (London and New York: Routledge, 2007).

Morgan, Jack, "The Irish in John Ford's Seventh Cavalry Trilogy—Victor McLaglen's Stooge-Irish Caricature," *Melus*, 22 (2), 1997, pp. 33–44.

Morley, David and Kevin Robins, "Techno-Orientalism: Japan Panic," in D. Morley and K. Robins (eds.), *Spaces of Identity: Global Media, Electronic Landscapes and Cultural Boundaries* (London: Routledge, 1995), pp. 147–73.

Morley, David and Kevin Robins (eds.), *Spaces of Identity: Global Media, Electronic Landscapes and Cultural Boundaries* (London: Routledge, 1995).

Morris, Meaghan, Siu Leung Li and Stephen Chan Ching-Kiu (eds.), *Hong Kong Connections: Transnational Imagination in Action Cinema* (Hong Kong: Hong Kong University Press, 2005).

Nan Huai-Chin, *The Story of Chinese Zen*, Trans. Thomas Cleary (Boston, MA, Rutland, VT, and Tokyo: Charles E. Tuttle Co., 1995).

Naremore, James, *The Magic World of Orson Welles* (New York: Oxford University Press, 1978).

Nash, Mark, "*Vampyr* and the Fantastic," *Screen*, 17 (3), 1976, pp. 29–67.

Nash, Mark, *Dreyer* (London: British Film Institute, 1977).

Neupert, Richard, *A History of the French New Wave Cinema*, Second Edition (Madison: University of Wisconsin Press, 2007).

Nishitani, Keiji, *Religion and Nothingness*, Trans. Jan Van Bragt (Berkeley, Los Angeles, and London: University of California Press, 1982).

Nitobe, Inazo, *Bushido: The Soul of Japan* (Tokyo: Tuttle Publishing, 1969).

Noguiera, Rui (ed.), *Melville on Melville* (London: Secker and Warburg, 1971).

Nolletti, Jr., Arthur, "Ozu's *Tokyo Story* and the 'Recasting' of McCarey's *Make Way for Tomorrow*," in D. Desser (ed.), *Ozu's Tokyo Story* (Cambridge: Cambridge University Press, 1997), pp. 25–52.

Oliver, Kelly and Benigno Trigo, *Noir Anxiety* (Minneapolis and London: University of Minnesota Press, 2003).

Palmieri, Rory, "*Straw Dogs*: Sam Peckinpah and the Classical Western Narrative," *Studies in the Literary Imagination*, 16 (1), 1983, pp. 29–42.

Parrain, Philippe, *Dreyer, cadres et mouvements*, Paris: Lettres Modernes, 1967.

Pearson, Jr., Sidney A. (ed.), *Print the Legend: Politics, Culture, and Civic Virtue in the Films of John Ford* (Lanham, MD: Lexington Books, 2009).

Peirse, Alison, "The Impossibility of Vision: Vampirism, Formlessness and Horror in *Vampyr*," *Studies in European Cinema*, 5 (3), 2008, pp. 161–70.

Pettey, Homer B. and R. Barton Palmer (eds.), *International Noir* (Edinburgh: Edinburgh University Press, 2014).

Peucker, Brigitte, "Aesthetic Space in Hitchcock," in T. Leitch and L. Poague (eds.), *A Companion to Alfred Hitchcock* (Chichester, West Sussex: Wiley-Blackwell, 2011), pp. 201–18.

Peucker, Brigitte, "Blood, Paint, or Red? The Color Bleed in Hitchcock," in J. Freedman (ed.), *The Cambridge Companion to Alfred Hitchcock* (Cambridge: Cambridge University Press, 2015), pp. 194–206.

Pierce, Anne R., "Modernity and the Destruction of Boundaries: John Ford's *The Grapes of Wrath*," in S. A. Pearson, Jr. (ed.), *Print the Legend: Politics, Culture, and Civic Virtue in the Films of John Ford* (Lanham, MD: Lexington Books, 2009), pp. 49–64.

Pipolo, Tony, *Robert Bresson: A Passion for Film* (New York: Oxford University Press, 2010).

Pippin, Robert, "Agency and Fate in Orson Welles's *The Lady from Shanghai*," *Critical Inquiry*, 37 (2), 2011, pp. 214–44.

Pollock, Dale, *Skywalking, The Life and Films of George Lucas* (London: Elm Tree Books, 1983).

Porter, John M., *The Tao of Star Wars* (Atlanta, GA: Humanics Trade Group Publications, 2003).

Powell, Anna, *Deleuze and Horror Film* (Edinburgh: Edinburgh University Press, 2005).

Prawer, S. S., *Caligari's Children* (Oxford: Oxford University Press, 1980).

Price, Brian, *Neither God nor Master: Robert Bresson and Radical Politics* (Minneapolis and London: University of Minnesota Press, 2011).

Prince, Stephen, *The Warrior's Camera: The Cinema of Akira Kurosawa* (Princeton, NJ: Princeton University Press, 1991).

Prince, Stephen, *Savage Cinema: Sam Peckinpah and the Rise of Ultraviolent Movies* (Austin: University of Texas Press, 1998).

Prince, Stephen (ed.), *Sam Peckinpah's* The Wild Bunch (Cambridge: Cambridge University Press, 1999).

Prince, Stephen, "Genre and Violence in the Work of Kurosawa and Peckinpah," in Y. Tasker (ed.), *Action and Adventure Cinema* (London and New York: Routledge, 2004), pp. 333–44.

Pu, Songling, *Strange Tales from a Chinese Studio*, Trans. John Minford (London: Penguin Books, 2006).

Pye, Michael and Linda Myles, "George Lucas," in S. Kline (ed.), *George Lucas Interviews* (Jackson: University Press of Mississippi, 1999), pp. 64–86.

Quandt, James (ed.), *Robert Bresson* (Toronto: Toronto International Film Festival Group, 1998).

Quandt, James, "Au Hasard Balthazar and Le Diable Probablement (The Devil Probably)," in M. L. Bandy and A. Monda (eds.), *The Hidden God: Film and Faith* (New York: Museum of Modern Art, 2003), pp. 17–28.

Raubicheck, Walter and Walter Srebnick (eds.), *Hitchcock's Rereleased Films: From Rope to Vertigo* (Detroit, MI: Wayne State University Press, 1991).

Rawitsch, Elizabeth, *Frank Capra's Eastern Horizons: American Identity and the Cinema of International Relations* (London and New York: I. B. Tauris, 2015).

Rees-Roberts, Nick and Darren Waldron (eds.), *Alain Delon* (London: Bloomsbury, 2015).

Rinzler, J. W., *The Making of Star Wars* (London: Ebury Press, 2007).

Rives, Rochelle, "'The Voice of an Animal': Robert Bresson and Narrative Form," *symplokē*, 24 (1–2), 2016, pp. 345–70.

Robinson (Ritoku), Walter, "The Far East of Star Wars," in K. S. Decker and J. T. Eberl (eds.), *Star Wars and Philosophy, More Powerful Than You Can Possibly Imagine* (Chicago and La Salle, IL: Open Court, 2005), pp. 29–38.

Roh, David S., Betsy Huang, and Greta A. Niu (eds.), *Techno-Orientalism: Imagining Asia in Speculative Fiction, History, and Media* (New Brunswick, NJ and London: Rutgers University Press, 2015).

Roh, David S., Betsy Huang, and Greta A. Niu, "Technologizing Orientalism: An Introduction," in D. S. Roh, B. Huang and G. A. Niu (eds.), *Techno-Orientalism: Imagining Asia in Speculative Fiction, History, and Media* (New Brunswick, NJ and London: Rutgers University Press, 2015), pp. 1–19.

Rohmer, Eric and Claude Chabrol, *Hitchcock: The First Forty-Four Films*, Trans. Stanley Hochman (New York: Continuum, 1988).

Rosemont, Jr., Henry and Roger T. Ames, *The Chinese Classic of Family Reverence: A Philosophical Translation of the* Xiaojing (Honolulu: University of Hawai'i Press, 2009).

Rosenbaum, Jonathan, "Vampyr: Der Traum des Allan Gray (Vampyr: The Strange Adventure of David Gray)," *Monthly Film Bulletin*, January 1976, p. 180.

Rosenbaum, Jonathan, "The Solitary Pleasures of Star Wars," *Sight and Sound*, 46 (4), 1977, pp. 208–09.

Rothman, William, "*The Goddess*: Reflections on melodrama East and West," in Wimal Dissanayake (ed.), *Melodrama and Asian Cinema* (Cambridge: Cambridge University Press, 1993), pp. 59–72.

Rothman, William, *The 'I' of the Camera: Essays in Film Criticism, History, and Aesthetics* (Cambridge: Cambridge University Press, 2004).

Rouyer, Philippe, "Le petit théâtre de Jean-Pierre Melville," *Positif*, December, 1995, pp. 100–03.

Rudkin, David, *Vampyr* (London: British Film Institute, 2005).

Sammons, Todd H., "*Return of the Jedi*: Epic Graffiti," *Science Fiction Studies*, 14 (3), 1987, pp. 355–71.

Sanderson, Jim, "American Romanticism in John Ford's *The Grapes of Wrath*: Horizontalness, Darkness, Christ, and F.D.R.," *Literature Film Quarterly*, 17 (4), 1989, pp. 231–44.

Schmenner, Will and Corinne Granof (eds.), *Casting a Shadow: Creating the Alfred Hitchcock Film* (Evanston, IL: Northwestern University Press, 2007).

Schrader, Paul, *Transcendental Style in Film: Ozu, Bresson, Dreyer* (New York: Da Capo Press, 1972).

Seabrook, John, "Letter from Skywalker Ranch: Why Is the Force Still with Us?," in S. Kline (ed.), *George Lucas Interviews* (Jackson: University Press of Mississippi, 1999), pp. 190–215.

Seaton, Jerome P. and Dennis Maloney (eds.), *A Drifting Boat: An Anthology of Chinese Zen Poetry* (Fredonia, NY: White Pine Press, 1994).

Sémolué, Jean, "Humour et ironie dans les films de Robert Bresson," *Positif*, February 2004, pp. 48–52.

Seydor, Paul, *Peckinpah The Western Films: A Reconsideration* (Urbana and Chicago: University of Illinois Press, 1999).

Sharrett, Christopher, "Make Way for Tomorrow," *Cineaste*, Fall, 2010, pp. 50–52.

Shaviro, Steven, *The Cinematic Body* (Minneapolis and London: University of Minnesota Press, 1993).

Shaviro, Steven, "A Note on Bresson," in S. Shaviro (ed.), *The Cinematic Body* (Minneapolis and London: University of Minnesota Press, 1993), pp. 241–52.

Silbergeld, Jerome, *Hitchcock with a Chinese Face: Cinematic Doubles, Oedipal Triangles, and China's Moral Voice* (Seattle: University of Washington Press, 2004).

Sobchack, Vivian, "*The Grapes of Wrath* (1940): Thematic Emphasis through Visual Style," *American Quarterly*, 31 (5), 1979, pp. 596–615.

Sontag, Susan, *A Susan Sontag Reader* (New York: Farrar, Strauss, and Giroux, 1982).

Stoker, Bram, *Dracula* (Oxford and New York: Oxford University Press).

Stone, Bryan P., *Faith and Film: Theological Themes at the Cinema* (St. Louis, MO: Chalice Press, 2000).

Suzuki, D. T., *Zen and Japanese Culture* (London: Routledge and Kegan Paul, 1959).

Suzuki, D. T., *Selected Works of D. T. Suzuki, Volume 1: Zen* (Oakland: University of California Press, 2015).

Tan, Sor-hoon, *Confucian Democracy: A Deweyan Reconstruction* (Albany: State University of New York Press, 2004).

Tasker, Yvonne (ed.), *Action and Adventure Cinema* (London and New York: Routledge, 2004).

Telotte, J. P., "Narration, Desire, and a Lady from Shanghai," *South Atlantic Review*, 49 (1), 1984, pp. 56–71.

Teo, Stephen, *Eastern Westerns, Film and Genre Inside and Outside of Hollywood* (London and New York: Routledge, 2017).

Todorov, Tzevetan, *The Fantastic: A Structural Approach to a Literary Genre*, Trans. Richard Howard (New York: Cornell University, 1975).

Trolle, Boerge, "The World of Carl Dreyer," *Sight and Sound*, 25 (3), 1955, pp. 122–27.

Trumpener, Katie, "Fragments of the Mirror: Self-Reference, Mise-en-Abyme, *Vertigo*," in Walter Raubicheck and Walter Srebnick (eds.), *Hitchcock's Rereleased Films: From Rope to Vertigo* (Detroit, MI: Wayne State University Press, 1991), pp. 175–88.

Versluis, Arthur, *American Transcendentalism and Asian Religions* (New York and Oxford: Oxford University Press, 1993).

Vincendeau, Ginette, *Jean-Pierre Melville: An American in Paris* (London: British Film Institute, 2003).

Wagner, Rudolf G., *The Craft of a Chinese Commentator: Wang Bi on the Laozi* (Albany: State University of New York Press, 2000).

Waldron, Darren, "On the Limits of Narcissism: Alain Delon, Masculinity, and the Delusion of Agency," in N. Rees-Roberts and D. Waldron (eds.), *Alain Delon* (London: Bloomsbury, 2015), pp. 13–29.

Warshow, Robert, "Movie Chronicle: The Westerner," *Partisan Review*, 21 (2), 1954, pp. 190–203.

Watkins, Raymond, "Robert Bresson's Modernist Canvas: The Gesture toward Painting in *Au hasard Balthazar*," *Cinema Journal*, 51 (2), 2012, pp. 1–25.

Watson, Burton, *The Analects of Confucius* (New York: Columbia University Press, 2007).

Weber, Johannes, "'Doctor! I'm Losing Blood!' 'Nonsense! Your Blood is Right Here': The Vampirism of Carl Theodor Dreyer's Film *Vampyr*," in D. Fischer-Hornung and M. Mueller (eds.), *Vampires and Zombies: Transcultural Migrations and Transnational Interpretations* (Jackson: University Press of Mississippi, 2016), pp. 191–212.

Weddle, David, *Sam Peckinpah "If They Move . . . Kill 'Em"* (New York and London: Faber and Faber, 1996).

Welles, Orson and Peter Bogdanovich, *This Is Orson Welles* (New York: Da Capo Press, 1998).

Wetmore, Jr., Kevin J., "The Tao of Star Wars, or, Cultural Appropriation in a Galaxy Far, Far, Away," *Studies in Popular Culture*, 23 (1), 2000, pp. 91–106.

White, Susan, "A Surface Collaboration: Hitchcock and Performance," in T. Leitch and L. Poague (eds.), *A Companion to Alfred Hitchcock* (Chichester, West Sussex: Wiley-Blackwell, 2011), pp. 181–97.

Wilhelm, Richard, *The Secret of the Golden Flower: A Chinese Book of Life*, Trans. Cary F. Baynes (London: Kegan Paul, Trench, Trubner and Co. Ltd., 1947).

Wilson, George M., *Narration in Light: Studies in Cinematic Point of View* (Baltimore, MD and London: The Johns Hopkins University Press, 1986).

Wood, Robin, "Democracy and Shpontanuity," *Film Comment*, January/February 1976, pp. 6–15.

Wood, Robin, "Leo McCarey and 'Family Values,'" in R. Wood (ed.), *Sexual Politics and Narrative Film: Hollywood and Beyond* (New York: Columbia University Press, 1998), pp. 141–73.

Wood, Robin, *Sexual Politics and Narrative Film: Hollywood and Beyond* (New York: Columbia University Press, 1998).

Wood, Robin, *Hitchcock's Films Revisited* (New York: Columbia University Press, 2002).

Wood, Robin, "From *Ruggles* to *Rally*; Or, America, America! The Strange Career of Leo McCarey," *Film International*, 5 (27), 2007, pp. 30–34.

Yamamoto, Tsunetomo, *Hagakure: The Secret Wisdom of the Samurai*, Trans. Alexander Bennett (Tokyo: Tuttle Publishing, 2014).

Yao, Zhihua, "Daoism and Buddhism," in Xiaogan Liu (ed.), *Dao Companion to Daoist Philosophy* (Dordrecht: Springer, 2015), pp. 513–26.

Young, John D., *Confucianism and Christianity: The First Encounter* (Hong Kong: Hong Kong University Press, 1983).

Zahlten, Alexander, *The End of Japanese Cinema: Industrial Genres, National Times, and Media Ecologies* (Durham, NC and London: Duke University Press, 2017).

Zeitlin, Judith, *Historian of the Strange: Pu Songling and the Chinese Classical Tale* (Stanford, CA: Stanford University Press, 1993).

Zhou, Zuyan, *Daoist Philosophy and Literati Writings in Late Imperial China: A Case Study of* The Story of the Stone (Hong Kong: Chinese University Press, 2013).

Žižek, Slavoj (ed.), *Everything You Always Wanted to Know About Lacan . . . But Were Afraid to Ask Hitchcock* (London: Verso, 1992).

Žižek, Slavoj, "'In His Bold Gaze My Ruin Is Writ Large'," in S. Žižek (ed.), *Everything You Always Wanted to Know About Lacan . . . But Were Afraid to Ask Hitchcock* (London: Verso, 1992), pp. 211–72.

Žižek, Slavoj, "*Vertigo*: The Drama of a Deceived Platonist," *Hitchcock Annual*, 12, 2003/2004, pp. 67–82.

Index

absent cause in *Vampyr*   156, 165, 172
alienation effect   90
Allen, Richard   50, 57
Alvis, J. David   245–6
Alvis, John E.   245–6
Analects of Confucius   7, 10, 90, 190, 206–7, 218, 220
Anders, Glenn   93
Art of War, The   245
Asian femme fatale   14, 79–82, 84–6, 88
Assassin, The (2015)   144–6
Au hasard Balthazar (1966)   14, 17, 129, 131–51
Auiler, Dan   50
Avatamsaka Sutra   3

Bainter, Fay   211
Bancroft, Anne   232
Barr, Charles   54, 61, 138
Barthes, Roland   107, 131
Bazin, André   80, 85–6, 94
Benesch, Oleg   110
Beynon, David   24
Bhabha, Homi K.   4, 84
Bierman, Joseph   243–4
Bishop, Jeffrey P.   211–12
bitter sea (samsaric suffering)   61, 75 n.44
Black and White Donkeys, The (*Heibai wei*)   144
Bliss, Michael   182–3, 192
Bogdanovich, Peter   88
Bond, Kirk   154
Bondi, Beulah   207, 221
Book of Balance and Harmony, The   257–8
Book of Rites (*Li ji*)   221, 259
Bordwell, David   154, 156, 162, 164–5, 170, 172
Borgnine, Ernest   191
Bourvil, Andre   116, 126 n.42
Brandon, Henry   245
Brenez, Nicole   110

Bresson, Robert   14–6, 105–6, 124 n.7, 129–52, 256
Bring Me the Head of Alfredo Garcia (1975)   186, 193–200
Britton, Andrew   82–3, 85–6, 94
Bronson, Charles   250
Browne, Nick   141, 149 n.13
Buddha's Palm (1964)   40
Buddhism   3, 8, 12–13, 23–4, 30, 45, 132, 195, 199, 207, 257
Bumstead, Henry   50–2
Burnett, Colin   148 n.5
Bushido   8, 103–5, 108–10, 112–13, 124 n.2, 125 n.22
Bushido, The Soul of Japan   103
Butler, Judith   70

Caan, James   179
Callow, Simon   80
Cameron, Sharon   147
Capra, Frank   208
Caputo, John D.   37, 40
Carrée, Roland   106
Carroll, Noël
   on *Vampyr*   156–7, 160, 166
   on *Vertigo*   50, 58–9
Castaneda, Carlos   23
Cavell, Stanley   53, 56, 73 n.16, 120, 139
Chabrol, Claude   62, 74
Chang, Chen   145
Chen, Kuan-Hsing   4
Cheyenne Autumn (1964)   245–6, 249
Chimes at Midnight (1965)   16, 83
Chinese opera   14, 80–1, 90–1, 96, 100 n.38
Chow, Rey   33–4
Chow, Yun-fat   126 n.42
Christianity   3
   in *Ballad of Cable Hogue*   185–6, 202 n.19
   Bresson   131–2, 136
   The Grapes of Wrath   246
   Hitchcock   62

McCarey   211
Matteo Ricci   210
Star Wars   23-4, 44 n.17
Vampyr   162-3, 172, 177 n.44
chuanqi   144
Classified History of Love, A (Qingshi leilüe)   58-9
   "The Story of Wang"   59
Cline, Erin   214, 216, 222
Coburn, James   194
Cohen, Tom   49, 51
Cohn, Harry   81
Coleman, Herbert   50-2, 54, 61, 67
Collet, Jean   140
Confucian gallant (*ruxia*)   69-70
Confucianism and Catholicism   209-11
Confucius   22, 206, 213-14, 240
Corkin, Stanley   236
Coward, Harold   158
Crippled Avengers (1978)   39-40
Crisp, Donald   239

Daidoji, Yuzan   103, 112, 123
dao (the path)   7, 22-4, 27, 30, 36-7, 42, 44, 47, 60, 130-3, 147, 159, 162, 164, 174, 183, 186, 189, 248
Daodejing   111, 181, 183, 202 n.21, 234
Daoism   7-8, 13-14, 24, 31, 37-8, 43-5, 101 n.50, 132-3, 137, 151 n.54, 159, 163, 168-9, 171, 181, 193, 201, 203 n.33
   fasting of the mind   138
   harmony   187
   principle of duality   257
   stillness (*jing*)   120
Darwell, Jane   248
Davidsen, Markus Altena   23
découpage technique of Melville   121
deimperialization   4
De Kosnik, Abigail   27-8
Deleuze, Giles   84, 134
Delon, Alain   14, 103, 108, 111-12, 117, 119-20
Delon, Nathalie   112
dianying   167
Dirlik, Arif   5, 11
Dostoevsky   148 n.5, 151 n.55
Doty, Alexander   72
Douchet, Jean   70

Dracula (1931)   163
Dream of the Red Chamber   57, 66
Dreyer, Carl   14-16, 129-30, 153-77, 256

Eastern Westerns: Film and Genre Inside and Outside Hollywood   2, 6, 12, 16, 231
East-West binary   3-4
Elliott, Paul   74 n.28
Emperor and the Assassin, The (1998)   199
epic graffiti   24-6, 28-9
essentialism
   Daoist   246
   European   25-6
   Western   155
Eurocentrism   5, 12, 22, 32-4, 43, 44 n.3, 255
European epic tradition   24-6

Fan, Victor, on Chinese film theory   12
fanying (reactions and responses)   10, 18 n.1
fascism   28
fate   81, 86-7, 89-90, 92, 95, 98, 112, 117-18, 133, 137, 146, 162, 170, 184, 187
   yuanfen   66
father and son   13, 41-2, 240
Feng, Menglong   58-9
Fernández, Emilio   190, 197
filial piety   16, 41-2, 70, 205-27, 229 nn.20, 21, 238, 253 n.18, 256
fish-bird imagery   159, 171
Flash Gordon   22, 29-30, 43 n.2
Fonda, Henry   232-3
Force, the   22-3, 26-7, 30, 36, 37-42
Ford, John   16-17, 231-54, 256
Forest of Dreams, The (Menglin xuanjie)   60
Fort Apache (1947)   238, 245
Franklin, J. Jeffery   3, 160
Friedlander, Eli   50, 64, 76 n.52
fuyun (floating cloud)   109, 118-19

Gabin, Jean   120
Gallagher, Tag   238-9
George, Susan   182
Gilda (1946)   81

Golden Ass, The 143
Golden Gate Bridge 51, 66
Gourlie, John M. 188
Graham, Mark 97–8
Grapes of Wrath, The (1940) 16, 232–5, 238, 246–9, 252 n.3
Grapewin, Charley 248
Gray, John 31, 92, 182, 193
Greene, Graham 107
Guigu Zi 1, 10, 18 n.1
Gunning, Tom 62–3

Hagakure (*In The Shadow of Leaves*) 103–5, 108, 110, 112, 119–20, 124 n.3, 124 n.4, 124 n.5
Hayward, Susan 120, 126 n.42
Hayworth, Rita 14, 79, 81–2, 85, 89
heart-mind (*xin*) 222–3, 225
Hellmann, John 35
Heraclitus 89
Hitchcock, Alfred 13–14, 49–77, 79, 87–8, 256
Hobson, John 11, 22, 29, 257
Hoffman, Dustin 182
Hogue, Peter 104, 114–15, 121
Holden, William 190
Hou, Hsiao-hsien 124 n.16, 144
How Green Was My Valley (1941) 16, 232–3, 235, 238–40, 249, 253 n.16
Huang, Betsy 36, 45 n.17
hun (spirit-soul or animus) 168–9, 173

ichinen (pure will) 103
Immortal Story, The (1968) 17, 83, 101 n.39
Inception (2010) 260

Jaglom, Henry 101 n.50
Jameson, Fredric 56
Jedi Knights 22–4, 29–30, 33, 36
jianghu 114–17
Jidaigeki (period drama) 13, 30, 179
Jing, Ke 199–200
Jones, Kent 138
Jones, L. Q. 196
Jung, Carl 5, 157–8, 169, 172, 175 n.17
Junior Bonner (1972) 201

Killer Elite, The (1975) 179, 180, 200

Kitses, Jim
 on Ford 231, 234–5, 241, 247–50
 on Peckinpah 182, 186
Kolker, Robert 28
Kurosawa, Akira
 The Hidden Fortress (1958) 30
 samurai films 193
 Seven Samurai (1954) 179–80, 189
 Yojimbo (1961) 197, 199
kusemono 105, 123

Ladd, Alan 107, 111
Lady from Shanghai, The (1947) 14, 17, 79–99
Lake, Veronica 118
Lancelot du Lac (1974) 16, 145
Lao Zi 22, 31, 132, 183
L'Argent (1983) 141–2
Last Hurrah, The (1958) 251
Leaming, Barbara 90
Leaves from Satan's Book (1921) 170
Le Cercle rouge (1970) 106, 116–17, 124 n.10
Lee, Danny 126 n.42
Le Fanu, Sheridan 154
Le Samouraï (1967) 8, 14, 103–27
Li, Bai 109
Li, Daochun 257
Li, Wai-yee 59
lingfu (spiritual talismans) 170
literary fantastic 156
Lost Patrol, The (1934) 232
Lü, Dongbin 158
Lucas, George 22–6, 28–30, 43 n.2

McCarey, Leo 16, 205–30, 256
McCrea, Joel 190
McDonald, Matthew 151 n.52
McGilligan, Patrick 80
McLaglen, Victor 241
McVeigh, Stephen 28, 35
Mair, Victor 31
Make Way for Tomorrow (1937) 8, 16, 17, 205–29
mandala (circle) 53–4, 73 n.17, 169
Man Who Shot Liberty Valance, The (1962) 232, 236–8, 251
materialism in *Balthazar* 131–3
Melville, Herman 105

Melville, Jean-Pierre 14, 103–27, 256
Mencius 7, 206, 216, 221–2, 224
miaoyong (effect of the marvelous) 122
Michael (1924) 153–4
Miles, Vera 236
Miller, D.A. 49
Milne, Tom 164
Misek, Richard 52
Mitchell, Thomas 213, 221
Miyamoto, Musashi 103, 115
Modleski, Tania 65, 68–9
Moeller, Hans-Georg 181
Møllgaard, Eske 31
Moore, Victor 207
Morgan, Jack 241–2
Myles, Linda 26–7
Murnau, F. W. 155
My Son John (1952) 211

Naremore, James 80, 85–6
Nash, Mark 156, 160, 162–3
Nazism 28
neidan (the inner elixir) 158
New Age 22, 24, 40
Nie, Yinniang 124 n.16, 144–6
Nishitani, Keiji 75, 113, 261 n.5
Nitobe, Inazo 103
Noguiera, Rui 105, 108, 112
Nolan, Christopher 260
Nolletti, Arthur Jr. 226
Notes of the Cinematographer 138
Novak, Kim 13, 55

Oates, Warren 190, 197
O'Hara, Maureen 235
Oliver, Kelly 80–1
Once Upon a Time in the West (1969) 250
One-Armed Swordsman, The (1967) 39, 180
Orientalism 5–6, 21–2, 24–30, 32–4, 36, 40–1, 43–4 n.3, 105–7
Oriental West 11, 13–15, 21–2, 25, 29–30, 32–7, 41, 43, 256
outer and inner 155, 158, 162
Ozu, Yasujiro 129, 205, 238

Palmieri, Rory 182
Parrain, Philippe 165

Passion of Joan of Arc, The (1928) 16, 153, 162–3
Pat Garrett and Billy the Kid (1973) 193–7
Peckinpah, Sam 15–16, 179–203, 256
Peirse, Alison 155
Peucker, Brigitte 50, 54–6, 58
Pickens, Slim 196
Pickpocket (1959) 130, 134, 140
Pierce, Anne R. 237
Pipolo, Tony 135–6
Pippin, Robert 87, 89, 92–3
piying 167
po (body soul or anima) 168
polar (police ganster thriller) 103–4, 114–15, 122
Pollock, Dale 24, 43 n.2
Powell, Anna 159
Prawer, S.S. 161
Prince, Stephen 186, 188, 197
proximate 2, 18 n.2
Pu, Songling 56, 62, 64
  "The Girl in Green" 56
  "The Painted Wall" 62–4
Pye, Michael 26–7

Qi 23, 38–40
Qualen, John 254 n.40
Quiet Man, The (1951) 16, 232–3, 235, 238, 241–4, 247

Ramayana 12, 231
rasa theory 8, 12, 167, 231
Rawitsch, Elizabeth 208, 228 n.13
Rear Window (1953) 68, 76 n.59
Recent Anecdotes and the Talk of the Age (*Shishuo xinyu*) 142
renqing 109, 113
Ride the High Country (1962) 179, 190
Robards, Jason 185
Robinson, Walter 23, 27, 30, 45 n.17
Rohmer, Eric 62, 74
Rosenbaum, Jonathan 29, 162
Rosier, Caty 112
Rothman, William 52, 73, 207
Rouyer, Philippe 110, 114–15
Ryan, Robert 191

Sammons, Todd H. 24–6
Samurai 14, 30, 103–4, 107–15, 117–24

Sanchez, Jaime 190
Sanderson, Jim 247
Satan Never Sleeps (1962) 209
Schrader, Paul 129–31, 134, 137, 147, 154–6, 163, 174
Scott, Randolph 190
Searchers, The (1956) 231–2, 235, 238, 245–50
Secret of the Golden Flower, The 158, 168, 173
Sémolué, Jean 136–7
Sergeant Rutledge (1960) 246
7 Women (1966) 232
Seydor, Paul 196
Shane (1953) 111, 250
Sharrett, Christopher 209
Shen, Xiu (Chan patriarch) 139, 198
shen ren 252
shenxian (Daoist transcendent) 164
She Wore a Yellow Ribbon (1949) 251
Silbergeld, Jerome 67
Simpson, Russell 248
Sjöström, Victor 155
Sloane, Everett 93
Sobchack, Vivian 234
Sontag, Susan 133
spiritual style in Bresson 133
Stagecoach (1939) 238
Star Wars Saga 5, 8, 13, 21–47
Stewart, James 13, 55, 68–9, 236–7
Stoker, Bram 160
Straw Dogs (1972) 180, 182–3
straw dogs (*chugou*) 15, 94, 181–4, 186–7, 189, 193–4, 199, 200–1, 202 n.17
Sun Zi 245, 248
Suzhou River (2000) 67
Suzuki, D.T. 110, 123, 125 n.22, 140
   Zen and Japanese Culture 110

techno-orientalism 27–8, 32, 34–6, 43
Telotte, J.P. 93
This Gun for Hire (1942) 107, 110–11, 117–18
Todorov, Tzevetan 156
Tokyo Story (1953) 205, 227 n.1
Touch of Zen, A (1970–71) 70
Tracy, Spencer 251
Trial of Joan of Arc (1962) 145

transcendentalism 104–6, 133, 147, 155, 207
transcendental style 103, 124 n.7, 129, 130–1, 133, 147, 154
Trigo, Benigno 80–1
Trolle, Boerge 153
Trumpener, Katie 73 n.12
Two Rode Together (1961) 249

Un Flic (1972) 106, 116, 126 n.42
unmarrying motif 217, 219, 230 n.38

vagueness in *Vampyr* 154–5, 161, 164
Vampyr (1933) 8, 14–15, 130, 153–77
Verhoeven, Paul 25
Vertigo (1953) 13–14, 17, 49–72, 79, 87–8
Vietnam war 28, 35, 188
Vincendeau, Ginette 105–6, 112–14, 121–2

Wagner, Rudolf 182
Waldron, Darren 112
wandering
   Daoist 1, 6, 60–1, 132–3, 147
   Ethan's 248, 250–1
   in *Vampyr* 159–61, 164–8, 170–5
Wang Yu, Jimmy 123
wan wu (ten thousand things) 37
Warner, David 185
Warshow, Robert 187
Water Margin, The 123, 190
wayang kulit 167
Wayne, John 232, 235–6, 245
Weddle, David 180
Welles, Orson 14, 16, 79–102, 152 n.57, 256
wenyi 70
West as realm of the dead, The 160–2
Western materialism in *The Lady from Shanghai* 91, 101 n.39
Wetmore, Kevin J. Jr. 22, 28, 38, 44 n.17
wheel symbolism 169–70, 173–4
White, Susan 68–9
Whitehead, O. Z. 248
Wilhelm, Richard 158, 175 n.17
Wilson, George M. 83, 99 n.14
Woo, John 14, 116

Wood, Robin
 on *Make Way for Tomorrow*   206, 208–9, 215, 217, 220, 223, 225
 on *Vampyr*   154, 157
 on *Vertigo*   53, 58, 65
wu (non-being, emptiness)   17, 36
wuwei (nonaction)   7, 173–4
wuxia   8–9, 13, 123

xia (knight-errant swordsman)   109, 111, 114, 117–19, 120, 122–3, 144, 189, 191, 200, 203 n.25
xiangbi (resemblance)   1, 8, 10, 18 n.1
xujing (void and quietude)   104, 111

Yama (God of Death)   196, 250
Yamamoto, Tsunetomo   103
yin-yang   23, 38, 42, 57, 93, 104, 110, 157, 248–9, 257–8
Young, John D.   210, 229 n.21

Zahlten, Alexander   18 n.2
Zeitlin, Judith   63
Zen
 Bresson   129, 139–40
 Chan   15, 139, 148 n.10, 193–200
 the Force   30

gong'an   195–7
Melville   14, 104, 109–10, 113, 119, 122, 125 n.17, 125 n.22
Peckinpah   140, 189–90, 193
Zhang, Che   39, 123
Zhang, Guo (Daoist immortal)   132
Zhuang Zi   7, 22, 23
 authentic being   247
 on being human   151 n.48
 and Bresson   15, 19 n.10, 137, 147–8
 carefree wandering   159, 171
 concept of no opposites   2, 26
 on death   38, 95–6, 142, 166, 168
 on dexterity   130
 discourse on swords   119–21, 144
 dream of the butterfly   57, 96–7, 135
 dream of the skull   168
 fate   90, 133
 father and son   42
 overlapping illusion   57
 re-incarnation   135, 142, 147
 in the Saga   27, 38, 42–3
 spatial dimension   37
 transformation of things   31, 97–8, 135, 151 n.54, 251
 the universe (*yuzhou*)   37
Žižek, Slavoj   56, 74 n.26, 75 n.46

www.ingramcontent.com/pod-product-compliance
Lightning Source LLC
Chambersburg PA
CBHW070019010526
44117CB00011B/1640